COMPUTER SKILLS WORKBOOK
to accompany

lawrence snyder

fluency4
WITH INFORMATION TECHNOLOGY   skills, concepts, & capabilities

SHARON SCOLLARD
Mohawk College of Applied Arts and Technology

Addison-Wesley

Boston Columbus Indianapolis New York San Francisco Upper Saddle River
Amsterdam Cape Town Dubai London Madrid Milan Munich Paris Montreal Toronto
Delhi Mexico City Sao Paulo Sydney Hong Kong Seoul Singapore Taipei Tokyo

Editor in Chief: *Michael Hirsch*
Acquisitions Editor: *Matt Goldstein*
Editorial Assistant: *Chelsea Bell*
Managing Editor: *Jeffrey Holcomb*
Senior Production Project Manager: *Marilyn Lloyd*
Director of Marketing: *Margaret Waples*

Senior Marketing Coordinator: *Kathryn Ferranti*
Senior Manufacturing Buyer: *Carol Melville*
Cover Designer: *Joyce Cosentino Wells/
    JWells Design*
Cover Image: © *2009 Josh Bernard/iStockphoto*
Composition: *Glyph International*

10 9 8 7 6 5 4 3 2 1—EB—14 13 12 11 10

Addison-Wesley
is an imprint of

ISBN 10: 0-13-214306-2
ISBN 13: 978-0-13-214306-6

Contents

About This Workbook

This workbook is for students who want to increase their knowledge of Computer Literacy and get started with the Microsoft® Office 2007, Windows Vista, and Mac OS X applications. It includes explanations, examples, and step-by-step exercises to help students become productive with Microsoft® Office tools, including Word, Excel, Access, and PowerPoint. The labs provide an excellent introduction to popular applications and bring students to a level where basic skills are mastered and an understanding of some of the more advanced capabilities of Microsoft Office are understood conceptually.

This workbook is specifically designed as a supplement to *Fluency with Information Technology: Skills, Concepts, and Capabilities* by Lawrence Snyder ("the FIT book"). Many people teaching or taking a traditional Computer Literacy course want to embrace the basic tenets of Computer Fluency, and this workbook, together with the FIT book, allows them to do so.

What's in This Workbook?

The workbook contains 14 modularized labs, suitable for self-study or instructor-guided lab classes:

- Lab 1   Introduction to Microsoft Windows
- Lab 2   File Management
- Lab 3   Word Processing Basics Using Microsoft Word
- Lab 4   Microsoft Word Layout and Graphics Features
- Lab 5   Spreadsheet Concepts Using Microsoft Excel
- Lab 6   Spreadsheet Concepts: Creating Charts in Microsoft Excel
- Lab 7   Debugging Concepts Using Microsoft Excel
- Lab 8   Database Concepts Using Microsoft Excel
- Lab 9   Database Concepts Using Microsoft Access
- Lab 10   Advanced Database Concepts Using Microsoft Access
- Lab 11   Presentation Concepts Using Microsoft PowerPoint
- Lab 12   Image Concepts
- Lab 13   The World Wide Web Using Microsoft Internet Explorer
- Lab 14   Email Using MSN Hotmail

Each lab includes an explanation of concepts within the step-by-step exercises and review material at the end of each lab that summarizes what was covered. This modularization allows students to focus their study on individual concepts; each lab or group of labs can be completed without prior labs as prerequisite material.

Each lab includes references to specific skills, concepts, and capabilities, as per the NRC's "Top Ten Skills, Concepts, and Capabilities" for Computer Fluency.

COMPUTER SKILLS WORKBOOK

to accompany

lawrence snyder

fluency4

WITH INFORMATION TECHNOLOGY   skills, concepts, & capabilities

How to Use This Workbook

- **Self-Study or "Pre-Fluency":** Students can complete the workbook prior to using *Fluency with Information Technology*, and they'll be prepared with all the "point and click" knowledge they need to focus fully on Fluency.

- **Instructor-Lead Lab Sections:** Each lab is designed in a suitable format for a traditional lab class (focused on computer skills).

Supplemental Materials

For Students:

- Starter files for use in each lab are available on the Fluency with Information Technology Companion Web site: http://www.aw-bc.com/snyder/.

- For students using Microsoft® Office XP, the labs and starter files from the previous edition of the workbook are also available on the Companion Web site.

For Instructors:

- Sample solution files are available to qualified instructors at Addison-Wesley's Instructor Resource Center. Register at http://www.pearsonhighered.com/irc/.

- All student supplements are also available for instructors at Addison-Wesley's Instructor Resource Center.

Introduction to Microsoft Windows

Objectives:

Upon successful completion of Lab 1, you will be able to

- Describe some of the basic functions of an operating system, and Windows in particular
- Describe the parts of the Windows desktop environment
- Use the Start menu to launch programs
- Effectively use the Windows applets WordPad and Calculator
- Maximize, minimize, size, and close a window
- Use the Windows Help feature

Resources required:

- A computer running the Windows Vista operating system or Mac OS X.

Starter files:

- None

Prerequisite skills:

- Basic familiarity with using a mouse to point, click, double-click, and drag, and basic familiarity with using a keyboard.

NRC's Top Ten Skills, Concepts, and Capabilities:

- Skills
  Use basic operating system facilities
  - Applets (WordPad, Calculator, or TextEdit)
  - Change the appearance of the desktop
  Use online help and instructional materials
  - Windows Help and Apple Help
- Concepts
  Fundamentals of computers—Windows as an operating system
  Limitations of Information Technology
- Capabilities
  Anticipate technological change

Lab Lesson

In order to be able to complete tasks such as **save** files, **print** documents, and **launch** programs, a computer requires software called an **operating system**. Two of the most popular operating systems are Windows and Mac. You have probably heard of different versions such as Windows XP, Windows Vista, Mac OS, and Mac OS X. Regardless of the version, they all have the same basic functionality.

The purpose of this hands-on lab is to provide an introduction to the Windows Vista and Mac OS X Operating Systems. Hands-on tasks will be identified by the ▶ symbol.

When a computer is powered on, you'll hear some beeping as it does some hardware checks, and then the operating system loads. A computer may display a login screen, or it may show the desktop immediately, depending on the setup. When you purchase software, you must be sure to check the system requirements and purchase software for the operating system, and version, you are using. For example, software purchased for the Windows Operating System will not work on an Apple MacBook. To confuse matters, Microsoft has developed Mac versions of some of their Office products. You would need to purchase a product developed for your specific Operating System.

Parts of the Windows Desktop

▶ Turn on your computer and sign in if necessary in order to display the Windows desktop. An example of the Windows desktop is shown in Figure 1.1a and the Mac desktop is shown in Figure 1.1b.

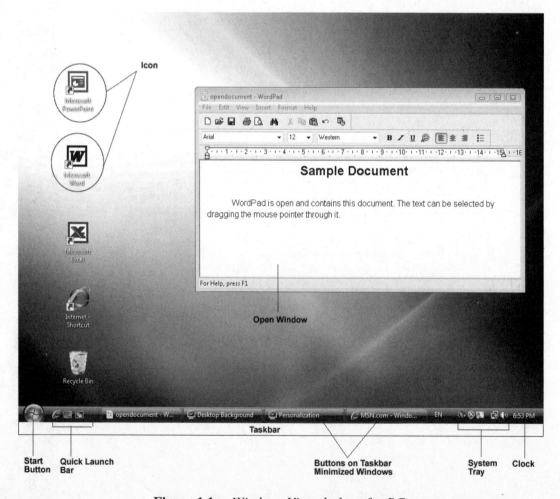

Figure 1.1a *Windows Vista desktop for PC.*

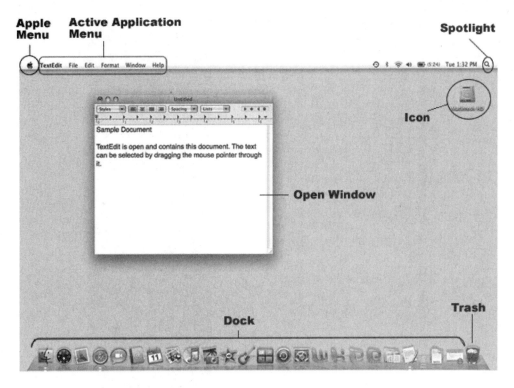

Figure 1.1b   *Windows OS X desktop for Mac.*

The desktops shown in Figures 1.1a and 1.1b have one or more icons on the desktop, icons on the bottom forming a Taskbar or Dock, and an open window, which contains a document. **Icons** are pictures that represent programs or files. Figure 1.1a shows a picture, which has been centered on the desktop. This picture is called "wallpaper" and any digital picture can be used as wallpaper.

> ► Look at your desktop. Identify the Taskbar or Dock and icons.
>
> ► Identify the **Start** button or Apple Menu button on your computer.
>
> ► Click once on the **Start** button or Apple Menu button to reveal the menu, similar to that shown in Figures 1.2a and 1.2b.

We will use this menu later to launch some programs or shut down.

> ► Click the **Start** button or Apple Menu button to close the menu.

The Windows **Start** button is used to display menu items that allow you to select and load applications programs, files, or options for changing the appearance and functionality of the Windows environment. **Applications programs** are programs that allow you to perform non-computer related tasks. This includes word processing, spreadsheet, image editing, games, and other programs. The **Start** button and Apple Menu button is also used to shut down the computer.

In Windows:

Quick Launch Bar

> ► Identify the **Quick Launch** bar on your computer. If you don't see it to the right of the **Start** button, it may not be visible on your computer. Some computers are configured so that the **Quick Launch** bar is not visible.
>
> ► If the **Quick Launch** bar is visible, move your mouse pointer over the icons and hover over each one for a second or two. You should see the name of the program or feature pop up.

Figure 1.2a *Start menu for PC.*

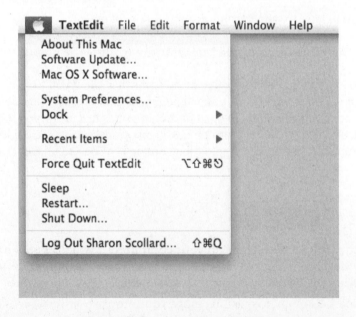

Figure 1.2b *Start menu for Mac.*

The **Quick Launch** bar contains icons that represent programs. You can click these icons to launch the programs as a shortcut method.

In Mac OS X:

    ► Identify the **Dock** on your computer.

The **Dock** contains icons that represent programs. You can click these icons to launch programs.

    System Tray

    ► Identify the **System Tray** (Windows) on your computer. On the Mac, look at the icons on the upper right corner of your screen. Notice that it contains the clock.

    ► If the clock is visible in the system tray, position your mouse pointer on top of the clock. On the Mac, click once on the date/time, to reveal the menu. Click on the date/time again to hide the menu.

The **System Tray** (Windows) and Menu Bar (Mac) displays icons for programs or processes that are currently running. You may see icons representing your network connection, anti-virus software, or speaker volume.

    ► In Windows, move your mouse pointer over icons in the **System Tray** and hover over each one for a second or two. You should see the name of the program or feature pop up.

    ► In Mac OS X, click once on each of the icons on the right-hand side of the menu bar. This will reveal a menu. Click again on the icon to hide the menu.

In Windows, if there are many items in the **System Tray**, only the active icons may be displayed and the inactive ones may not be visible.

    ► In Windows, click the **Show Hidden Icon** arrow on the **System Tray** to display all icons, as shown in Figure 1.3. You may not see this icon if all items are active and displayed.

Notice that all icons in the system tray are visible. After a few seconds, the **System Tray** should collapse to show only the active icons.

Show Hidden Icons

Figure 1.3 *Windows System Tray.*

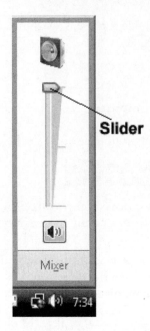

Figure 1.4a *Volume Control dialog box for PC.*

Let's select an active feature and make some changes.

▶ In Windows, double-click the **volume icon** on the **System Tray** as shown in Figure 1.4a.

▶ In Mac OS X, click once on the volume icon in the right-hand side of the Menu Bar, as shown in Figure 1.4b.

▶ Position the mouse pointer on the slider and drag it up and down to adjust the volume.

▶ Click once on the desktop to close the **Volume Control** box.

Applets—Calculator

There are a variety of small application programs available in the Windows environment. These small application programs are called **applets**. Applets perform just a few tasks and are not nearly as robust as the large application packages such as Word and Excel. As examples of applets, let's explore Calculator and WordPad (Windows) or TextEdit (Mac).

Figure 1.4b *Volume Control dialog box for Mac.*

Figure 1.5a *Start Menu with Calculator selected for PC.*

In Windows:

▶ Click the **Start** button to reveal the **Start** menu.

▶ Click the **All Programs** menu to reveal the list of programs on your computer. Your list will be similar to the list shown in Figure 1.5a.

Figure 1.5b *Start Menu with Calculator selected for Mac.*

▶ Click the **Accessories** menu item.

▶ Click the **Calculator** menu item to open the Calculator applet.

In Mac OS X:

▶ Click the **Finder** as shown in Figure 1.5b.

▶ Click the **Applications** option as shown in Figure 1.5b.

▶ Double-click the **Calculator** option as shown in Figure 1.5b. If Calculator is not visible in the list, use the up and down arrows on the keyboard to scroll through the list.

Notice that the Calculator has opened and there is a corresponding button on the Taskbar or Dock as well. The Calculator applet is exactly what your intuition is telling you. You can click each of the buttons to enter a number and perform math functions. The buttons that may not be intuitive are * for multiplication and / for division.

▶ Take a few minutes to use the calculator to perform some quick calculations. For instance try 99 + 199 = and the answer will appear in the display. To perform calculations you can click the number and symbol buttons on the Calculator applet or you can press the keys on the keyboard.

An open window will also contain a text menu that can be used to select features.

▶ In Windows, in the **Calculator** window, click the menu items **View**, **Scientific**, as shown in Figure 1.6a.

▶ In Mac OS X, click the menu items **View**, **Scientific**, as shown in Figure 1.6b.

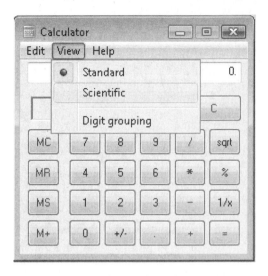

Figure 1.6a *Windows Calculator menu for PC.*

Notice that the calculator is now displayed as a scientific calculator.

▶ Click the menu items **View**, **Standard** (Windows) or **View**, **Basic** (Mac) to return the calculator view to a standard calculator.

Minimizing and Closing Open Windows

Now that the **Calculator applet** is open, it is a good time to review minimizing and closing windows. The **Window Navigation** buttons are located in the upper-right corner of each open window on a Windows system, and on the upper-left corner of each window on a Mac system. The Windows Navigation buttons on the Mac (Close, Minimize, and Expand) are shown in Figure 1.6b.

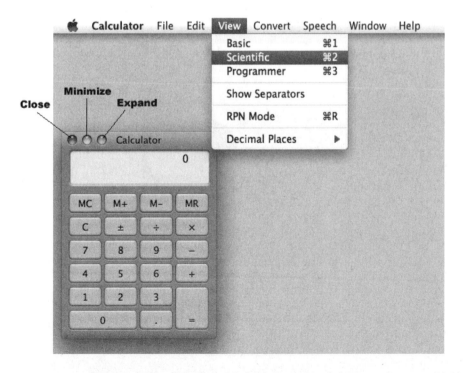

Figure 1.6b *Windows Calculator menu for Mac.*

Title Bar

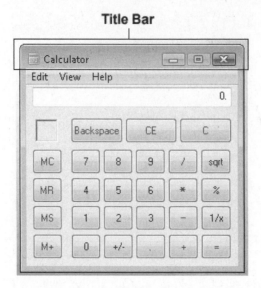

Figure 1.7a *Calculator title bar for PC.*

Sometimes the Expand or Maximize/Restore button is disabled. In the case of the **Calculator applet (Windows)**, the **Maximize/Restore** button is disabled because this window cannot be sized. When a button is disabled, clicking on it will have no effect. There are many instances when a button or other element is disabled because a feature is not available at a particular time.

▶ Click the **Minimize** button.

Notice that the **Calculator** disappears from the desktop and a button appears on the Taskbar or Dock.

▶ Click the **Calculator** button on the Taskbar or Dock to restore the **Calculator** dialog box to the desktop.

You can also use the mouse to drag a window from one position to another on the desktop. The title bar of a window is at the top of the window, as shown in Figures 1.7a and 1.7b.

▶ Drag the **Calculator** title bar to move the **Calculator** window around the desktop.

Title Bar

Figure 1.7b *Calculator title bar for Mac.*

If there are other open or minimized windows, those icons will be displayed on the Taskbar or Dock as well.

Let's close the **Calculator applet**.

▶ Click the **Close** button on the **Calculator applet** to close the window.

Notice that the **Calculator** icon has disappeared from the Taskbar or Dock.

Let's open the **Calculator applet** again in order to work with multiple windows.

▶ In Windows, click the **Start** button and select the menu items **All Programs**, **Accessories**, **Calculator**.

▶ In Mac OS X, click the **Finder**, select **Applications**, and double-click on **Calculator** as before.

Using WordPad or TextEdit

Windows and Mac OS include a small word processing applet. The Windows applet is WordPad and the Mac OS applet is TextEdit. It allows you to create and edit a small document such as a memo or essay. Let's open WordPad or TextEdit and save a document.

▶ In Windows, click the **Start** button to open the **Start** menu and click the menu items **All Programs**, **Accessories**, **WordPad**.

▶ In Mac OS X, click the **Finder**, and select **Applications, and double-click on TextEdit.** If you do not see TextEdit in the list, use the up and down arrow keys on the keyboard to scroll through the list.

You should notice the **WordPad** or TextEdit window is open on the desktop, as shown in Figures 1.8a and 1.8b. You also have the **Calculator** window open as well. In Mac OS, you also have the Finder window open. Feel free to drag on the title bar to move windows around the desktop.

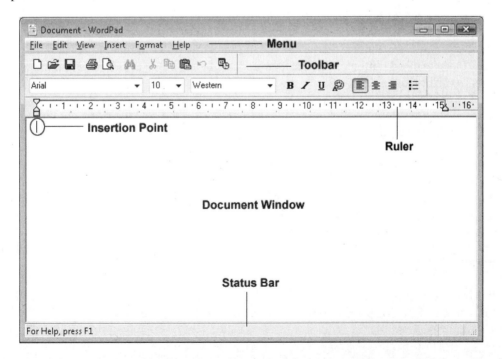

Figure 1.8a *WordPad Window for PC.*

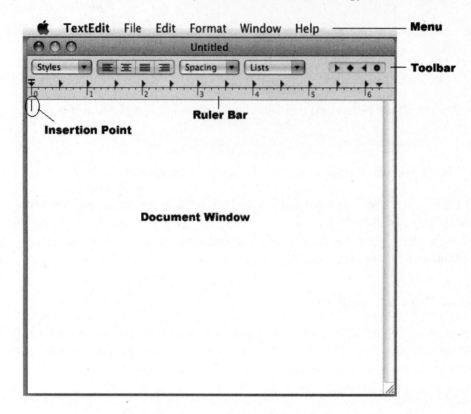

Figure 1.8b *WordPad Window for Mac.*

When there are several windows open, the active window generally has a darker title bar and possibly a flashing insertion point or other indicator.

▶ Click the **Calculator** window to activate it.

Notice that the title bar is darker, and the **Calculator** button on the Taskbar appears to be pressed.

▶ Click the **WordPad** or TextEdit window to activate it.

Notice that the title bar is darker, there is a flashing insertion point in the document window. In Windows, the **WordPad** button on the Taskbar appears to be pressed. In Mac OS, there is a dot under the TextEdit icon in the Dock.

You can activate a window by clicking inside the window on the desktop or by clicking on the corresponding button on the Taskbar or Dock.

Let's look at a few of the WordPad or TextEdit features and save a file.

▶ Make sure the **WordPad or Text Edit** window is active.

The buttons on the toolbars may look a little confusing, but you can determine what each one is by hovering your mouse pointer over each button. A pop-up label with the name of the button will appear.

▶ Move your mouse pointer over one of the buttons on the toolbar and hover for a second. The pop-up label should appear under the button.

Figure 1.9a   *Help dialog box for PC.*

Let's add some text.

► Type your name in the document window. To do this, you can hold the **Shift** key down while you press letters for uppercase. You can also press the **Caps Lock** key to turn on uppercase. Pressing the **Caps Lock** key again will return to lowercase. In Windows, you can use the **Backspace** key to delete characters to the left of the insertion point, and the **Delete** key to delete characters to the right. In Mac OS, you can use the **Delete** key to delete characters to the left and **hold the fn key while you tap the Delete key** to delete characters to the right.

► Press the **Enter** key on the keyboard to move the insertion point to the next line. Press the **Enter** key again to move the insertion point to the next line.

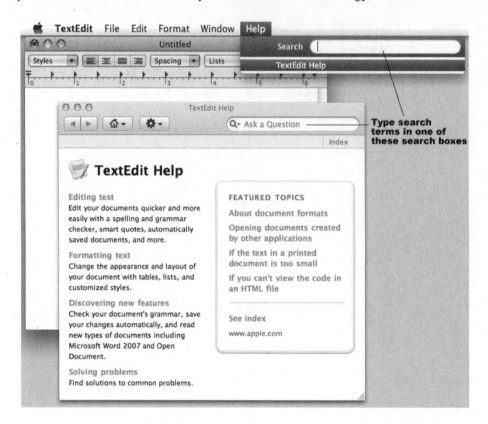

Figure 1.9b *Help dialog box for Mac.*

There are many instances when it is useful to find information using the built-in **Help** feature. Let's use the **Help** feature to learn how to center the text.

▶ In Windows, click the menu options **Help**, **View Help**.

▶ In Mac OS, click the menu options Help, TextEdit Help, as shown in Figure 1.9b.

The **Help** dialog box should appear, as shown in Figures 1.9a and 1.9b. Notice there are a variety of topics you can select if you wish. We will search for a specific topic.

In Windows:

▶ Click in the **Search** box as shown in Figure 1.9a.

We will use the keywords "WordPad center text" to search for information about the center feature.

▶ Type: WordPad center text

▶ Press the **Enter** key to display the Help information for the center feature.

In Mac OS:

▶ Click the Search box as shown in Figure 1.9b.

▶ In the search box type: center text

▶ Press the Enter key to display the Help information for the center feature.

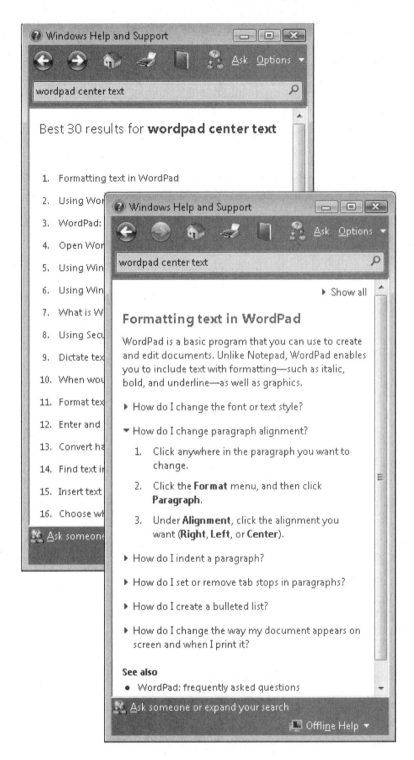

Figure 1.10a *Help search results for PC.*

The **Help** window displays options that may contain helpful information as shown in Figures 1.10a and 1.10b.

▶ In Windows, click the option "Formatting text in WordPad" as shown in Figure 1.10a. Click the option "How do I change paragraph alignment?" A description of the steps required to center the paragraph will be displayed, as shown in Figure 1.10a.

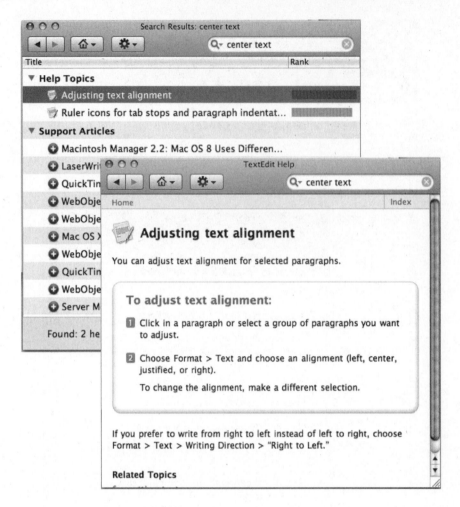

Figure 1.10b *Help search results for Mac.*

▶ In Mac OS, double-click the option "Adjusting text alignment" as shown in Figure 1.10b.

▶ Following the directions in the **Help** window, click anywhere in your name text. Move the help window out of the way if necessary.

In Windows:

> ▶ Click the menu items **Format**, **Paragraph**.
>
> ▶ Click the drop-down for Alignment and select **Center** as shown in Figure 1.11a.
>
> ▶ Click the **OK** button.

In Mac OS:

> ▶ Click the menu items **Format**, **Text**.
>
> ▶ Click the menu option **Center**.

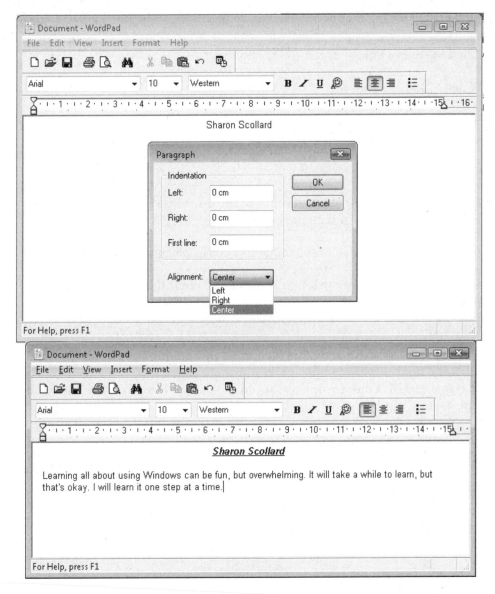

Figure 1.11a *WordPad paragraph format dialog box and formatted document for PC.*

The text should be centered horizontally.

> ▶ Click the **Close** button in the Help window.
> ▶ Position the mouse pointer at the end of your name text and click to position the insertion point.
> ▶ Press the **Enter** key twice.

Notice that the insertion point is centered. Let's left-align it so that the next paragraph will be left-aligned.

In Windows:

> ▶ Click the menu items **Format, Paragraph**.
> ▶ Click the drop-down for Alignment and select Left.
> ▶ Click the **OK** button.

In Mac OS:

► Click the menu items **Format, Text, Align Left.**

In both Windows and Mac OS:

► Type the following paragraph:

Learning all about using Windows can be fun, but overwhelming. It will take a while to learn, but that's okay. I will learn it one step at a time.

► Do not press the **Enter** key at the end of the line of text. WordPad automatically wraps the text to fit the ruler.

We can use the formatting toolbar to add formatting enhancements to the text.

► Drag the mouse pointer through your name to highlight it. Hold the **left mouse** button down (Windows) or mouse button (Mac) while you drag the pointer through your name, and release the **mouse** button once your name is highlighted.

► In Windows, click the **Underline** button ⊔ to underline your name. Feel free to click the **Bold** and **Italics** buttons to add those formatting enhancements to your name as well. Your document should look something like that shown in Figure 1.11a.

► In Mac OS, click the drop-down arrow for Styles, and select Underlined, as shown in Figure 1.11b. Feel free to click the Styles drop-down again and select Bold and Italic.

Figure 1.11b *WordPad paragraph format dialog box and formatted document for Mac.*

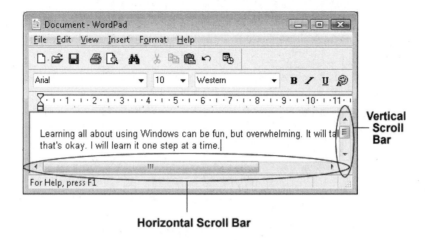

Figure 1.12a   *WordPad with scroll bars for PC.*

Sizing an Open Window

Most open windows can be adjusted in size and maximized to fit the full desktop. Let's play with the size of the **WordPad** and TextEdit windows.

► In Windows, move your mouse pointer along any of the edges of the **WordPad** window until a double arrow appears. Once the double arrow appears, drag the mouse pointer in either direction of the arrow to change the size of the window. When you release the mouse pointer the size will be set.

► In Mac OS X, move your mouse pointer to the bottom-right corner of the window as shown in Figure 1.12b. Drag the mouse pointer to change the size of the window.

If you size a window so that the document is not completely visible, scroll bars will appear as shown in Figure 1.12a. TextEdit does not display scroll bars, however. You will see the scroll bars in other applications, as shown in Figure 1.12a.

► Once your window is sized to display scroll bars, click the arrow buttons at either end of the scroll bars to scroll through the document.

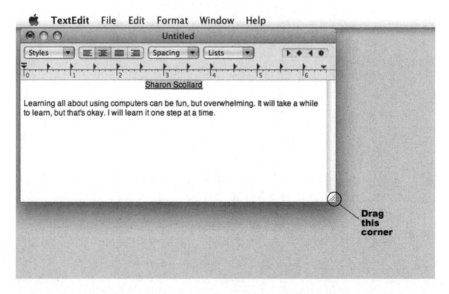

Figure 1.12b   *WordPad with scroll bars for Mac.*

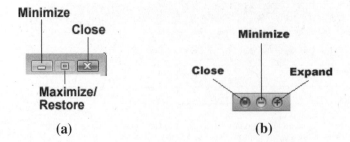

(a)   (b)

Figure 1.13 (a) *Windows buttons: Minimize, Maximize/Restore, Close.*
(b) *Mac buttons: Minimize, Expand, Close.*

The window can be maximized to fit the full size of the monitor using the **Maximize/Restore** button at the top-right corner of the window (Windows) or the **Expand** button in the top-left corner (Mac).

▶ In Windows, click the **Maximize/Restore** button to maximize the **WordPad** window, as shown in Figure 1.13a.

▶ In Mac, click the **Expand** button to maximize the **TextEdit** window, as shown in Figure 1.13b.

Notice that the **WordPad** or **Text Edit** window has been sized to fit the full screen.

▶ In Windows, click the **Maximize/Restore** button to restore the WordPad window.

▶ In Mac OS X, click the **Expand** button to restore the **TextEdit** window.

Notice that the **WordPad** or **TextEdit** window has been restored to the size it was before it was maximized to the full screen size.

Let's save the document as a **Rich Text Format (RTF)** document. Word processing applications, regardless of the version, are able to read Rich Text documents. If you are sending your resume via email, RTF is a good file format choice.

▶ Click the menu items **File, Save As**. The **Save As** dialog box should appear as shown in Figures 1.14a and 1.14b.

▶ In the File name box, type: test

By default, WordPad will save your file as a Rich Text file, in the **Documents** folder.

▶ Click the **Save** button to save your file.

Figure 1.14a *File Save As box in WordPad for PC.*

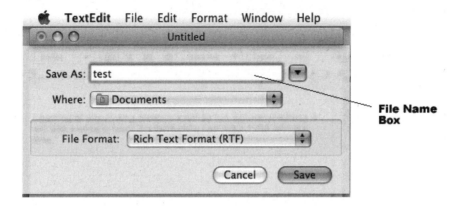

Figure 1.14b *File Save As box in WordPad for Mac.*

Notice that the name of the file, test now appears in the title bar of the **WordPad** window.

▶ Make a change to the document by adding your middle name.

▶ In Windows, click the **Save** button 🖫 to save the change.

▶ In Mac OS X, click the menu options **File**, **Save** to save the change.

Let's close the file, and then reopen it.

▶ Click the **Close** to close the window and close the file.

▶ In Windows, click the **Start** button and the menu options **All Programs**, **Accessories**, **WordPad** to reopen WordPad.

▶ In Mac OS X, click the **Finder**, **Applications** and **double-click on TextEdit** to reopen TextEdit.

▶ Click the menu items **File**, **Open**.

▶ Click the **test** file name and click the **Open** button to open the file. You may not see the .rtf extension; it depends on your Windows configuration.

The test.rtf document file should now be visible in the **WordPad** window.

Changing the Appearance of the Windows Desktop

In addition to manipulating open windows and using applets, the Windows Operating System allows us to adjust the appearance of the desktop and set some configuration features such as screen savers and energy saving options. We will use a shortcut menu to access the properties of the desktop. In Windows, right-clicking the mouse reveals a shortcut menu. The method is to click the **right-mouse** button instead of the **left-mouse** button. In Mac OS X, the method is to **hold the function key while you click the mouse button**.

▶ Close the **WordPad** and **Calculator** windows.

Figure 1.15a   *Windows desktop shortcut menu for PC.*

In Windows:

▶ Move your mouse pointer to an empty area on the desktop, and right-click to reveal the shortcut menu, as shown in Figure 1.15a.

▶ Click the **Personalize** menu item with either the **right-** or **left-mouse** button to reveal the **Personalization** dialog box.

▶ Click the **Screen Saver** option, as shown in Figure 1.16a.

In Mac OS X:

▶ Hold the function key while you click the **mouse** button to reveal the shortcut menu, as shown in Figure 1.15b.

▶ Click the menu item **Change Desktop Background** as shown in Figure 1.15b.

▶ Click the **Screen Saver button** as shown in Figure 1.16b.

Figure 1.15b   *Windows desktop shortcut menu for Mac.*

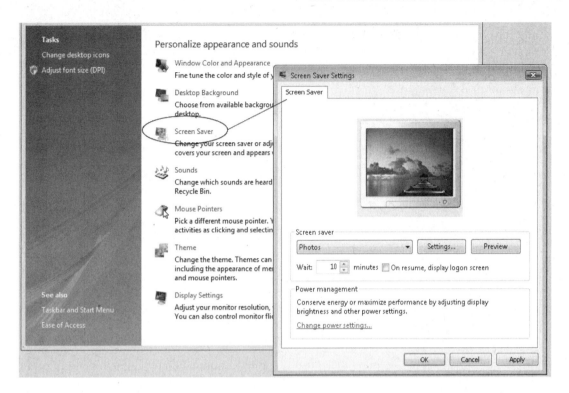

Figure 1.16a   *Windows desktop Display Properties dialog box for PC.*

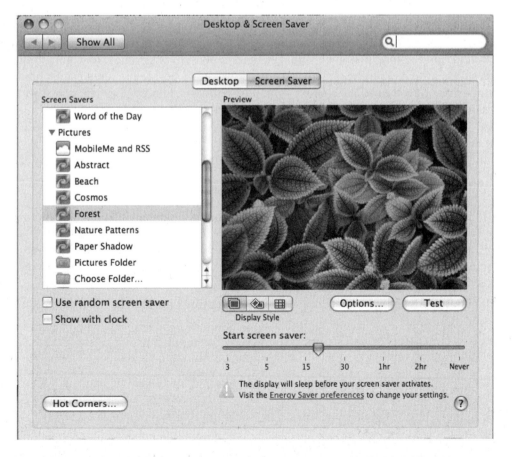

Figure 1.16b   *Windows desktop Display Properties dialog box for Mac.*

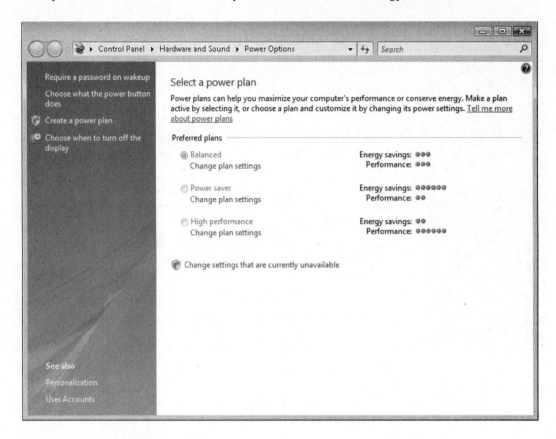

Figure 1.17   *Windows desktop Power Options dialog box.*

The purpose of a screen saver is to prevent burning an image into the monitor screen if the screen does not change over a long period of time. Feel free to take a few minutes to explore the variety of screen savers available by clicking on the drop-down arrow beside the screen saver name (Windows) or the screen saver name itself (Mac). In Windows, choose a screen saver by clicking on a screen saver name and clicking the **Preview** button to view a sample of the screen saver. Click again when the screen saver is in preview mode to return to the desktop. In Mac OS X, click the screen saver name and close the window.

In Windows only:

> ▶ Click the "Change Power Settings" link to view the power options, as shown in Figure 1.17. Feel free to take a few minutes to read the assorted options for conserving power. The power options will be tailored to the type of computer you are using. If you are using a laptop, options will include features to conserve battery power.
>
> ▶ Click the **Close** button to accept the power options and return to the **Screen Saver** dialog box.
>
> ▶ Click the **Cancel** button to close the Screen Saver window without changes.

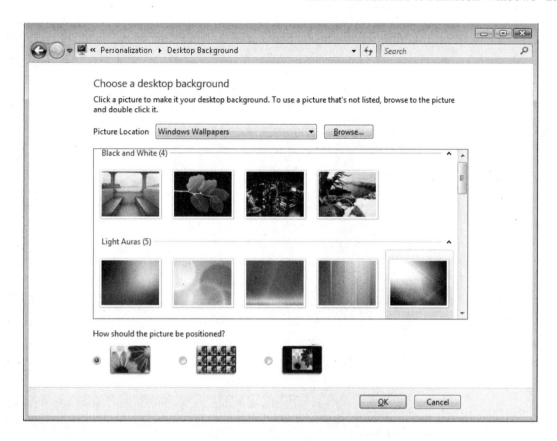

Figure 1.18 *Windows desktop background properties.*

▶ In the **Personalization** box, click the **Desktop Background** option to display the properties for wallpaper, as shown in Figure 1.18.

▶ You can scroll through the Background list and click each background type. Some backgrounds are large pictures. You can adjust the position of a large picture to center or stretch. If a small picture is stretched, you will find that it becomes out of focus.

▶ After you've finished making selections, click the **OK** button to accept the Display Background options.

▶ Close the **Personalization** window.

Using Help

Most software, including the Windows and Mac Operating Systems, contain extensive help information. If you're wondering how to use a feature, or are interested in more information about the features of the software you're using, the Help feature is the first place to look. Let's use the Windows or Mac Help feature to learn how to set up a printer.

▶ In Windows, click the **Start** button and click the **Help and Support** menu item.

▶ In Mac OS, click the **Help** menu item.

▶ In the **Search** box, type: "setting up a printer," as shown in Figures 1.19a and 1.19b.

▶ In Windows, click the **Search Help** button.

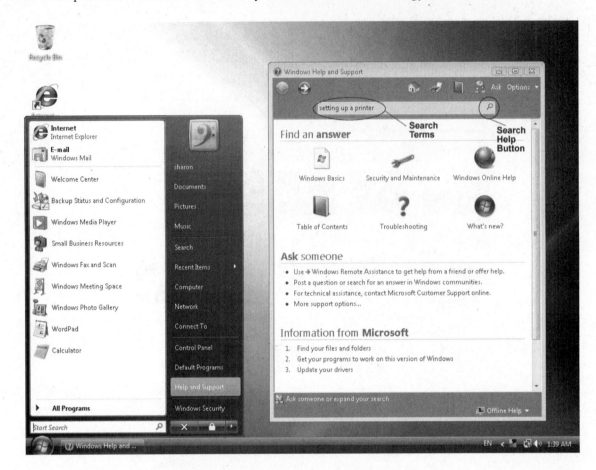

Figure 1.19a *Windows Help and Support for PC.*

You should see a list of results appear in a new window, as shown in Figures 1.19b and 1.20.

> ▶ Click the task "Getting started with printing" (Windows) or "About setting up printers" (Mac). If your version reveals other tasks, feel free to choose one.
> ▶ Close the **Help and Support Center** window (Windows) or **Mac Help** window (Mac) after you have completed your search.

Shutting Down Your Computer

When you have finished using your computer, it is important to shut it down properly. Windows will close any open applications, save settings, and remove temporary files that have been stored.

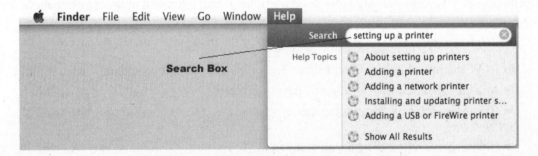

Figure 1.19b *Windows Help and Support for Mac.*

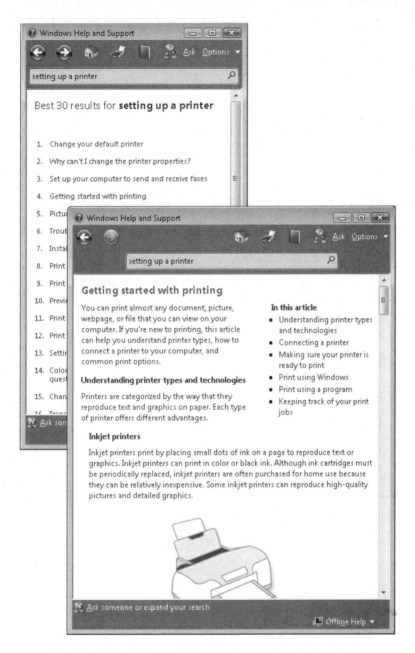

Figure 1.20 *Help and Support for setting up a printer.*

When you're ready, take the following steps to shut down your computer.

▶ In Windows, click the **Start** button. Click the arrow next to the **Lock** button, as shown in Figure 1.21a.

▶ In Mac OS X, click the Apple menu as shown in Figure 1.21b.

▶ Click the **Shut Down** option to turn off the computer.

Figure 1.21a *Windows Turn off computer buttons for PC.*

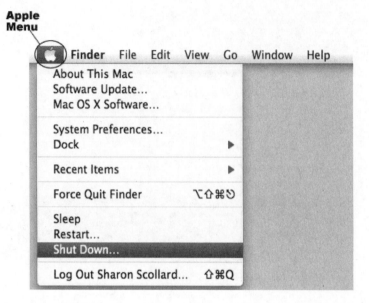

Figure 1.21b *Turn off computer buttons for Mac.*

The **Sleep** feature can be used when you wish to conserve energy. It will power down the hard drive and monitor and retain information in memory. If there is a power interruption, information in memory will be lost, so it is wise to save your documents before you use the **Sleep** feature.

Review

This has been a busy lab! We have covered the following topics:
- The Windows and Mac families of operating systems
- Parts of the desktop
  - Icons
  - Taskbar/Dock
  - Quick Launch bar
  - System Tray
  - Start button, Apple menu
- Opening Windows
  - Minimize
  - Size
  - Maximize/Restore, Expand
  - Close
  - Taskbar button, Dock buttons
- Applets
  - Calculator
  - WordPad/TextEdit
- Changing the appearance of the desktop
  - Screen savers
  - Power saving options
  - Desktop wallpaper
- Windows and Mac Help
- Shutting down your computer

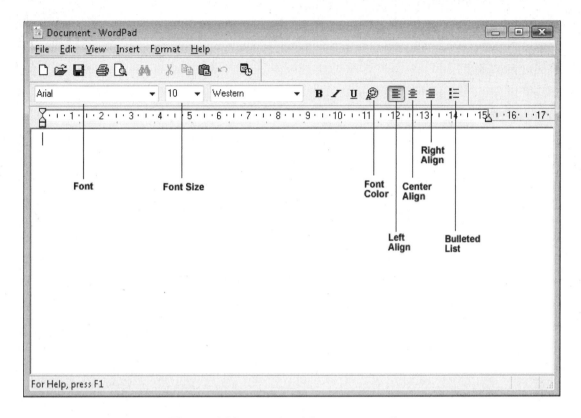

Figure 1.22 *WordPad formatting toolbar.*

Exercises

1. In Windows, right-click the desktop and select the **Personalize** menu item from the shortcut menu. Click the **Window Color and Appearance** option. You can select a color scheme from the drop-down arrow on the **Color Scheme** box. You can also click the **Advanced** button to select custom colors. Feel free to experiment!

2. In Windows, open WordPad. You can open the test.rtf file or start a new file with text of your choice. Experiment with the buttons on the formatting toolbar to add color and change the font and font size. Formatting buttons are shown in Figure 1.22. Drag to select text, and then click the formatting buttons to apply the formatting feature to the highlighted text. Use the **Alignment** buttons to align titles or paragraphs.

3. In Mac OS X, open TextEdit. You can open the test file or start a new file with text of your choice. Experiment with the menu items Format, Font and Format, Text. Drag to select text, and then use the Format menu to apply the formatting feature to the highlighted text. Use the Format, Text menu to align titles or paragraphs.

File Management

Objectives:

Upon successful completion of Lab 2, you will be able to

- Define the terms file and folder
- Understand file and memory storage capacity concepts including byte, kilobyte, megabyte, and gigabyte
- Create a folder in the **Save As** dialog box in an application and save a file in the folder
- Create folders
- Copy and move files and folders
- Understand the concepts of file extensions and associations
- Delete files and folders permanently and recover files and folders from the Recycle Bin or Trash before they have been deleted

Resources required:

- A computer running Windows Vista or Mac OS X

Starter files:

- None

Prerequisite skills:

- Basic familiarity with using a mouse to point, click, double-click and drag, and basic familiarity with using a keyboard
- Windows manipulation skills—open, close, size, drag, maximize, minimize, restore

NRC's Top Ten Skills, Concepts, and Capabilities:

- Skills
  Use basic operating system facilities.
  - Save files and create folders in an applet (WordPad or TextEdit)
  - Copy and move files and folders
- Concepts
  Fundamentals of computers—File Management using Windows Vista or Mac Finder
  Structuring information
- Capabilities
  Manage complexity

31

Lab Lesson

Files are everywhere! Documents such as a memo to your boss or a letter to your cousin are stored as files on your computer. A file can also contain a digital image, a Web page, a piece of music, a movie, or your family budget spreadsheet. Files can be stored on your computer's hard drive, on a DVD, or on a USB memory stick, and sent as attachments to email messages. So it's unavoidable. If you are using a computer, you are also using files to store your data. And as soon as you start working with files, you also need to organize them so that you can find them later. Files are organized using folders. Folders can contain many files and other folders as well, as we will see. You can think of a folder as a container. A folder can also contain other containers; like a tackle box contains drawers and compartments.

The purpose of this hands-on lab is to provide an introduction to file management using Windows Vista and Mac OS X. Hands-on tasks will be identified by the ▶ symbol.

We'll need to create some files so that we can also copy them and move them around. Let's start by creating some files using WordPad (Windows) or TextEdit (Mac).

Saving Files

▶ Open WordPad. In Windows, you should find it in **Start**, **All Programs**, **Accessories**, **WordPad**. In Mac OS X, you should find it in **Finder**, **Applications**.

▶ Type: your name. Your name should appear at the insertion point.

▶ Click the menu items **File**, **Save**. The **Save As** dialog box should appear as shown in Figures 2.1a and 2.1b. In Windows, if the dialog box does not display folders, click the **Browse Folders button** to see the folders.

▶ In the **File name** box, delete the current file name and type: myname, as shown in Figures 2.1a and 2.1b.

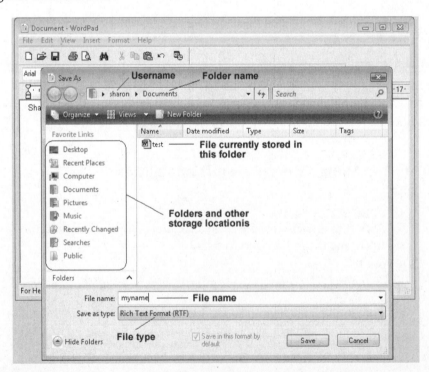

Figure 2.1a *WordPad Save As dialog box showing myname.rtf.*

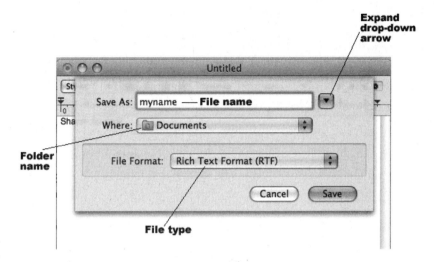

Figure 2.1b *TextEdit Save As dialog box showing myname file name.*

Notice that the **Save As** dialog box identifies the **Documents** folder as the location for the file, as shown in Figures 2.1a and 2.1b.

▶ Click the **Save** button to save the file.

The new file, myname.rtf, has been saved in the **Documents** folder.

Let's edit the myname.rtf file and save the changes as a different file.

▶ Press the **Enter** key to move the flashing insertion point to the next line.
▶ Type your address, pressing the **Enter** key each time you need to move the insertion point to the next line.
▶ Click the **File**, **Save As** menu commands. The **Save As** dialog box should appear as shown in Figure 2.2.

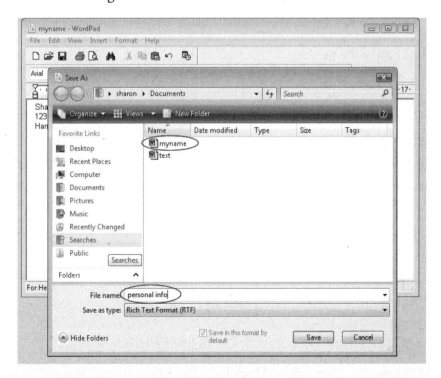

Figure 2.2a *WordPad Save As dialog box showing myname.rtf.*

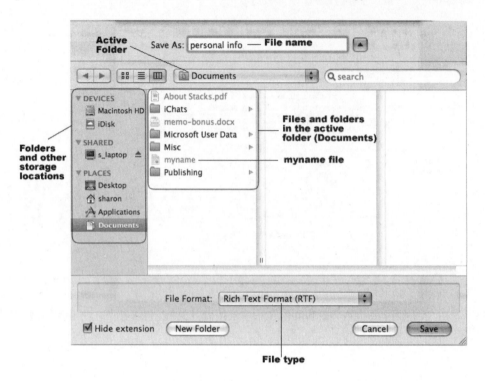

Figure 2.2b   *TextEdit Save As dialog box showing myname file name.*

The difference between **File**, **Save** and **File**, **Save As** might be a bit confusing! Use File, **Save** when you wish to save the editing changes to a file, keeping the same file name. Use File, **Save As** when you wish to save the file as a different name, preserving the "old" file and saving the newly edited file using this new file name.

►In the **File name** box, delete the current file name (myname.rtf) and any other characters that appear.

►Type: personal info

►In Mac OS X, click the Expand drop-down arrow to reveal the folders as shown in Figure 2.2b.

Notice in Figures 2.2a and 2.2b that the myname.rtf file appears in the **Documents** folder list. You may not see the .rtf extension if your system is configured to hide file extensions.

►Click the **Save** button to save the personal info file in the **Documents** folder.

Organizing files and folders is as much of an art as a science. Your folder organization will evolve as you use your computer more. You may find that you need folders for personal correspondence, folders for each of the courses you are taking, folders for business dealings, and so forth. You will find yourself moving files into different folders as you decide on improved organization. Sometimes folder organization ideas occur to you as you're saving a file. Let's look at creating a folder as we save a file.

Creating a Folder in WordPad or TextEdit

We will edit the current file and save it in a new folder using a different file name.

►In WordPad or TextEdit, press the **Enter** key twice to move the insertion point below the address.

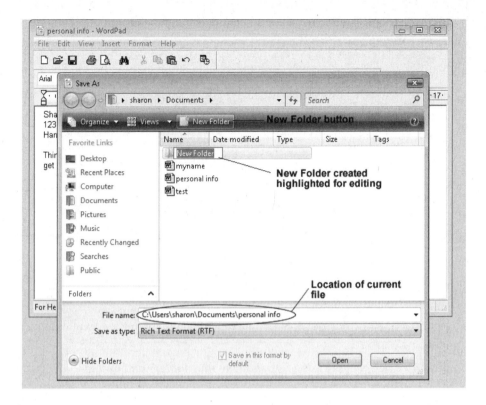

Figure 2.3a *WordPad Save As dialog box with the new folder created.*

▶ Type: Things To Do Today

▶ Press the **Enter** key and type: get groceries

▶ Feel free to add more items to the "To Do" list, but for this exercise, the data is not important.

Let's save this new file in a folder called "personal."

▶ Click the **File**, **Save As** menu commands. The **Save As** dialog box should appear, as we have seen previously.

This time, we will create the folder first, and then save the file in the new folder.

▶ Click the **New Folder** button, as shown in Figures 2.3a and 2.3b.

In Windows, a new folder will be created, with the name "New Folder," and it will be highlighted as shown in Figure 2.3a. In Mac OS X, the New Folder dialog box will appear as shown in Figure 2.3b.

Now we will edit the New Folder name.

▶ In Windows, the New Folder is selected and highlighted. In Mac OS X, the New Folder dialog box is displayed and the default folder name is highlighted. Type: personal

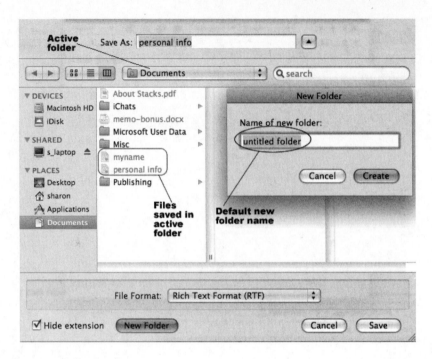

Figure 2.3b *TextEdit Save As dialog box showing new folders and create folder dialog box.*

▶ In Windows, press the **Enter** key to set the folder name and open the new folder.

▶ In Mac OS X, click the **Create** button as shown in Figure 2.3b.

You should notice the **personal** folder is open, as shown in Figures 2.4a and 2.4b.

▶ Delete the current file name and type: todo

▶ Click the **Save** button to save the file.

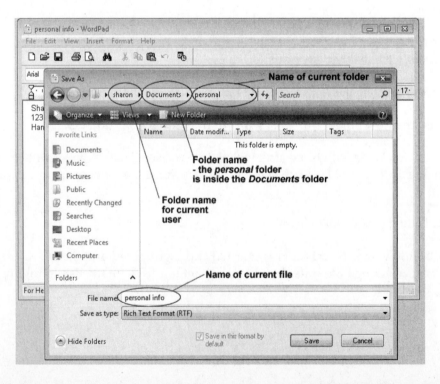

Figure 2.4a *WordPad Save As dialog box with the personal folder in Documents list.*

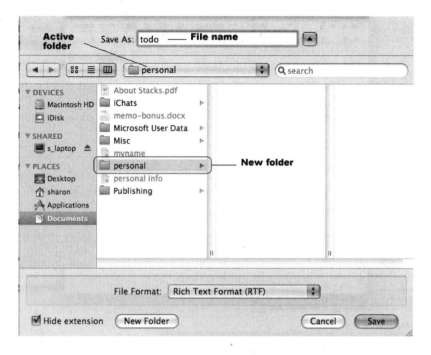

Figure 2.4b *TextEdit Save As dialog box with personal folder in Documents list.*

Let's open one of our saved files.

▶ Click the menu items **File**, **Open**.

You should see the **Open** dialog box appear as shown in Figures 2.5a and 2.5b. Notice that the previously used folder listing is open.

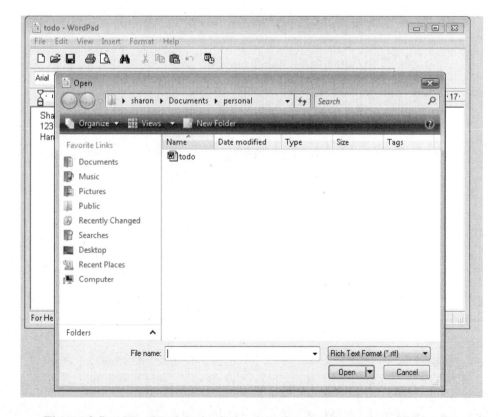

Figure 2.5a *WordPad Open dialog box showing the personal folder list.*

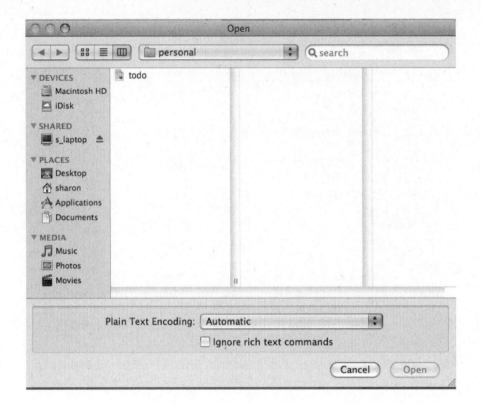

Figure 2.5b *TextEdit Open dialog box showing the personal folder list.*

Let's choose one of the files we saved in the **Documents** folder.

▶ Click the **Documents** folder name to select it and list the files as shown in Figures 2.6a and 2.6b.

▶ Click the file name myname to select it as shown in Figures 2.6a and 2.6b. In Mac OS X the file information will be displayed after you click on the file name.

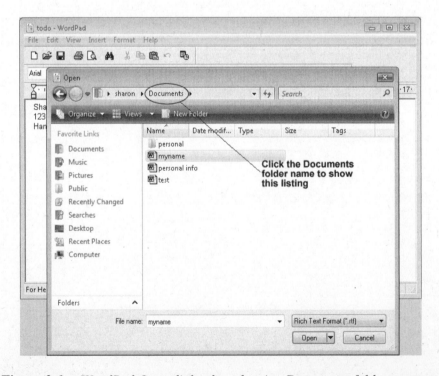

Figure 2.6a *WordPad Open dialog box showing Documents folder contents.*

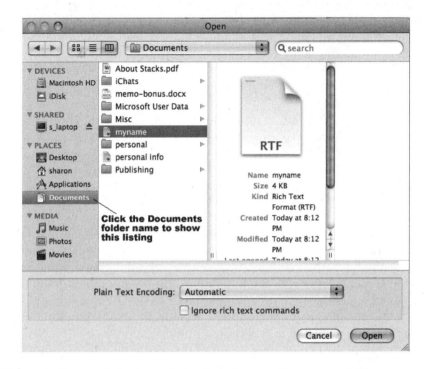

Figure 2.6b *TextEdit Open dialog box showing Documents folder contents.*

▶ In Windows, click the **Open** button to open the myname file in the Documents folder.

▶ In Mac OS X, **double-click the file name myname** to open the file.

▶ Close the WordPad or TextEdit window. We're finished creating files.

Using Windows File Explorer or Mac's Finder

We created data files using WordPad and also created a folder in which data files can be stored. This method was convenient because we were already using WordPad or TextEdit when we decided to create a folder. However, when organizing and copying files, it is not necessary to be using the application software in which the data files were created. Windows and Mac OS X provide several methods for creating folders and copying and moving files and folders. One method is to use Windows File Explorer or Mac's Finder to view and manage files and folders.

▶ In Windows, click the **Start** button and click the **Documents** menu item. The Windows File Explorer window should open, as shown in Figure 2.7a.

▶ In Mac OS X, click the Finder icon in the Dock. Finder should open as shown in Figure 2.7b.

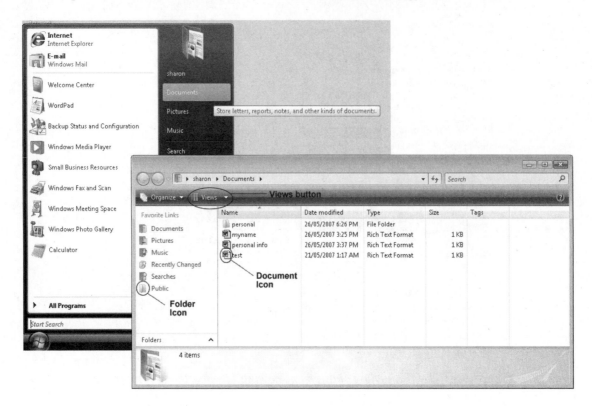

Figure 2.7a *Windows File Explorer.*

In both Windows File Explorer and Finder, you will see a list of folders on your computer system. The list in the right-hand column shown in Figures 2.7a and 2.7b shows the details display of the documents and folders.

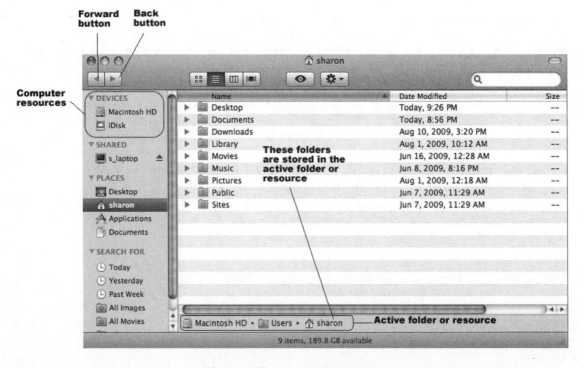

Figure 2.7b *Mac OS X Finder.*

Lab 2: File Management **41**

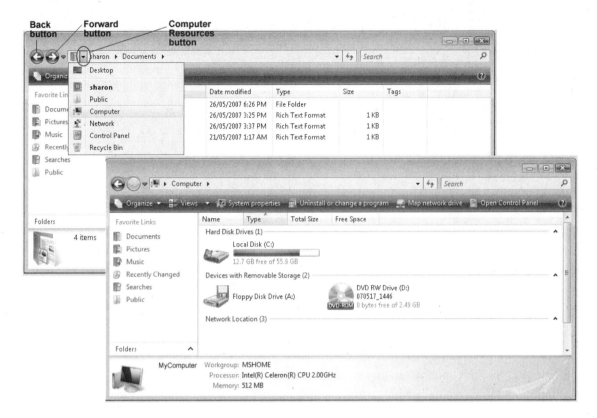

Figure 2.8a *Windows File Explorer showing the Computer selection.*

▶ In Mac OS X, **click on the Macintosh HD device**, as shown in Figure 2.8b.

In Windows, the hard drive is usually labeled as the "C:" drive. In Mac OS X, the hard drive is usually labeled as "Macintosh HD". The hard drive list should appear as shown in Figures 2.8a and 2.8b. Your list of folders will be different because it is unique to your computer system. If the folders in the pane on the right side of the window display differently, don't worry. We'll be changing that shortly and you'll see the options available.

Let's have a look at the resources available on the computer.

▶ In Windows, click the drop-down arrow to the left of your username as shown in Figure 2.8a to reveal the computer resources.

▶ In Windows, click the **Computer** option as shown in Figure 2.8a.

In Windows, notice that the computer storage devices are listed such as **Hard Disk Drives** and **Devices with Removable Storage**. Also notice that the various drives are assigned letter names. The hard disk drive is often assigned the drive letter C. In Figure 2.8a the computer also has a DVD RW Drive, which is assigned the letter D. Some computer systems have multiple hard drives, removable drives, USB memory stick, and other devices. Letters are assigned to those devices as well. In Mac OS X, the devices are listed as Macintosh HD and iDisk.

You can click the **Back** and **Forward** buttons to navigate through the previously viewed selections.

▶ Click the **Back** button to view the previous folder contents previously viewed.

▶ Click the **Forward** button to view the Hard Drive listing again.

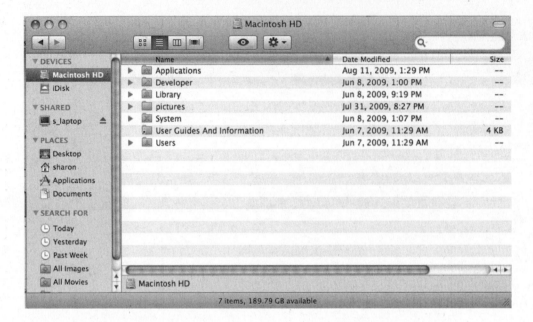

Figure 2.8b *Mac OS X Finder showing Macintosh HD selection.*

Let's look at the files and folders listing on the hard drive.

▶ In Windows, double-click on the **Local Disk** icon. The listing will appear as shown in Figure 2.9a.

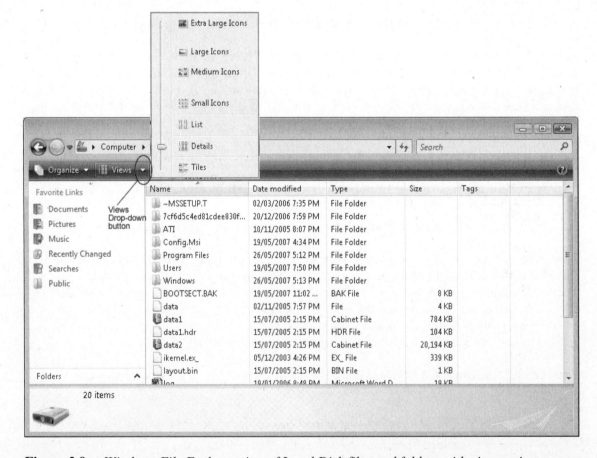

Figure 2.9a *Windows File Explorer view of Local Disk files and folders fwith view options menu.*

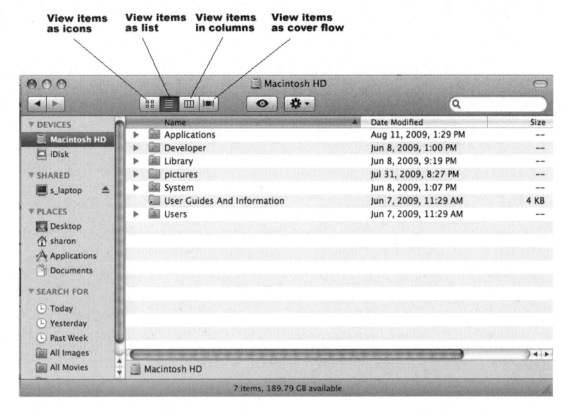

Figure 2.9b *Mac OS X Finder showing file listing options.*

Let's explore different methods available to view the listing.

> ▶ In File Explorer, click the **Views** button.

Notice that the slider indicator is pointing to the **Details** view. If your view is not **Details**, the slider will point to your current view. In Mac OS, notice that the current view is the List view. If your view is not the List view, click on the List button as shown in Figure 2.9b.

> ▶ In File Explorer, click the **Details** menu option to see the **Details** view.

Views are simply alternate ways of displaying files and folders. Let's look at the other views. In File Explorer, the **Tiles** and **Icons** views display the list with various sizes of icons. In Mac OS X, the icons view displays the items as icons.

> ▶ In File Explorer, click the **Views** button and click the **Tiles** menu option.
> ▶ In Mac OS X, click the icon view as shown in Figure 2.9b.

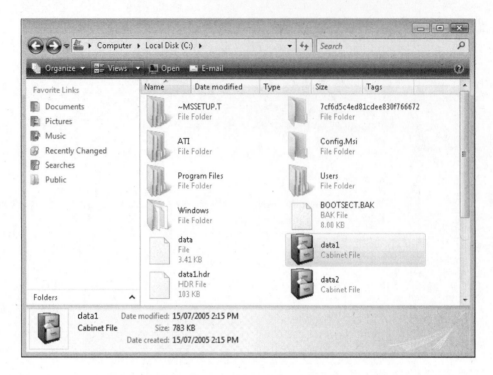

Figure 2.10a *Windows File Explorer Tiles view.*

The **Tiles** view is shown in Figure 2.10a and the icons view is shown in Figure 2.10b.

In File Explorer, notice that some of the files in the **Tiles** list display the date and time the file was created and the file size. We will discuss file size later.

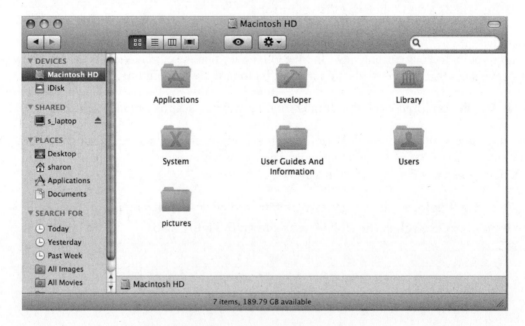

Figure 2.10b *Mac OS X Finder Icons view.*

Figure 2.11a *Windows File Explorer Medium Icons view.*

▶ In File Explorer, click the **Views** button click the **Medium Icons** menu item. You should notice icons that represent folders and files in this list, as shown in Figure 2.11a.

▶ In Mac OS X, click the Cover Flow button. You should notice that the icons display above the listing as shown in Figure 2.11b. You can drag the "covers" to scroll through the file listing as well as click on the file and folder names in the listing below the "covers."

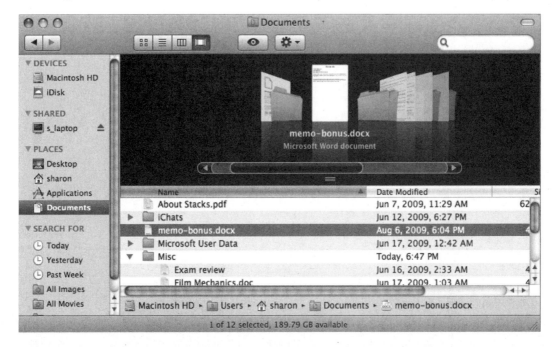

Figure 2.11b *Mac OS X Finder Cover Flow view.*

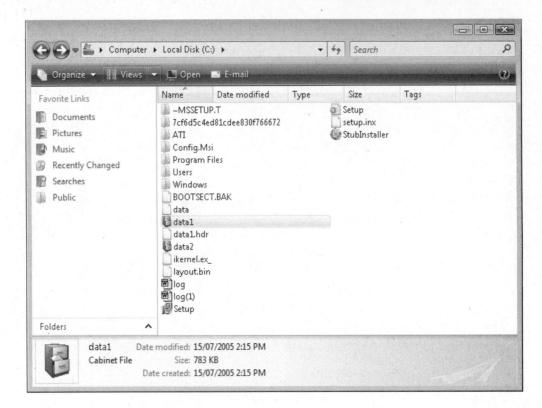

Figure 2.12a *Windows File Explorer List view.*

Icons are the small images such as the image of the folder, which represent files and folders.

▶ In File Explorer, click the **Views** button click the **List** menu item. You should notice that the folders and files are displayed in a vertical list, as shown in Figure 2.12a. This is similar to the icons view in Mac OS X.

▶ In Mac OS X click the Columns button. You should notice that the folders and files are displayed in columns as shown in Figure 2.12b.

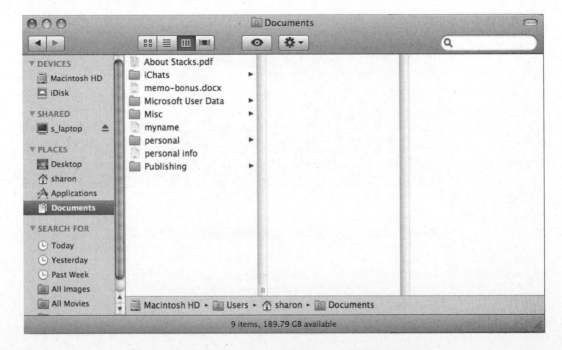

Figure 2.12b *Mac OS X Finder Columns view.*

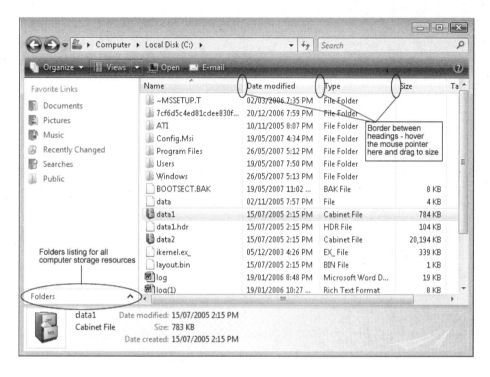

Figure 2.13a *Windows File Explorer Details view.*

Finally, let's look at the **Details** view.

► In File Explorer, click the **Views** button and click the **Details** menu item.
► In Mac OS X, click the **Details** button.

You should notice that the files and folders are displayed in a list, with information about file size, file type, and modified date, as shown in Figures 2.13a and 2.13b. If you cannot see all of the columns, drag the lower corner of the window to increase its size. The **Details** view provides a lot of information about the files and folders. Let's use this view and take a look at some of the other folders on the hard drive.

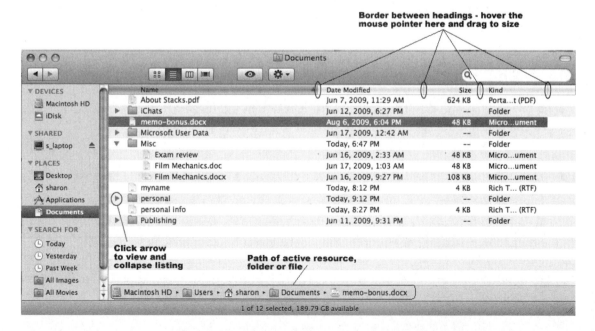

Figure 2.13b *Mac OS X Finder List view.*

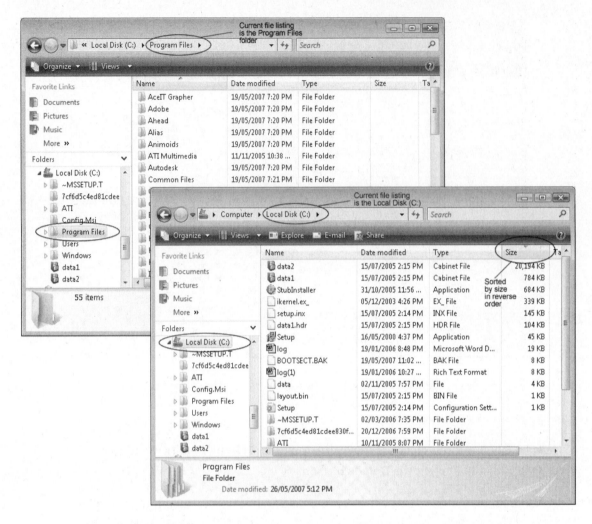

Figure 2.14a *Windows File Explorer showing Program Files folder listing.*

You can change the widths of the columns by positioning the mouse pointer at the border between headings in the pane on the right side of the window, as shown in Figures 2.13a and 2.13b.

> ▶ Move the mouse pointer so that it is resting on the border between two headings in the pane on the right side of the window. The mouse pointer should change to a double arrow symbol.
>
> ▶ When the mouse pointer is a double arrow symbol drag it to change the width of the column. Release the **mouse** button when you have adjusted the width of the column to your liking.

Folders that contain other folders are indicated by an arrow symbol to the left of the folder name.

> ▶ In File Explorer, click the **Program Files** folder in the left-hand pane if it is available. If the **Program Files** folder is not in your listing, click one of the other folder names. The **Program Files** listing will be displayed as shown in Figure 2.14a.
>
> ▶ In File Explorer, take a few minutes to click individual folder names to see the list of files in the folders you select.

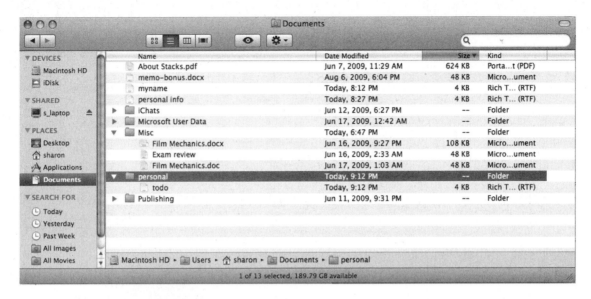

Figure 2.14b *Mac OS X Finder showing Documents folder listing.*

▶ In Mac OS X, take a few minutes to click on the arrow to the left of a folder to see a listing of files in the folder as shown in Figure 2.13b. Click the arrow again to collapse the folder listing.

▶ In File Explorer, click the Local Disk (C:) option in the Folders listing in the left-hand pane to see the listing for the Local Hard Drives as shown in Figure 2.14a.

At this point, we are simply viewing the contents of the folders and not affecting them. Occasionally you may find that you click on a folder and an error message indicates that you do not have permission to access the contents. Some folders contain system files that affect programs or the operating system. If this happens, simply select a different folder.

You can change the sort order of any column by clicking on the column heading. If the list is already sorted by that heading, clicking on the column heading again will reverse the sort order.

▶ Click the Name heading to reverse the sort order of file and folder names.

▶ Click the Size heading to list the folders and files by size. If your selected folder does not contain any files, you will not see any sizes listed.

▶ Click the Size heading again to list the folders and files by size, in reverse order. Your list should look something like that shown in Figures 2.14a and 2.14b.

▶ Similarly, click the other headings: Name, Type, and Date Modified, to change the list order.

File Size and Hard Drive Capacity

File size and hard drive capacity are measured in bytes. A byte contains a single character. Notice that some of the files in your file list indicate KB. A Kilobyte (KB) is 1,024 bytes, or roughly 1,000 characters. Hard drives, RAM memory, USB memory sticks, CDs, and DVDs hold data and their capacities are also measured in terms of bytes. However these media hold so much data, that we talk about storage in terms of Megabytes (MB) (millions of bytes) and Gigabytes (GB) (billions of bytes).

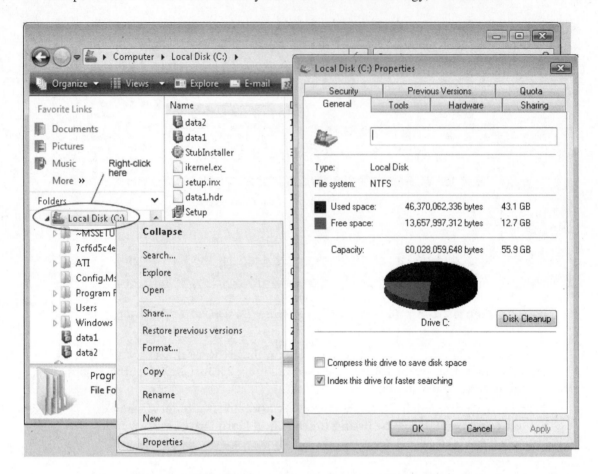

Figure 2.15a *Windows Vista Local Disk (C:) properties.*

Let's look at the capacity of your hard drive.

> ▶ In File Explorer, right-click the Local Drive (C:) icon in the Folders pane to reveal the short-cut menu, as shown in Figure 2.15a, and click the **Properties** menu item.
>
> ▶ In Mac OS X, click the Macintosh HD device and **hold the function key while you click the mouse** to reveal the shortcut menu. Click the **get info menu item** as shown in Figure 2.15b.

A dialog box should appear indicating the Local Disk C: or Macintosh HD properties, as shown in Figures 2.15a and 2.15b.

The hard drive properties in Figure 2.15a indicate that this drive has a total capacity of 55.9 GB. There is 43.1 GB of storage used and 12.7 GB of free space, which is storage available for storing more files. The hard drive properties in Figure 2.15b indicate that this drive has a total capacity of 232.57 GB. There is 42.78 GB of storage used. You may notice rounding errors in the calculation of storage capacity as is the case in Figure 2.15a. The total capacity indicated 55.9 GB yet the sum of Used and Free space is 55.8 GB. The difference of 0.1 GB is a rounding error caused by rounding Bytes to Gigabytes.

> ▶ In Windows, click the **OK** button to close the **Properties** dialog box.
> ▶ In Mac OS X, click the close button on the Macintosh HD Info window.

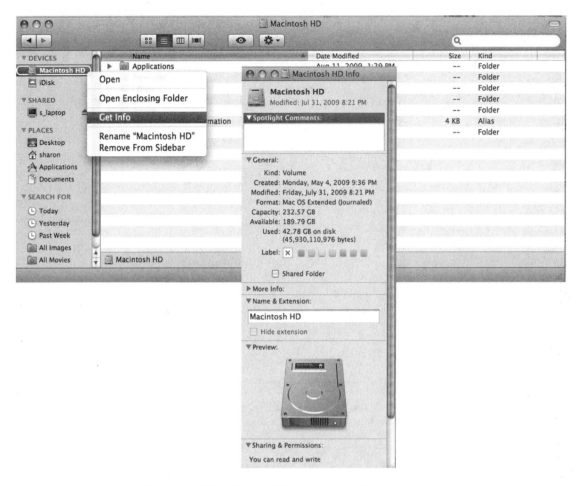

Figure 2.15b *Mac OS X Macintosh HD properties.*

Searching for Files

We've looked through folders on the hard drive and displayed the folders and file names in various ways. Let's look for a specific file.

At the beginning of this lab, we created several files. Where are they? We don't need to browse through folders until we find a specific file. We can use the Search feature to do the searching for us. Let's look for the personal info file we created at the beginning of this lab. Keep the File Explorer or Finder window open since we will use it to find the file.

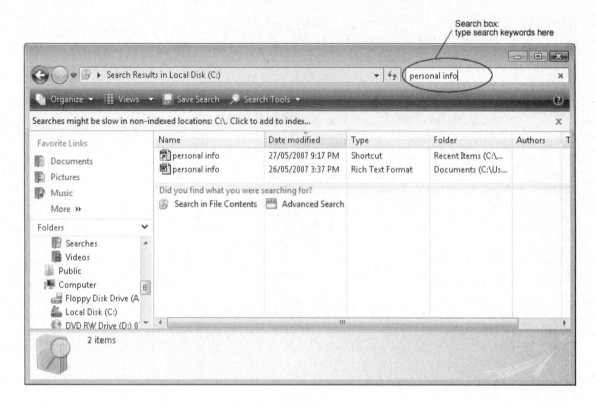

Figure 2.16a *Search Results in File Explorer.*

▶ In the **Search** box in the upper right corner of File Explorer or Finder, type: personal info. This is shown in Figures 2.16a and 2.16b.

As you type, notice that search items are displayed. As you type more characters, the search results become more specific.

There are several options available for searching.

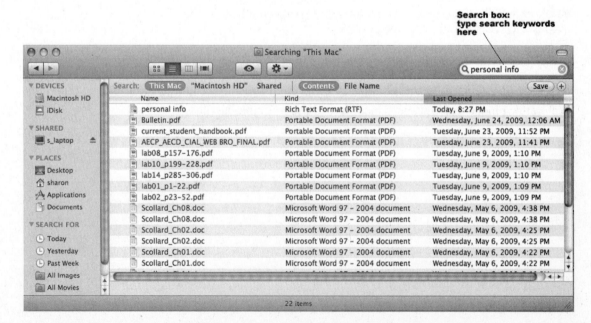

Figure 2.16b *Search Results in Finder.*

Figure 2.17 *Search option from the Vista Start menu.*

Let's look at another method for Windows only.

In Windows Only:

> ▶ Close the File Explorer window.
> ▶ Click the **Start** button as shown in Figure 2.17.

This search feature allows us to limit the search to specific types of files.

Let's search for a picture of a flower.

> ▶ Click the **Picture** button as shown in Figure 2.18 to confine the search to picture files.

You may notice that picture files appear already in the search results. Let's narrow this to pictures of flowers.

> ▶ Click in the search box and type: flower, as shown in Figure 2.18.

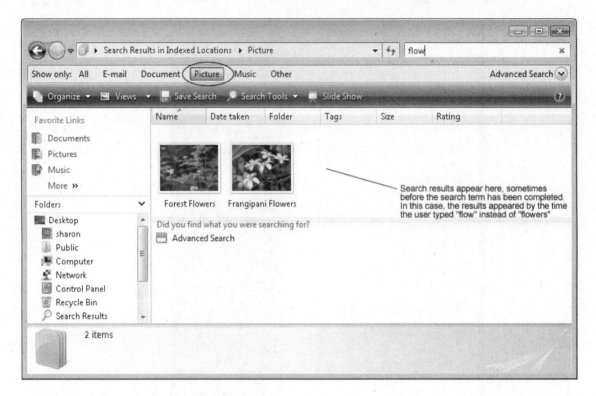

Figure 2.18 *Windows search Results window with flower picture search results.*

You may find the search results appear before you have completed typing the search term. The search results in Figure 2.18 appear using the **Medium Icon** view. Your search results may appear using other views as well.

When viewing files and folders, you can double-click a file to open it. Let's give that a try.

▶ Double-click one of the pictures.

Depending on the configuration of your computer, an image editing application will launch and the picture file will be displayed. The Windows operating system allows us to double-click a file name and the application package associated with that file type will open and the file will be displayed.

▶ Close the image editing application.

Let's close the **Search** Results window and return to the **File Explorer** window to view the **Documents** folder list.

▶ Close the **Search Results** window.

Opening Files Using File Explorer or Finder

▶ In Windows, click the **Start** button and the **Documents** menu choice to open the Documents listing in **Windows File Explorer**. Click the **Views** button and select the **Details** view.

▶ In Mac OS X, click the **Finder icon in the Dock.** Click **Documents** in the Places listing to list the files and folders in the Documents folder as shown in Figure 2.19b.

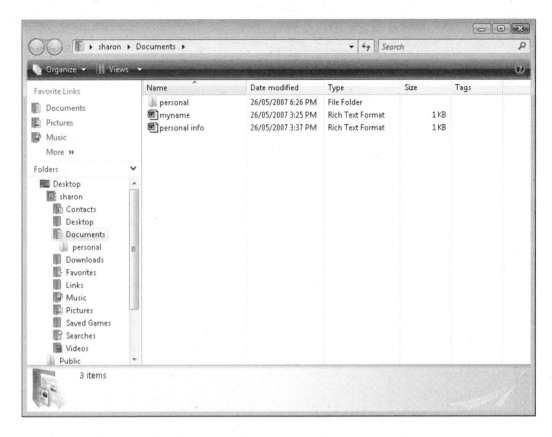

Figure 2.19a *Windows File Explorer displaying My Documents.*

You should see the **Documents** list as shown in Figures 2.19a and 2.19b.

In File Explorer we can see the folders in the pane on the right and the files in the pane on the left. In Finder, we can see a listing of folders and if the folders are expanded, we see the files listed below each folder.

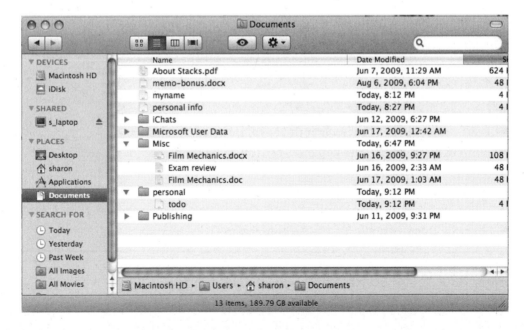

Figure 2.19b *Mac OS X Finder displaying Documents.*

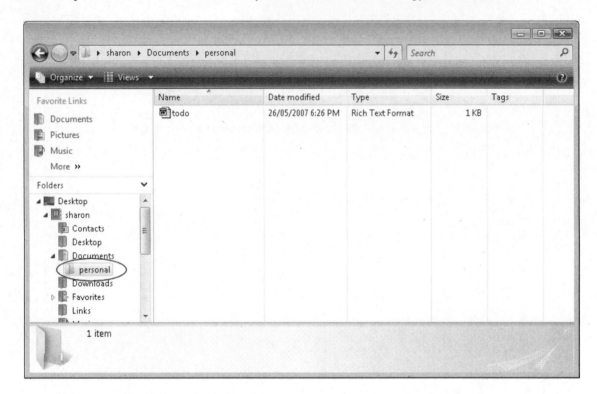

Figure 2.20 *Windows File Explorer displaying the personal folder.*

▶ In File Explorer, click the personal folder in the folder list pane on the left. You should see the todo file listed in the file list on the right, as shown in Figure 2.20.

▶ In Finder, if you cannot see the todo file in the listing, click the arrow to the left of the Personal folder to expand the folder listing.

Copying Files

It's useful to be able to copy and move files and folders. Regardless of how organized you think your files and folders are, at some point you'll want to reorganize some of them. We'll start by copying and moving files. The same techniques apply to folders.

Let's copy the todo.rtf file to the **Documents** folder. Currently it is in the personal folder only.

▶ In File Explorer or Finder, click the todo file once to select it.
▶ In File Explorer, click the **Organize** button to reveal a drop-down menu, as shown in Figure 2.21a.
▶ In File Explorer, click the **Copy** menu option.
▶ In Finder, click the menu options **Edit, Copy "todo"** as shown in Figure 2.21b.
▶ Click the **Documents** folder in the folder pane to activate it.

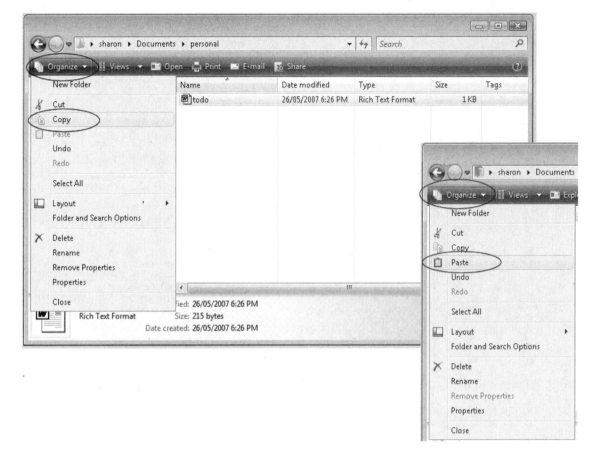

Figure 2.21a   *Windows File Explorer showing Organize menu options.*

▶ In File Explorer, click the **Organize** button to reveal a drop-down menu as shown in Figure 2.21a.

▶ In Finder, click the menu options **Edit, Paste Item** as shown in Figure 2.21b.

▶ In File Explorer, click the **Paste** menu option, as shown in Figure 2.21a.

You should notice that there is a copy of the todo file in the **Documents** folder.

Now we have two copies of the todo file. One copy is in the **Documents** folder and another copy is in the personal folder.

▶ In File Explorer, click the personal folder to verify that the original is still there.

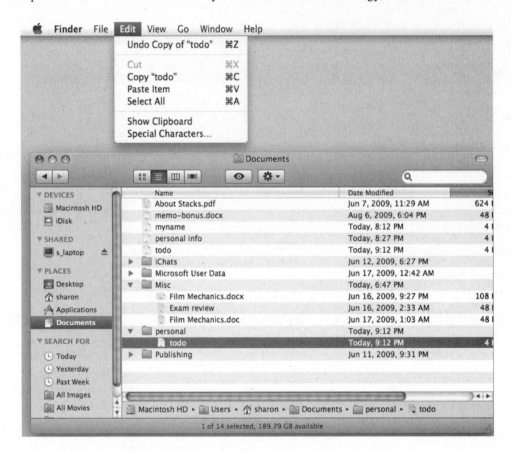

Figure 2.21b *Mac OS X Finder and File menu.*

Deleting Files

Let's delete the original todo file, which is in the personal folder.

> ► Click the todo file in the Personal folder once to select it.
> ► In File Explorer, press the **Delete** key on the keyboard.

A confirmation box will appear, as shown in Figure 2.22.

When we delete a file from the hard drive, Windows places it in the Recycle Bin. In Mac OS X, you need to drag the file to the Trash bin in order to delete it. This gives us a chance to recover it or delete it permanently later. In Windows, we'll send the todo file to the Recycle Bin, recover it, and then permanently delete it. In Mac OS X, we'll drag the file to the Trash bin, then drag it out of the Trash bin to recover it.

> ► In Windows, click the **Yes** button to send the todo file to the Recycle Bin.
> ► In Mac OS X, drag the todo file from the Finder window to the Trash as shown in Figure 2.22b.

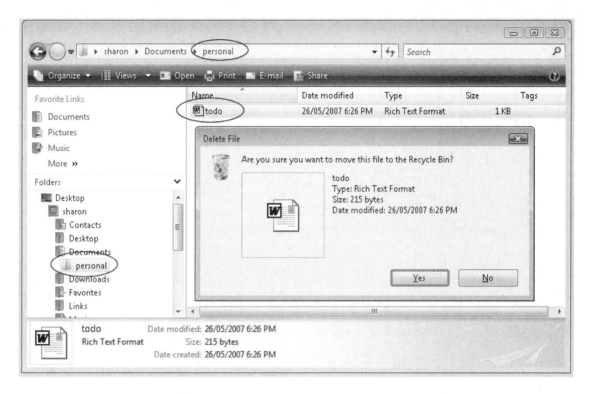

Figure 2.22a   *Windows File Explorer Delete File confirmation.*

You should notice that the todo file has been removed from the personal folder list. Let's find it in the Recycle Bin or Trash list. The Recycle Bin is available as an icon on the Windows desktop as well as in the File Explorer list. The Trash icon is on the Dock.

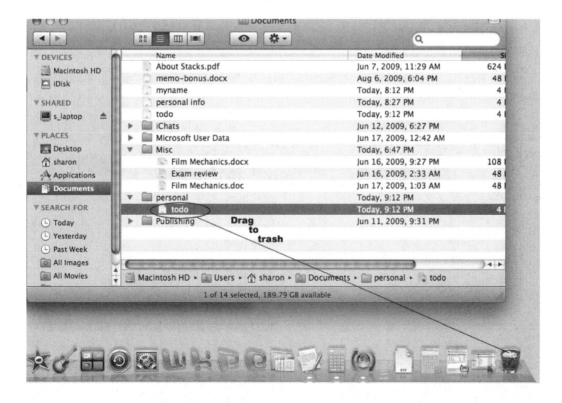

Figure 2.22b   *Mac OS X Finder and Trash.*

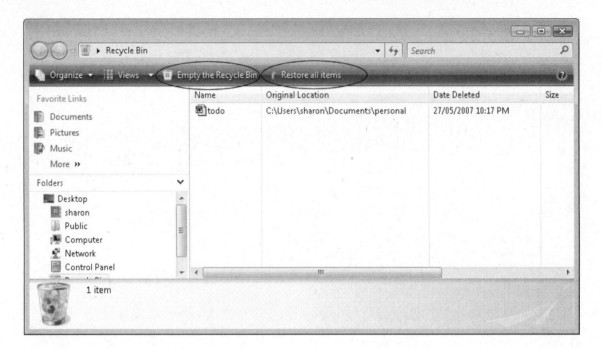

Figure 2.23a *Windows Recycle Bin list.*

► Minimize or move the windows so you can see the Recycle Bin or Trash icon.

► In Windows, double-click the Recycle Bin icon to open it.

► In Mac OS X, click the Trash icon on the Dock.

The Recycle Bin list should be similar to that shown in Figure 2.23a. The Trash list should be similar to that shown in Figure 2.23b.

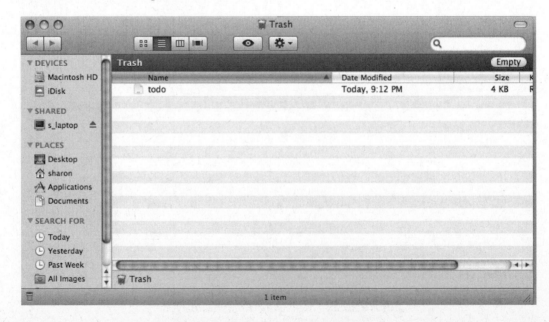

Figure 2.23b *Mac OS X Trash listing.*

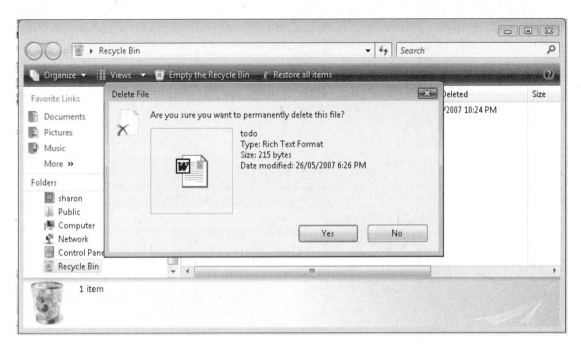

Figure 2.24a *Windows Recycle Bin Confirm Delete box.*

Restoring Files from the Recycle Bin in Windows

In Windows only, notice that there are options available in the Recycle Bin Tasks list that include "Empty the Recycle Bin" and "Restore all items." You can perform these tasks that apply to all files in the Recycle Bin, or you can select individual files to restore or delete permanently.

▶ Click the todo file in the file list pane.

Notice that the "Restore all items" option has changed to "Restore this item."

▶ In Windows, click the "Restore this item" option in the Recycle Bin Tasks list.

Notice that the todo file has disappeared from the list. It's back in the personal folder as before. It has been restored to its original location and removed from the Recycle Bin. Let's verify this.

▶ Close the Recycle Bin window.
▶ Activate the File Explorer window and click the personal folder in the **Documents** list. Notice that the todo file has been restored to the personal folder.

Restoring Files from the Trash in Mac OS X

In Mac OS X, you can drag the files in the Trash to other folders. Let's drag the todo file back to the Personal folder.

▶ Position the Finder and Trash windows so you can see the file listings, as shown in Figure 2.24b.
▶ **Drag the todo file** from the Trash window to the personal file in the Finder window as shown in Figure 2.24b.

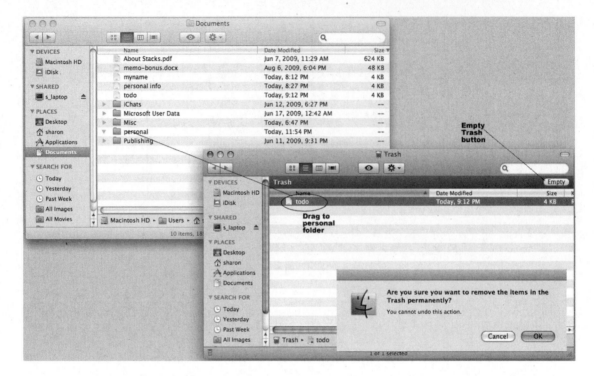

Figure 2.24b *Mac OS X dragging file from Trash and emptying Trash.*

Deleting Files Permanently from the Recycle Bin in Windows

Let's delete the todo file again, but this time we will remove it permanently.

▶ In File Explorer or Finder, click the todo file once to select it.

▶ Press the **Delete** key on the keyboard. In Windows, the **Confirm File Delete** box should appear again, as shown in Figure 2.22.

▶ In Windows, click the **Yes** button to send the todo file to the Recycle Bin.

▶ In Windows, double-click the Recycle Bin icon on the desktop to open the Recycle Bin.

▶ In Mac OS X, click the Trash on the Doc to open the Trash window.

Again, notice that the todo file appears in the Recycle Bin list or Trash window.

▶ In Windows, click the "Empty the Recycle Bin" option in the Recycle Bin Tasks. The **Confirm File Delete** box will appear as shown in Figure 2.24a.

▶ In Mac OS X, click the Empty button in the Trash window as shown in Figure 2.24b. A confirmation box will appear as shown in Figure 2.24b.

▶ In Windows, click the **Yes** button to empty the Recycle Bin.

▶ In Mac OS X, click the **OK** button to empty the Trash.

The todo file is now deleted permanently from the personal folder.

▶ Close the Recycle Bin or Trash window.

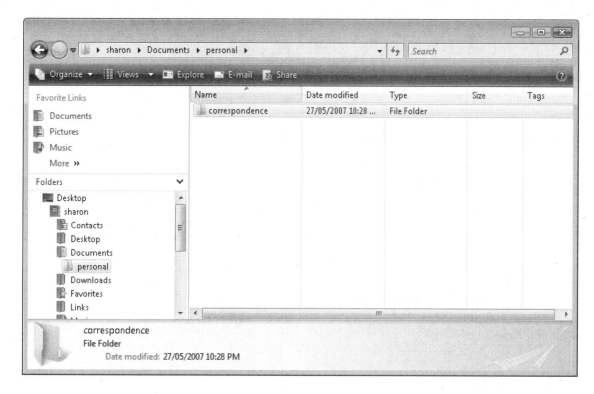

Figure 2.25a   *Windows File Explorer showing the personal folder and correspondence subfolder.*

You can delete and restore folders using the same method used to delete files. When you delete a folder, you also delete all of the contents in the folder. If the folder includes subfolders, they are deleted, as well as the files that are contained within them.

Creating Folders and Moving Files

Let's finish this lab by creating some folders and moving some files.

▶ In the File Explorer or Finder window, click the personal folder to activate it. The personal folder may be activated already.

▶ In File Explorer, click the **Organize** button and select the menu item **New Folder**.

▶ In Mac OS X, double-click the personal folder to view the personal folder listing, as shown in Figure 2.25b.

▶ In Mac OS X, click the menu items File, New Folder, as shown in Figure 2.25b.

This creates a new folder inside the active folder. In this case, the new folder is created in the personal folder. The new folder will be selected and we can edit the name. This same technique was used when we created the personal folder while saving a file using WordPad or TextEdit.

▶ Type: correspondence.

▶ Press the **Enter** key on the keyboard.

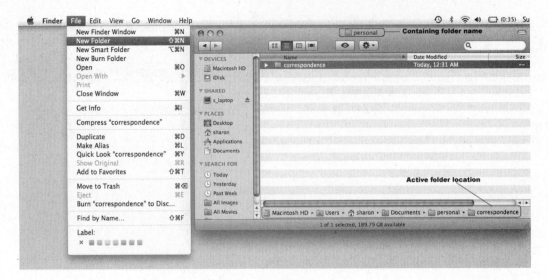

Figure 2.25b *Mac OS X Finder and new folder.*

You have created a new folder called "correspondence," which is a subfolder of "personal," as shown in Figures 2.25a and 2.25b.

Let's move some of the files into the personal and correspondence folders.

Moving Files Using Cut and Paste in File Explorer Only

Let's move the myname file into the correspondence folder.

▶ Click the **Documents** folder in the Folders pane to activate it.
▶ Click the myname file in the file list pane to activate it.
▶ Click the **Organize** button and select the **Cut** option, as shown in Figure 2.26a.

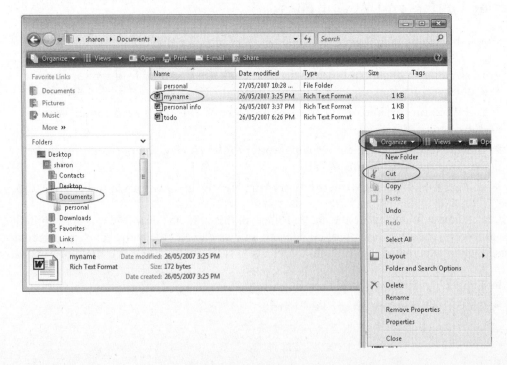

Figure 2.26a *Windows File Explorer showing the Documents folder and the Organize button drop-down menu.*

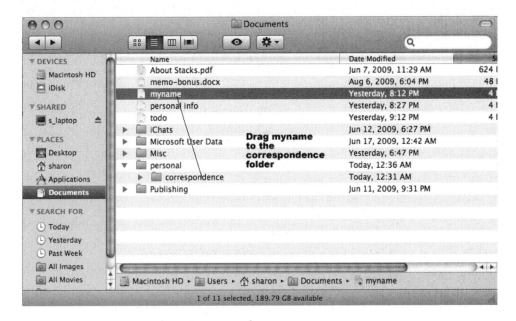

Figure 2.26b *Mac OS X Finder showing file dragging technique.*

▶ Double-click the personal folder to open it.

▶ Double-click the correspondence folder to open it.

▶ Click the **Organize** button and select the **Paste** option.

Notice that the myname file now appears in the correspondence folder list. You can click the **Documents** folder name to verify that the myname file is no longer in the list of **Documents**.

Moving Files Using Drag and Drop in Mac OS X Only

Let's move the myname file using a drag and drop technique. This technique will also work in Windows File Explorer.

▶ In Finder, click on Documents to view the Documents file and folder listing as shown in Figure 2.26b.

This lab has demonstrated some basic features and methods for viewing folder contents and file lists. It has also demonstrated some simple methods for copying and moving single files. It's also possible to select multiple files and move and copy them as a group but this is beyond the scope of this lab.

Review

This has been a busy lab! We have covered the following topics:

- Saving files to a specific folder location in an application (WordPad or TextEdit)
- Creating a folder in the **Save As** window
- Using Windows File Explorer and Mac Finder
    - Choosing different views: tiles, icons, list, and details
    - File size and hard drive capacity
- Using the search feature to find files and folders
- Using Windows File Explorer and Finder to create folders

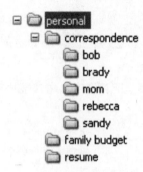

Figure 2.27 *Folders and subfolders.*

- Using copy and paste to copy a file to a different folder location
- Using cut and paste to move a file to a different folder location
- Using the Recycle Bin and Trash
      Restoring files that have been deleted
      Deleting files permanently

Exercises

1. Create the following folder structure. You can use Windows File Explorer or Mac Finder to create the folders and subfolders shown in Figure 2.27. You have already created the personal and correspondence folders.

2. Copy the myname file into the following folders: bob, mom, sandy.

3. Move the myname file from the bob folder to the resume folder.

4. Delete the myname file from the sandy folder.

5. In Windows, restore the myname file using the Recycle Bin restore feature. In Mac OS X, restore the myname file by dragging it back to the sandy folder.

Word Processing Basics Using Microsoft Word

Objectives:

Upon successful completion of Lab 3, you will be able to

- Use Word to create a simple word processing document
- Understand the concept of word wrapping and when it is appropriate to press the **Enter** key for a new line
- Format text fragments and paragraphs
  Bold, italic, underline, font face, font size, and font color
  Paragraph alignment options: left, center, right, and justify
- Use the Search and Replace feature to find text and replace it with substitute text
- Use the Spell Check feature to correct misspelled words
  Understand that proper names and other correctly spelled words are not in the Spell Check dictionary

Resources required:

- A computer running any version of Microsoft Word for PC or Mac

Starter files:

- None

Prerequisite skills:

- Basic familiarity with using a mouse to point, click, double-click and drag, and basic familiarity with using a keyboard
- Windows manipulation skills—open, close, size, drag, maximize, minimize, and restore
- Basic familiarity with saving, finding, and opening files

NRC's Top Ten Skills, Concepts, and Capabilities:

- Skills
  Use a word processor to create a document
  - Data entry
  - Formatting—text/paragraphs
  - Search/replace
  - Spell Check

- Concepts
  Fundamentals of computers—word processing
- Capabilities
  Think abstractly about Information Technology—building generic word processing concepts

Lab Lesson

Most people who use a computer daily use word processing skills. Word processing skills allow us to prepare text documents such as letters, memos, and other correspondence. In the past we would have used a typewriter. In the 1970s, the typewriter evolved into a word processing system, which could be as simple as an electric typewriter with a small screen display, or an old fashioned green screen computer. Today, the term "word processing" basically means creating a text document and using a computer and word processing software such as Word. Just to make things a little more confusing, most modern word processing software allows us to create text documents that include pictures and drawings.

Let's use Word to learn some basic word processing skills.

▶ Open Word, as shown in Figures 3.1a and 3.1b.

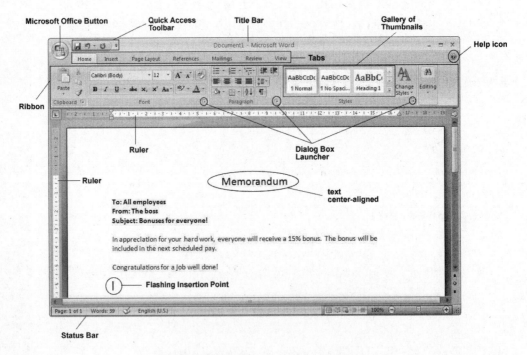

Figure 3.1a *Word window for PC.*

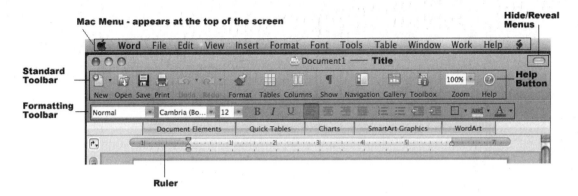

Figure 3.1b *Word window for Mac.*

Figures 3.1a and 3.1b show the Word window for PC and Mac. This view displays rulers at the top and along the left side which indicate the size of the page. The document is displayed as it will look when printed. This type of display is referred to as **WYSIWYG** (What You See Is What You Get). Older versions of word processing software displayed the text only without proper formatting, but modern word processing software displays the document as it will look when it is printed.

The ribbon and tabs are positioned at the top of the window. The position of these can be changed, so your window may look slightly different. If you are using a Mac and the toolbars are not displayed, click the Hide/Reveal Menus button as shown in Figure 3.1b. If the formatting toolbar is not displayed, click the View, Toolbars, Formatting menu items.

▶ Position the mouse pointer over one of the toolbar buttons.

After a moment, you should see the name of the toolbar button and a description pop up. This way you don't have to remember which button is which.

The ruler may be visible or hidden so you may not see it in your window. The status bar indicates the page number and other information about the document. The flashing insertion point indicates where the text will appear when typed. Some people refer to this as the **cursor**.

Let's create the document shown in Figure 3.1. First, let's ensure that the document is displayed in the print layout view so that the margins are displayed.

▶ Click the **View** tab.
▶ Click the **Print Layout** button (PC) or menu item (Mac) as shown in Figures 3.2a and 3.2b.

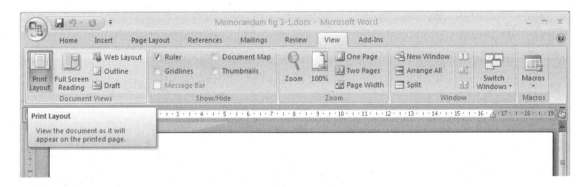

Figure 3.2a *Word View menu for PC.*

Figure 3.2b *Word View menu for Mac.*

If your window was already in **Print Layout** view, you will not see a change.

The flashing insertion point should be positioned in the upper left corner of the document area of the Word window, as shown in Figures 3.3a and 3.3b.

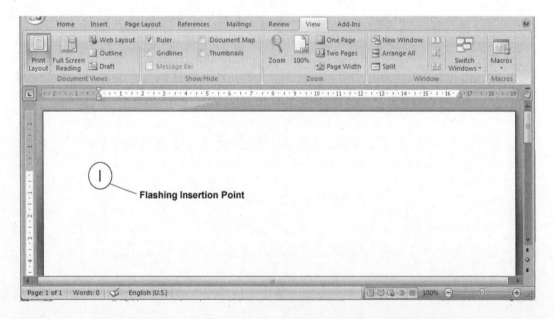

Figure 3.3a *Windows showing flashing insertion point for PC.*

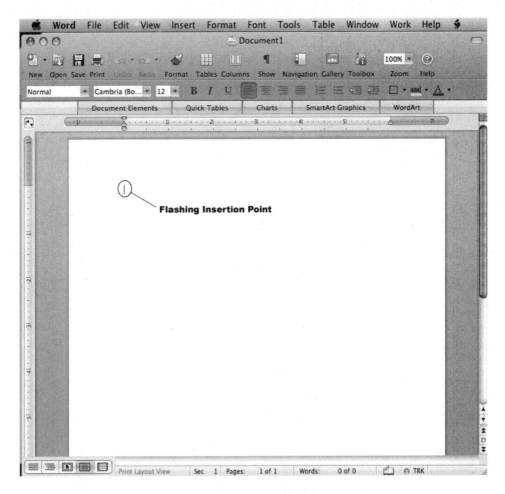

Figure 3.3b *Windows showing flashing insertion point for Mac.*

You will find that the text appears at the flashing insertion point when you type. If you make a mistake while you're typing, you can press the **Backspace** key (PC) or **Delete** key (Mac) to delete characters to the left of the flashing insertion point. Let's try some quick keyboard skills. If you're already comfortable using the **Backspace**, **Delete**, **Shift**, **Caps Lock**, and **Arrow** keys, feel free to skip the Keyboard Skills section and continue to the Data Entry section.

Keyboard Skills

No need to worry about typing errors! We can fix them all. Let's look at some techniques to edit text.

▶ Type your name. To type an uppercase letter, hold the **Shift** key down while you type the letter. If you type an incorrect letter, press the **Backspace** key (PC) or **Delete** key (Mac) to delete it.

▶ Press the **Enter** key to move the flashing insertion point down one line.

▶ Press the **Caps Lock** key. You may see a light on your keyboard indicating that the **Caps Lock** key is active.

▶ Type your name. Notice that your name has been typed in all uppercase letters.

▶ Press the **Caps Lock** key to turn off the caps lock feature.

▶ Press the **Backspace** key (PC) or **Delete** key (Mac) a few times. Notice that the characters to the left of the flashing insertion point are deleted.

▶ Press and hold down the letter "a" on the keyboard for a few seconds. It will repeat the letter. This repeat feature is available for most of the keys on the keyboard, including the **Backspace** key (PC) or **Delete** key (Mac).

▶ Press the **Enter** key twice to move the flashing insertion point down.

▶ Type your address.

▶ Move the mouse pointer to your name and highlight it to select it. You can highlight it by dragging (hold the **left mouse** button while you move the mouse, and release the button to finish).

When text is highlighted in this way, it is selected.

▶ Press the letter "a" on the keyboard.

Notice that your name was replaced with the letter "a".

▶ Move the mouse pointer to your address, between the number and the street name.

▶ Click the **left mouse** button once to position the flashing insertion point at the mouse pointer position. Using this method we can position the flashing insertion point anywhere in a document.

▶ Press the letter "a" key on the keyboard.

Notice that the letter "a" is automatically inserted to the left of the insertion point.

▶ Press the left **Arrow** key on the keyboard.

Notice that the flashing insertion point moves one character to the left but does not delete. The arrow keys can be used to move the flashing insertion point through the document without affecting the text.

▶ On the PC, press the **Delete** key on the keyboard. On the Mac, hold the **fn** key while you tap the **Delete** key on the keyboard.

Notice that the character to the right of the flashing insertion point was deleted.

▶ Press the left, right, up, and down arrows on the keyboard to see how the flashing insertion point moves through the text. Feel free to hold the arrow keys down for a few seconds and notice that the movements repeat.

Now that we've learned or reviewed a few keyboard skills, let's delete all of the text.

▶ Drag through all of the text to select it. You can start at the top-left or the bottom-right and drag to the opposite corner to select all of the text.

▶ Press the **Delete** key to delete all of the selected text.

Data Entry

Let's create a sample document.

▶ Type: Memorandum

▶ Press the **Enter** key.

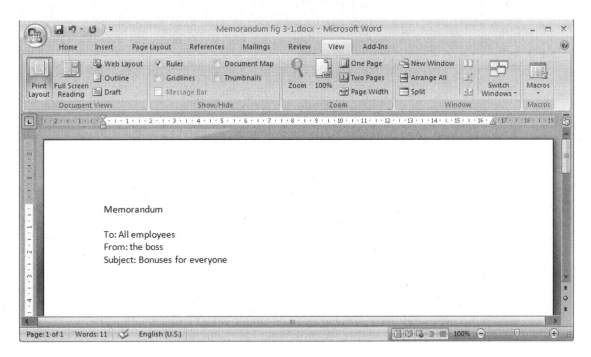

Figure 3.4 *Word, Memorandum document data entry.*

Notice that the flashing insertion point is now positioned under the Memorandum text. Pressing the **Enter** key moves the insertion point down to the next line.

▶ Press the **Enter** key.

Notice that the flashing insertion point has moved down another line. This gives us a blank line between the Memorandum title and the rest of the text.

▶ Type: To: All employees
▶ Press the **Enter** key.
▶ Type: From: the boss
▶ Press the **Enter** key.
▶ Type: Subject: Bonuses for everyone
▶ Press the **Enter** key.

Your document should look something like that shown in Figure 3.4.

▶ Press the **Enter** key twice.

Next, we will type a paragraph. When typing a paragraph, do not press the **Enter** key while you type the paragraph. The words will automatically wrap to the next line as appropriate. If you press the **Enter** key at the end of each line in a paragraph, and later decide to change the page margins, you will find that the paragraph will not wrap properly. The **Enter** key should be pressed only when you are entering a title or short line as we have done already, or when you need a blank line between paragraphs.

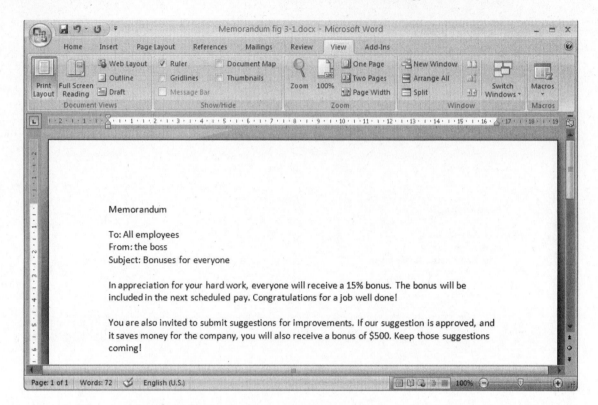

Figure 3.5 *Word, Memorandum document with paragraphs.*

▶ Type the following paragraph:

> In appreciation for your hard work, everyone will receive a 15% bonus. The bonus will be included in the next scheduled pay. Congratulations for a job well done!

▶ Press the **Enter** key twice. We will add another paragraph.

▶ Type the following paragraph:

> You are also invited to submit suggestions for improvements. If your suggestion is approved, and it saves money for the company, you will also receive a bonus of $500. Keep those suggestions coming!

Your document should look something like that shown in Figure 3.5.

The information in our document is very plain. Let's use some formatting features to add some interest and clarity.

Alignment

Let's start by centering the Memorandum title.

▶ On the PC, click the **Home** tab. On the Mac, do nothing.

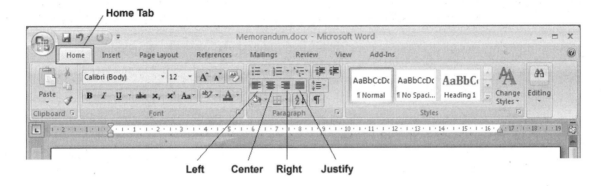

Figure 3.6a *Word alignment buttons for PC.*

You will find the alignment buttons on the toolbar, as shown in Figures 3.6a and 3.6b.

We can use the alignment buttons to align titles, single lines of text, whole paragraphs, and pictures.

> ▶ Position the flashing insertion point anywhere in the Memorandum title. You can position the flashing insertion point using the arrow keys on the keyboard, or by moving the mouse pointer and clicking once.
> ▶ Click the **Center** alignment button to center the Memorandum title.

> > The other alignment options include Left, Right, and Justify. Text is left-aligned by default. This means that the left edge of the text is flush with the left margin. This paragraph is left-aligned.
> >
> > A paragraph that is right-aligned has the right edges of each line flush with the right margin. This paragraph is right-aligned. It is a bit more difficult to read, and this type of alignment is generally used for a small amount of text.
> >
> > Justify alignment adds spaces between the words in the paragraph so that both the right and left edges are flush with the margins. This paragraph is justify-aligned. This type of alignment is popular for newspapers and newsletters.
> >
> > > An entire paragraph can also be center-aligned. This paragraph is center-aligned. Notice that each line of the paragraph is centered. A paragraph that is center-aligned is also difficult to read. Most often center-alignment is used for short lines of text, such as titles.

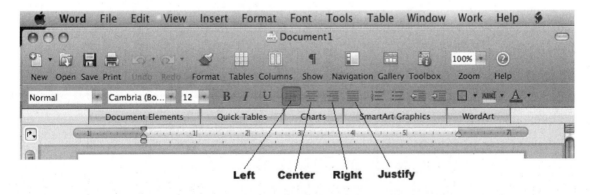

Figure 3.6b *Word alignment buttons for Mac.*

Let's look at the alignment options using one of the paragraphs in the Memorandum document.

> ► Position the flashing insertion point anywhere in the paragraph that begins with "In appreciation . . ."
> ► Click the **Right-align** button.

Notice that the paragraph is now right-aligned. Notice also that the other text in the document was not affected.

> ► Click the **Center-align** button.

Notice that the paragraph is now center-aligned, and the rest of the text in the documents is not affected.

> ► Click the **Justify-align** button.

Notice that the paragraph is now justify-aligned and looks more like a newspaper column. Again, none of the other text is affected.

> ► Click the **Left-align** button.

Notice that the paragraph is left-aligned once again.

The Ribbon (for PC only)

In Word 2007 for PC, you can minimize the ribbon. The ribbon is not available in other versions of Word. In other versions, only the menu is available. Let's minimize the ribbon and display it again.

> ► On the PC, right-click anywhere along the ribbon. The menu should appear as shown in Figure 3.7.
> ► On the PC, click the menu item: **Minimize the Ribbon**.

Notice that the ribbon has disappeared and only the menu remains.

> ► On the PC, right-click on one of the menu tabs to reveal the shortcut menu.
> ► On the PC, click the menu item: **Minimize the Ribbon**.

The ribbon should be visible again.

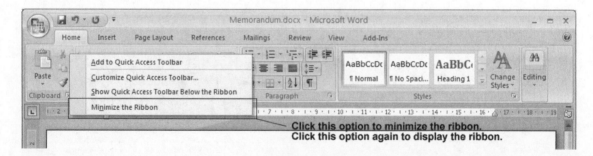

Figure 3.7 *Word toolbar customize dialog box.*

Undo and Redo

The undo feature will allow you to undo a task such as formatting. It will also allow you to undo several tasks, effectively rolling back the document task by task.

> ▶ Click the **Undo** button . located in the upper-left corner of the Word window (PC) or on the standard toolbar (Mac).

Notice that the paragraph is justify-aligned again. The Undo feature "undid" the previous task, which had left-aligned the paragraph. Clicking on the drop-down arrow beside the **Undo** button will reveal a task list. If you select one of the tasks, Word will undo all tasks up to and including the one selected.

> ▶ Click the Redo button , located in the upper-left corner of the Word window (PC) or on the standard toolbar (Mac).

Notice that the paragraph alignment is "redone" so that it is left-aligned again.

The undo and redo features are tremendously useful, but despite these features it's important to save your document often.

Save a Document

Let's save our memorandum document.

> ▶ Click on the **Save** button located in the upper-left corner of the Word window (PC) or on the standard toolbar (Mac).

The **Save As** dialog box should appear as shown in Figures 3.8a and 3.8b.

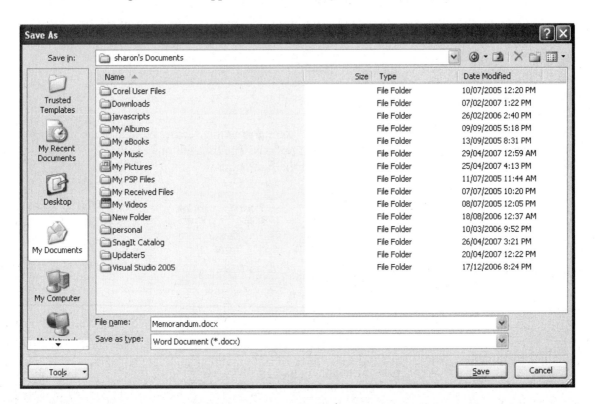

Figure 3.8a *Word Save As dialog box for PC.*

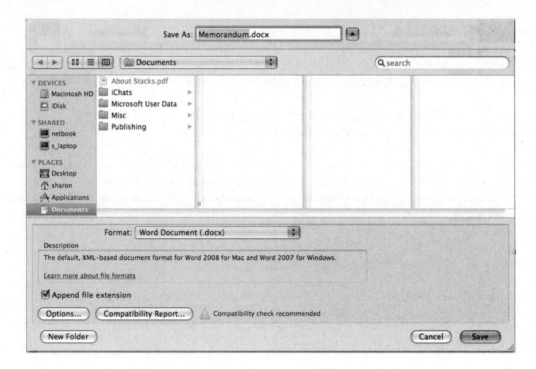

Figure 3.8b   *Word Save As dialog box for Mac.*

Notice that Word has used the first line of text from the document as a suggestion for the file name. The file save location in this example is the **Documents** folder, in both the PC and the Mac.

▶ Delete the Memorandum.docx name from the **File name** box.

▶ In the **File name** box type: memo-bonus

▶ Click the **Save** button to save the file. It will be saved as memo_bonus.docx

As you would expect, you can save changes to the file by clicking on the **Save** button.

Text Formatting

The text in our document is very plain. Let's add some formatting features to add some interest and emphasis. We've already used the alignment buttons. The font buttons are displayed in Figures 3.9a and 3.9b. We will use only a few of the font features.

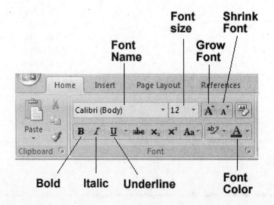

Figure 3.9a   *Word formatting toolbar for PC.*

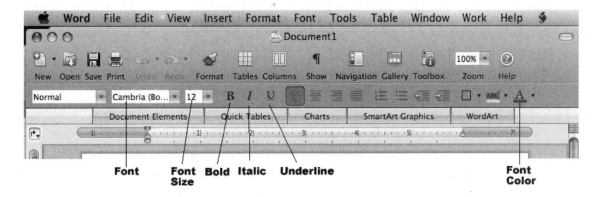

Figure 3.9b   *Word formatting toolbar for Mac.*

► Use the mouse to drag through the Memorandum title to select the title.

► Click the **Bold** button to add bold formatting. Since the text is selected, you may notice that the text appears dark and slightly larger.

► Move the mouse pointer to one of the paragraphs and click to position the flashing insertion point away from the Memorandum title.

Clicking somewhere else in the document removes the selection highlighting. Notice that the Memorandum title is darker.

You can use the **Bold** button to remove the bold formatting as well.

► Drag through the Memorandum title to select it.

► Click the **Bold** button to remove bold formatting.

► Deselect the text as before by moving the mouse pointer to one of the paragraphs and click to position the flashing insertion point away from the Memorandum title.

Notice that the text has returned to normal without bold formatting. Let's use the undo feature to re-apply the bold formatting.

► Click the **Undo** button to undo the last task. Notice that the text is bold again.

We can apply formatting to a large block of text rather than to one word or line at a time.

► Drag through the To: From: and Subject: text to select it. The selected text is shown in Figure 3.10.

Memorandum

To: All employees
From: the boss
Subject: Bonuses for everyone

In appreciation for your hard work, everyone will receive a 15% bonus. The bonus will be included in the next scheduled pay. Congratulations for a job well done!

Figure 3.10   *Word Memorandum document with selected text.*

▶ Release the mouse button and move the mouse pointer to the right. On the PC you should see a toolbar appear, as shown in Figure 3.10. On the Mac, use the buttons on the standard toolbar.

▶ Click the **Bold** button on the toolbar to add bold formatting.

Similarly we can add italic and underline. Let's add these formatting enhancements to other parts of the document.

▶ Drag through "hard work" in the first paragraph to select it.

▶ Click the **Italic** button on the ribbon bar, standard toolbar or on the shortcut toolbar to add italic style to the text. Notice that the text is slanted to the right.

Italic formatting slants the characters. Use this sparingly in documents. It is suitable for emphasis, but it slows down the reader.

▶ Drag through "15% bonus" in the first paragraph to select it.

▶ Click the **Underline** button to add underlining to the text. Notice that the text has a thin underline.

As we saw with the **Bold** formatting, the italic and underline formatting can also be applied or removed by clicking again on the corresponding buttons. Formatting can also be combined. Let's add italic formatting to the Memorandum title.

▶ Drag through the Memorandum title to select it.

▶ Click the **Italic** button to apply italic formatting. Notice that the Memorandum title is slanted.

Font

In addition to adding style enhancements such as bold and italic to the text, we can also change the typeface and the size. The typeface (character set) is referred to as the **font**. You will have a variety of fonts available to choose from. Some are installed with Word, and others are installed by other applications packages you may have. There are also free fonts available for download from Web sites. Although there are a few fonts common to most computer systems, the list of available fonts varies greatly from one computer system to another. No need to worry, though. You will see the list, and examples of the fonts from which you can choose! Let's change the font for the Memorandum title.

▶ If the Memorandum title is not already selected, drag through it to select it.

▶ Click the drop-down arrow on the **Font** box, as shown in Figure 3.11, to see the available font listing.

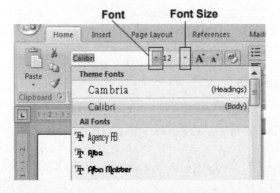

Figure 3.11a *Word Font and Font Size for PC.*

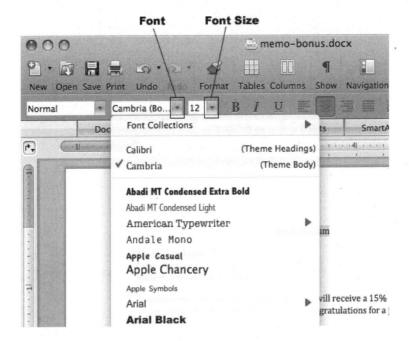

Figure 3.11b *Word Font and Font Size for Mac.*

The Memorandum title uses Cambria. You will notice that each font name is also a sample of the font itself. So you don't have to wonder what the font looks like before you select it.

> ► Feel free to take a few minutes to explore the font list available on your system. Use the scroll bar or move the mouse pointer up and down to scroll through the list. Select a few different fonts, one at a time, and they will be applied to the Memorandum title.
>
> ► After you've finished exploring, select Arial from the font list. If Arial is not available, feel free to select a font you like.

Let's increase the size of the title as well, since it's an important part of the document. Font size is measured in points. An inch is 72 points, so a font that is 72 points has characters that are one inch tall. A good size for readable text is 10 or 12 point. Headings might be 16 or 20 point.

> ► If the Memorandum title is not already selected, drag through it to select it.
> ► Click the drop-down arrow for Font Size.
> ► Select 16 from the Font Size list.

Notice that the font is larger.

In addition to size and font, we can also change the color. In order to print in color, the document must be printed using a color printer. Let's add a splash of color to our document.

> ► Drag through the text "Congratulations for a job well done!" to select it.
> ► Click the drop-down arrow for Font Color as shown in Figures 3.12a and 3.12b.

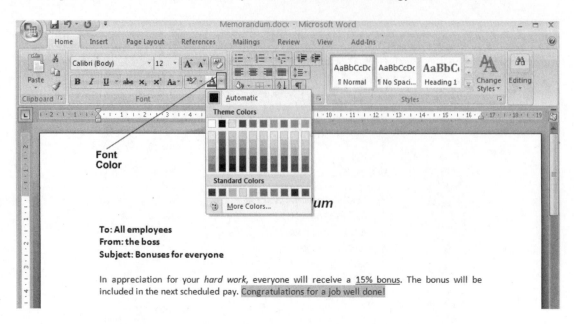

Figure 3.12a *Word Font Color and color palette for PC.*

This reveals a color palette, which is also displayed in Figures 3.12a and 3.12b.

▶ Click on one of the red swatches from the color palette.

Since the text is selected, the characters may appear red or may appear highlighted. We will see the red color when the text is no longer selected.

▶ Click somewhere else in the document to deselect the text. Now you should see the red color has been applied to the text.

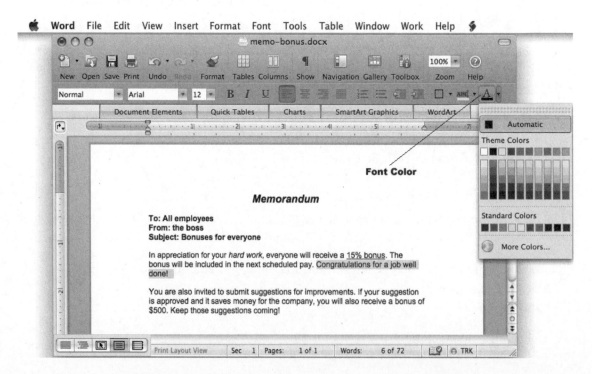

Figure 3.12b *Word Font Color and color palette for Mac.*

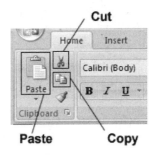

Figure 3.13a *Word Cut, Copy, and Paste buttons for PC.*

Cut, Copy, and Paste

One of the strengths of using word processing software to compose a document is the ability to edit. We have practiced using the **Delete** and, **Backspace** (on the PC), keys, which are useful for editing as we type. If we wish to copy or move blocks of text we can do this using the **Cut**, **Copy**, and **Paste** methods.

Let's move the "Congratulations for a job well done!" text to the bottom of the document. We can move an item using the cut and paste method. On the PC, we will use the **Cut**, **Copy**, and **Paste** buttons as shown in Figure 3.13a. These buttons are located on the standard toolbar. On the Mac, we will use the Edit menu, and options Cut, Copy, and Paste, as shown in Figure 3.13b. The PC version also has the Edit menu with the options Cut, Copy and Paste. You can use this menu method on the PC version as well as the Mac version.

▶ Select the text "Congratulations for a job well done!" by dragging through it.

▶ On the PC, click the **Cut** button, and on the Mac select the menu items Edit, Cut.

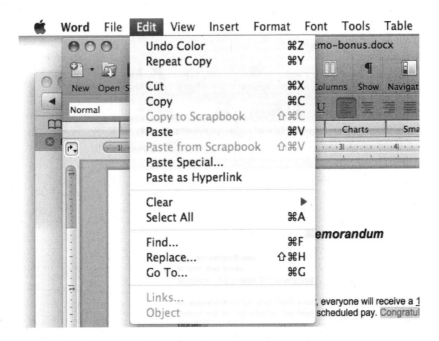

Figure 3.13b *Word Cut, Copy, and Paste buttons for Mac.*

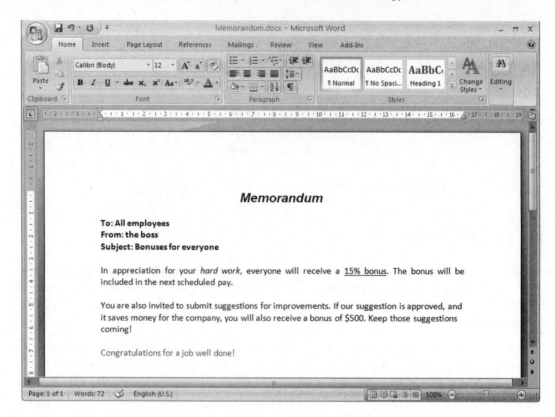

Figure 3.14   *Word Memorandum document.*

Notice that the text has disappeared. Don't worry, it's in the clipboard waiting to be pasted to its new location. The clipboard is a temporary holding location for data when you use copy or cut.

▶ Move the mouse pointer to the end of the document and click to place the flashing insertion point at the end of the document.

▶ Press the **Enter** key twice to move the flashing insertion point below the text, adding a blank line.

▶ On the PC, click the **Paste** button, and on the Mac, select the **Edit, Paste** menu items to paste the text at the end of the document.

▶ Depending on the version of Word you are using, a little clipboard icon may appear beside the pasted text. We will not use this feature here. If you see the clipboard icon, press the **Esc** key on the keyboard to remove it.

The document should look something like that shown in Figure 3.14.

Let's copy some text as well.

▶ Select the text, "Bonuses for everyone."

▶ On the PC, click the **Copy** button, as shown in Figure 3.13a, and on the Mac, select the Edit, Copy menu items.

▶ Move the mouse pointer to the end of the document, after "Congratulations for a job well done!" and click to position the flashing insertion point.

▶ Press the **Enter** key twice to move the flashing insertion point below the text and insert a blank line.

▶ On the PC, click the **Paste** button, and on the Mac, select the Edit, Paste menu items to paste a copy of the text at the end of the document.

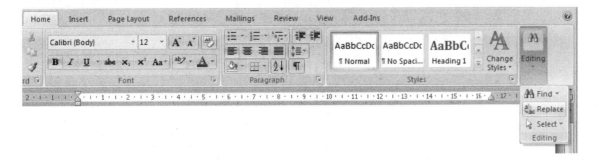

Figure 3.15a   *Word Expand menu indicator for PC.*

Again, if Word has placed a clipboard icon after you have pasted, press the **Esc** key to remove it.

A feature of using Copy and Paste is that you can paste multiple times.

► Press the **Enter** key to move the flashing insertion point down one line.

► On the PC, click the **Paste** button, and on the Mac select the Edit, Paste menu items to paste another copy of the text at the end of the document.

Again, if Word has placed a clipboard icon after you have pasted, press the **Esc** key to remove it.

Find and Replace

The boss has reviewed the document and decided that the word "everyone" is a bit too general. You've been asked to use "all employees" instead of "everyone." Since "everyone" has been used several times in the document, the quickest way to replace it and ensure that we catch all instances, is to use the find and replace feature.

► On the PC, click the **Editing** button on the ribbon bar to reveal the edit options as shown in Figure 3.15a. The Edit options may be visible already if your Word window is large enough to support them. Click the **Replace** menu item.

► On the Mac, click the Edit, Replace menu item, as shown in Figure 3.15b.

Figure 3.15b   *Word Expand menu indicator for Mac.*

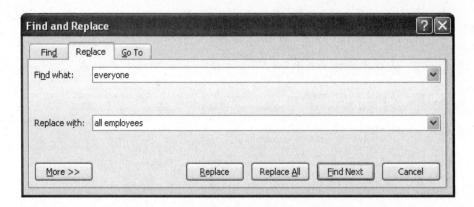

Figure 3.16a   *Word Find and Replace dialog box for PC.*

The **Find and Replace** dialog box should appear as displayed in Figures 3.16a and 3.16b, with the **Replace** tab selected.

> ► As indicated in Figures 3.16a and 3.16b, in the **Find what** box, type: everyone
>
> ► As indicated in Figures 3.16a and 3.16b, in the **Replace with** box, type: all employees
>
> ► Click the **Replace All** button to replace all instances of "everyone" with "all employees"
>
> ► A dialog box will appear indicating the number of replacements made. Click the **OK** button.

Word will search for all instances of "everyone" and replace each one with "all employees." If you think this type of global replace is risky, you can use the **Replace** button to approve each replacement. This same dialog box is used for the **Find** feature, which allows you to search for text in the document.

> ► Click the **Close** button to close the **Find and Replace** dialog box if it is still open.

Notice that all instances of "everyone" have been replaced with "all employees" and formatting has been preserved.

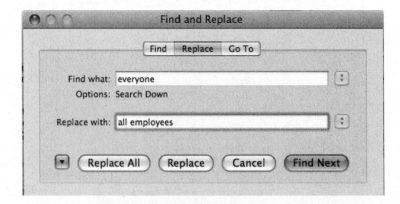

Figure 3.16b   *Word Find and Replace dialog box for Mac.*

Spell Checking

Most word processing software includes a spell checking feature. It can be configured to check your spelling as you type, or you can manually check the document when you're ready. There are a wide variety of spell checking dictionaries available. American English is likely installed as the default dictionary on your computer. Other possible options include British English, French, Spanish, and other languages. If spelling is checked as you type, you will see a red wavy line underlining words that are not found in the dictionary. You should be aware that many proper names are not found in the dictionary, so a word may be spelled correctly even though it has a wavy line under it. You can add custom words to the dictionary, or ignore the misspelling indicator.

Let's add some spelling errors to our document and use the spell checking feature to correct them.

▶ Position the flashing insertion point at the end of the document. As before, you can move the mouse pointer to the end of the document and click to position the flashing insertion point.

▶ Press the **Enter** key twice to move the flashing insertion point below the last line, adding a blank line.

Since the last line had bold formatting, you should notice that the **Bold** button looks pressed. If you begin typing, the new characters will also be bold. Let's turn the bold feature off.

▶ Click the **Bold** button to turn the bold feature off.

▶ Type: Lokin forwardd to a grate year!

If the spelling is checked as you type, you should notice a red wavy line under the word "Lokin" as shown in Figure 3.17. Depending on the configuration for your version of Word, you may also notice that the word "forward" has been corrected automatically.

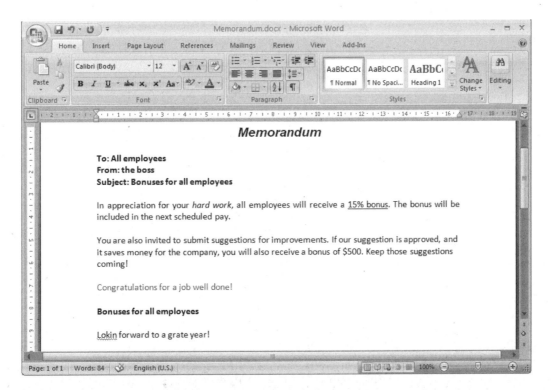

Figure 3.17 *Word Spell Checking.*

You can correct the spelling errors by manually editing, or you can right-click on the misspelled word and a short-cut menu will contain suggestions for possible corrections. On the Mac, you would "right click" by holding down the Control key and click.

Notice that the word "grate" does not have a wavy red line under it. In fact, this word is spelled correctly, but the usage is incorrect. It should be "great." This illustrates one of the pitfalls of relying on the spell checking feature. Words may be spelled correctly, but not used correctly. Even though the spell checking feature is available, it is still important to read your work carefully for errors.

Let's correct the mistakes.

▶ Position the mouse pointer over the word "Lokin." On the PC, right-click to reveal the shortcut menu. On the Mac, press the Command button while you click. The shortcut menu is displayed in Figures 3.18a and 3.18b.

Notice that Word has suggested a variety of words to replace "Lokin."

▶ Click on the menu item "Looking" to replace the misspelled word.

▶ Correct the word "grate," replacing it with "great." Use your editing skills to manually make the change.

▶ Click the **Save** button to save the document and we're done!

▶ On the PC, click on the Microsoft Office button to reveal the drop-down menu. Click the Close menu option to close Microsoft Word.

▶ On the Mac, click the Close button to close the window.

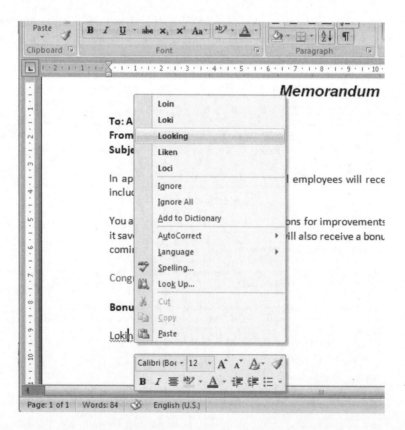

Figure 3.18a *Word shortcut menu for PC.*

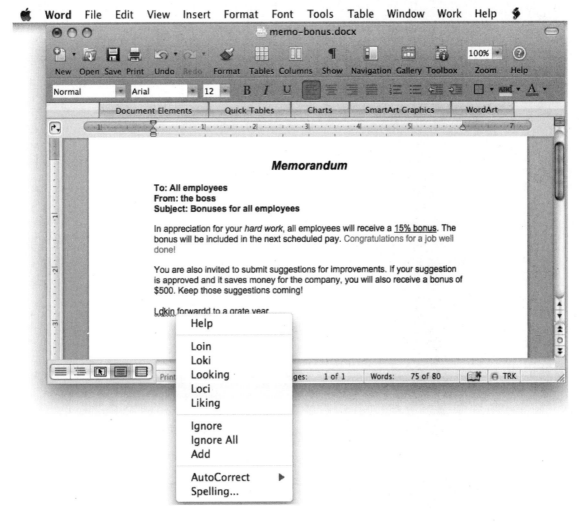

Figure 3.18b *Word shortcut menu for Mac.*

Many methods can be used to perform the tasks we have performed in this lab. The overview provided touched on using the ribbon bar (PC version) for some tasks and the shortcut menu as well. As you continue learning more about Word, you will find yourself choosing a particular method. There is no single "right way" of doing things, so choose the method you like the best. The purpose of this lab was to expose you to a variety of methods to accomplish some basic tasks.

Review

This has been a busy lab! We have covered the following topics, using both the PC and Mac versions of Word:

- Parts of Word
- Keyboard skills
    - Repeat keys
    - Shift
    - Caps Lock
    - Delete
    - Backspace
    - Arrow keys

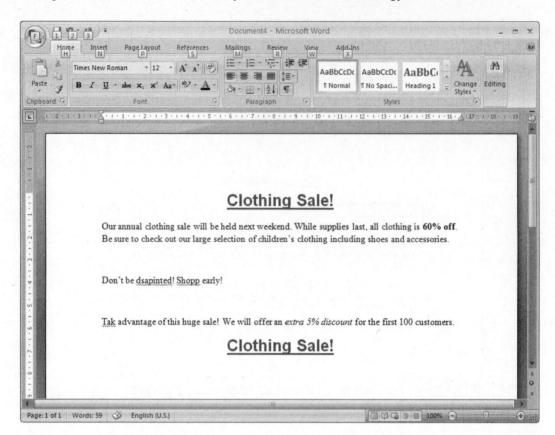

Figure 3.19 *Word Exercise 1 document complete.*

- Data entry
    Using word wrap for paragraphs
    Pressing the **Enter** key at the end of a paragraph or a short line of text
- Undo and Redo
- Saving a Document
- Cut, Copy, and Paste using the standard toolbar
- Formatting
    Text
    - Bold, italic, font, font size, and font color using the ribbon bar
    Paragraph
    - Alignment including left, center, right, and justify
- Search and Replace
- Spell Check

Exercises

1. Use Word to create the following document. The completed document is shown in Figure 3.19 and the formatting enhancements are indicated in Figure 3.20. Spelling errors are included purposely to be corrected later.

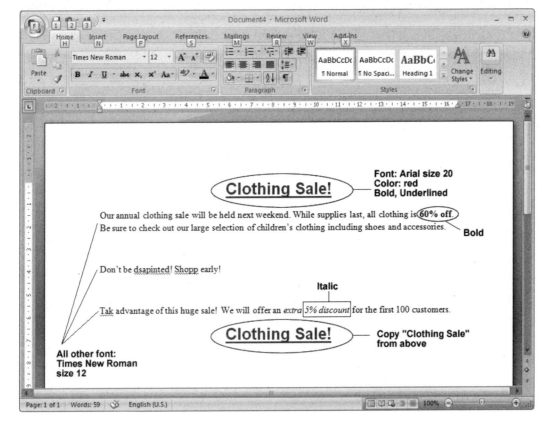

Figure 3.20 *Word Exercise 1 document showing formatting enhancements.*

2. Use the Spell Checking feature to correct the spelling mistakes in the document that was created in Exercise 1.

3. Save your document and close the Microsoft Word window.

Microsoft Word Layout and Graphics Features

Objectives:

Upon successful completion of Lab 4, you will be able to use Word to perform the following tasks

- Set page margins
- Set the ruler measurement (inches, centimeters) and display the ruler
- Set paragraph line spacing, margins, first line, and hanging indentation
- Understand the concepts of tabs and tab alignment
    Use the ruler to set tabs
- Create bulleted lists
- Insert clip art and set alignment options
- Insert Word art

Resources required:

- A computer running any version of Word

Starter files:

- band_biographies.doc
- lab04_exercise_1.doc

Prerequisite skills:

- General keyboarding skills; familiarity with editing keys such as Delete, Backspace, Shift, Caps Lock, and Arrow keys
- Familiarity with Word for editing a simple document
- Open, Close, and Save a Word document
- Ability to find files using Windows Explorer or Windows search feature

NRC's Top Ten Skills, Concepts, and Capabilities:

- Skills
    Use a word processor to create a document
    - Page formatting, including margins
    - Paragraph and text alignment options—line spacing, margins, indents

- • Bulleted lists
- • Clip art
- • Word art
- Concepts
  Fundamentals of computers—word processing
- Capabilities
  Think abstractly about Information Technology—building generic word processing concepts

Lab Lesson

Once you've learned the skills necessary to create a basic word processing document, soon you'll want to be able to position the text by adjusting margins, adding tabs, and using bulleted lists. You may also wish to add some interest to the document with images and text art. The focus of this lab is to introduce all of these features. There are a variety of methods that can be used to accomplish these tasks; first we will focus on the **Ruler** buttons. Be sure to save your document periodically throughout this lab exercise.

Let's use the print layout view so that we can see the margins and page edges, and display the ruler.

▶ On the PC, click the **View** tab and click the Ruler checkbox as shown in Figure 4.1a.

▶ On the Mac, select the menu items **View, Ruler,** as shown in Figure 4.1b.

The Word window should look something like that shown in Figures 4.1a and 4.1b.

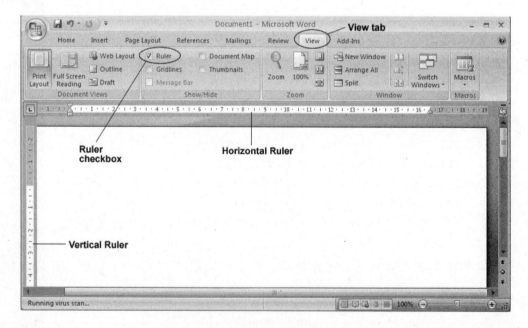

Figure 4.1a *Word showing rulers for PC.*

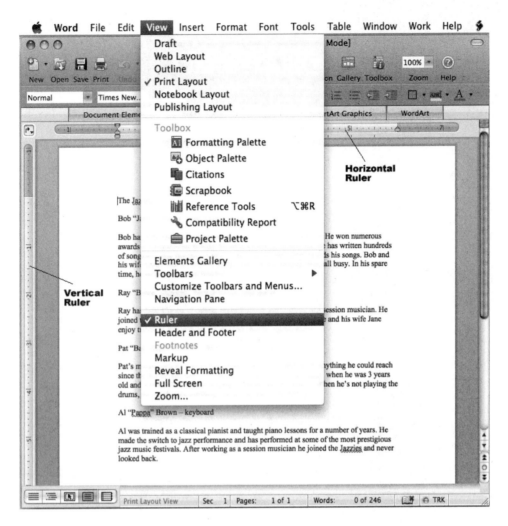

Figure 4.1b *Word showing rulers for Mac.*

Notice the dark margin area at the top of the page on the ruler. This is the header area, and you will find a similar shaded area on the ruler at the bottom of each page called the **footer** area. The ruler measurement is often displayed in centimeters by default. Let's change that to display in inches.

On the PC:

▶ Click the **Office** button located at the top left corner of the Word window.

▶ Click the **Word Options** button located at the bottom of the menu window, as shown in Figure 4.2a.

▶ Click the **Advanced** button in the Word Options dialog box, as shown in Figure 4.2a.

▶ Scroll down to the **Display** options and click the drop-down box for measurements to select inches, as shown in Figure 4.2a.

▶ Click the **OK** button to apply the measurement units change.

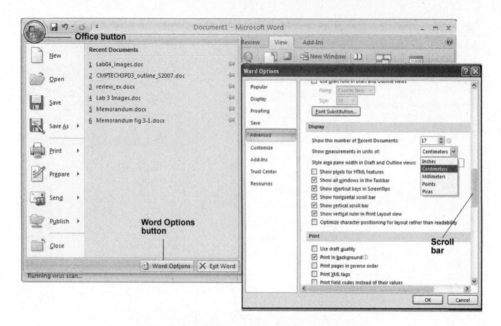

Figure 4.2a *Word Options dialog box for PC.*

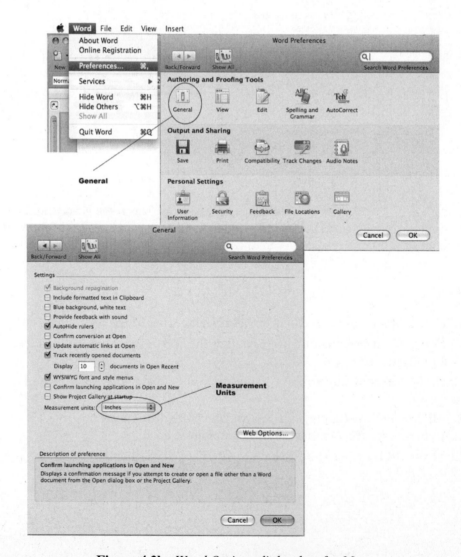

Figure 4.2b *Word Options dialog box for Mac.*

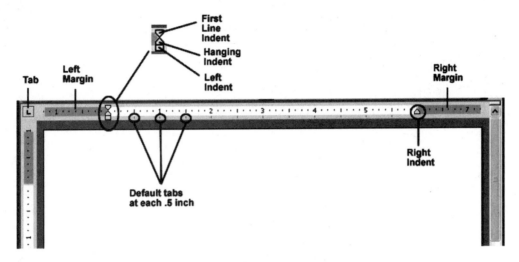

Figure 4.3 *Word horizontal ruler.*

On the Mac:

▶ Click on the Word, Preferences menu items as shown in Figure 4.2b.

▶ Click on the General preference option as shown in Figure 4.2b.

▶ Click the drop-down box for Measurement Units to select inches, as shown in Figure 4.2.

▶ Click the **OK** button to apply the measurement units change.

This change will affect page margins as well as the rule.

Let's take a closer look at the horizontal ruler area, as shown in Figure 4.3.

The horizontal ruler indicates the left and right margin with shaded areas. As you type, the characters will appear between the margins and automatically wrap at the right margin. There are preset tabs at each .5". Notice the small lines below .5", 1 inch, 1.5", and so forth. When you press the **Tab** key, the flashing insertion point will jump from one tab to the next. Let's give this a try.

▶ Press the **Tab** key.

Notice that the flashing insertion point has jumped to the .5" location, corresponding to the horizontal ruler indicator.

▶ Press the **Tab** key several times.

Notice that each time the flashing insertion point jumps another .5" to the right.

▶ On the PC, press the **Backspace** key. On the Mac, press the **Delete** key.

Notice that the flashing insertion point moves one tab to the left.

▶ Press the **Backspace** key (PC) or **Delete** key (Mac) several times until the flashing insertion point is at the beginning of the line.

Notice that the flashing insertion point jumps to the left .5" each time you press the **Backspace** (PC) or **Delete** (Mac) key.

We will find that when we set tabs manually, the new tabs will override these default tabs.

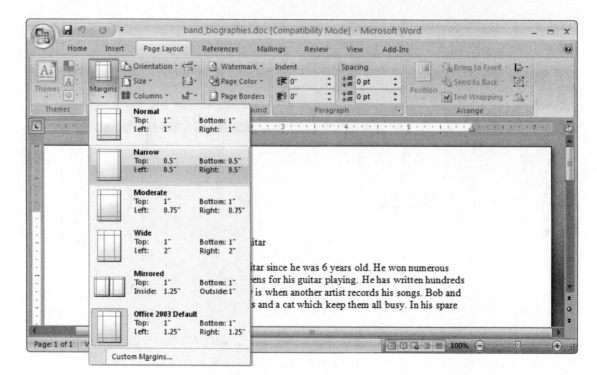

Figure 4.4 *Margin options.*

We can use the ruler to set tabs and we can also use it as a guide to align paragraphs. Let's do some exercises with paragraph alignment. In this lab we will create a biography page for members of a jazz band.

▶ Open the band_biographies.doc file.

There is a paragraph for each member of the band. Let's experiment with some paragraph formatting options, using different formatting for each paragraph.

Setting Margins for the PC Version

First, let's look at the page margins.

▶ Click the **Page Layout tab**.
▶ Click the **Margins** button as shown in Figure 4.4.

Notice the variety of margin settings.

▶ Click the **Narrow** option as shown in Figure 4.4.

If you wish to use specific margins that are not available in the menu list, you can customize the margins.

▶ Click the **Margins** button.
▶ Click the **Custom Margins** menu option.

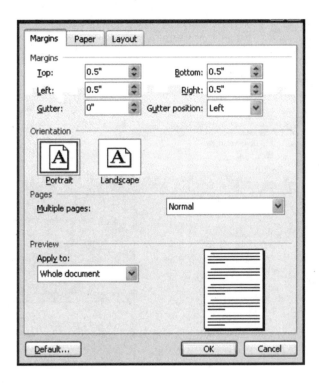

Figure 4.5a *Word Page Setup dialog box with margins set to .5" for PC.*

The Page Setup dialog box should appear as shown in Figure 4.5a.

Notice that there are margin options for top, bottom, left, and right. Since we changed the unit of measurement to inches, these margins are also measured in inches. The standard page is 8.5 inches wide and 11 inches long.

As you can see, margins can be set individually.

▶ Click the **Cancel** button to retain the margins.

Setting Margins for the Mac Version

First, let's look at the page margins.

▶ Click on the menu items View, and Formatting Palette, as shown in Figure 4.5b.

The Formatting Palette will be displayed, as shown in Figure 4.5b. You can drag the palette to any location on your screen.

▶ Click the Document Margins drop-down to reveal the margin measurements.
▶ Change the top, and bottom, margins to 1" and the left, and right margins to .5".

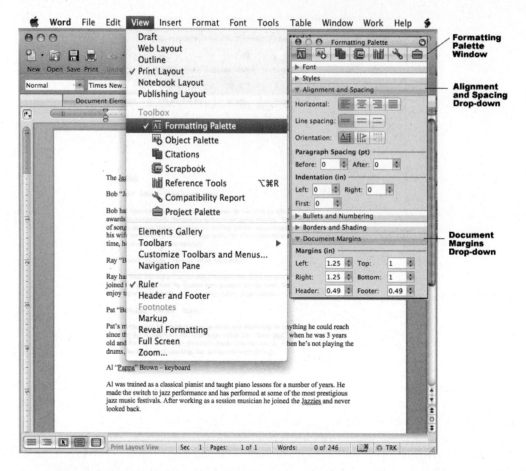

Figure 4.5b *Word Page Setup dialog box with margins set to .5" for Mac.*

Paragraph Margins

Notice that the text has rewrapped and the top, left, and right margins are much narrower than they were previously. Let's experiment with some paragraph margins.

First, we have to select a paragraph. We can do this by simply positioning the flashing insertion point anywhere in the paragraph. You can drag through the whole paragraph to select it but this is not necessary. The margins will be applied only to the paragraph that contains the flashing insertion point.

▶ Position the flashing insertion point anywhere in Bob's biography paragraph. You can do this by moving the mouse pointer to a position in the paragraph and clicking the **left mouse** button.

▶ Drag the Right Margin pointer to the left and position it at the 6.5" mark as shown in Figure 4.6.

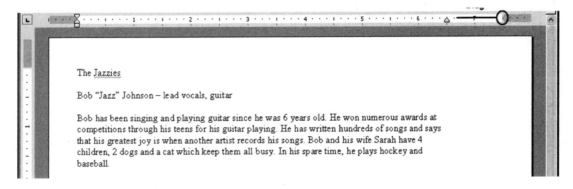

Figure 4.6   *Word Right Margin position at 6.5".*

Notice that only Bob's paragraph has been affected by the paragraph margin.

Let's adjust the left margin for Bob's paragraph as well.

▶ Drag the Left Margin pointer to the 1" mark. Be very careful to position the mouse pointer on the small box at the bottom of the Left Margin pointer, as shown in Figure 4.7.

Again, only Bob's paragraph is affected by this margin setting.

Paragraph Indents

Let's add a first line indent to Bob's paragraph as well.

▶ Drag the First Line Indent pointer to the 1.5" marker, as shown in Figure 4.8. Again, be very careful to drag only the top triangular marker and not the lower one.

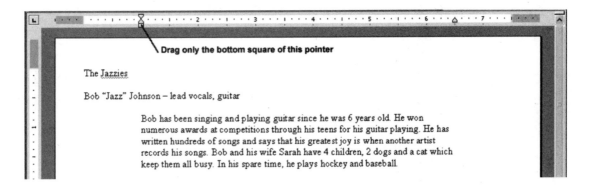

Figure 4.7   *Word Left Margin pointer at 1".*

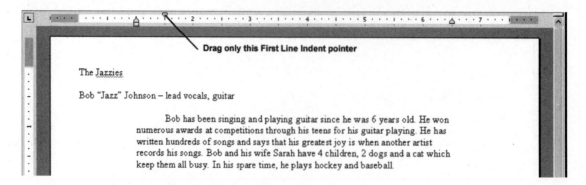

Figure 4.8 *Word First Line Indent pointer at 1.5".*

Let's also adjust the paragraph spacing for Bob's paragraph. Let's create a double-spaced paragraph.

▶ On the PC, click the **Paragraph Dialog Box Launcher icon** as shown in Figure 4.9a. On the Mac, click the Alignment and Spacing drop-down on the Formatting Palette as shown in Figure 4.9b.

Notice that the indentation is indicated. We set the indentation using the margin pointers on the ruler bar, and the corresponding settings are shown in the **Paragraph** dialog box (PC) or **Formatting** Palette (Mac). Left and right paragraph margins are shown as 1" and the first line indent at .5" is also indicated. We could have set paragraph margins using this dialog box instead of dragging pointers on the toolbar.

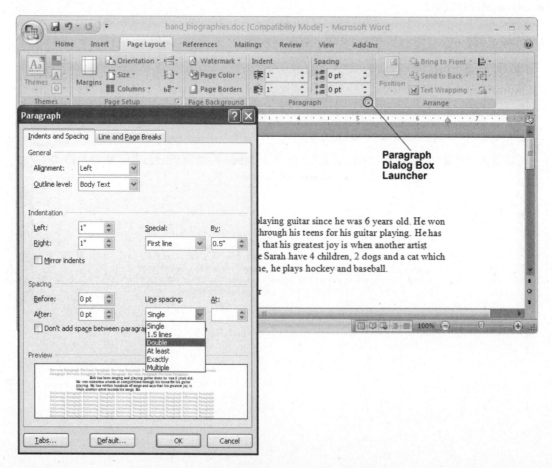

Figure 4.9a *Word Paragraph dialog box for PC.*

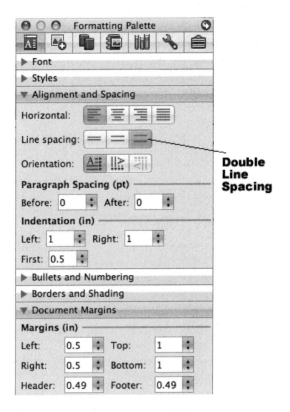

Figure 4.9b *Word Paragraph dialog box for Mac.*

▶ For the PC, set the paragraph spacing to Double, as shown in Figure 4.9a and click the OK button.

▶ For the Mac, set the Line spacing to Double Space as shown in Figure 4.9b.

Bob's paragraph should now look something like that shown in Figure 4.10.

Let's set up a hanging indent for Ray's paragraph. A paragraph formatted with a hanging indent has the first line hanging to the left of the rest of the paragraph. To achieve this effect, we will drag the Hanging Indent pointer to the right.

▶ Select Ray's paragraph by positioning the mouse pointer anywhere in Ray's paragraph and click the **left mouse** button.

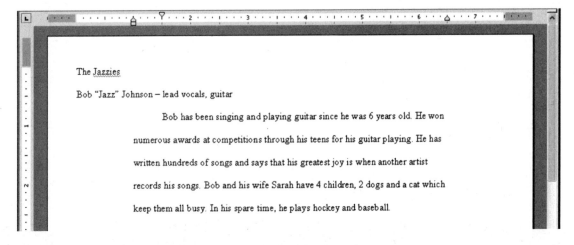

Figure 4.10 *Word displaying double-spaced paragraph.*

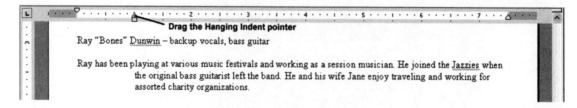

Figure 4.11 *Word displaying hanging indent.*

▶ Drag the Hanging Indent pointer to the 1" mark as shown in Figure 4.11. Be careful to drag the lower triangular marker and not the lower box or upper triangular marker.

Notice that Ray's paragraph shows the first line hanging over the rest of the paragraph. The rest of the paragraph is indented 1".

Let's adjust the left and right paragraph margins for Ray's paragraph.

▶ Drag the Right Margin pointer to the 6.5" mark, as shown in Figure 4.12.

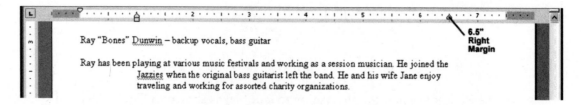

Figure 4.12 *Word displaying hanging indent and right margin change.*

When we drag the Left Margin pointer, Word preserves first line and hanging indent settings.

▶ Drag the Left Margin pointer to the 2" marker, as shown in Figure 4.13. Be careful to drag the small box, which is the Left Margin pointer, and not the triangular Hanging Indent pointer.

We can also use the **Tab** key to change the left margin of a paragraph.

▶ Drag through Pat's entire paragraph to select it. This method requires that the entire paragraph is selected.

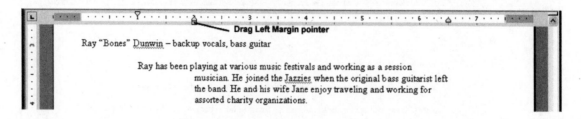

Figure 4.13 *Word displaying hanging indent and left margin change.*

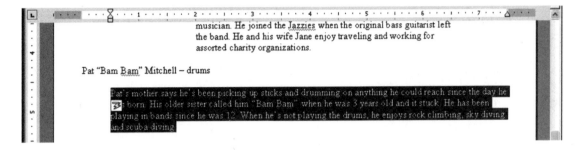

Figure 4.14 *Word displaying paragraph left margin after tab.*

▶ Press the **Tab** key to move the left margin .5" to the right, as shown in Figure 4.14.

Let's use the **Tab** key to indent the first line only.

▶ Position the flashing insertion point at the beginning of Al's paragraph, to the left of "Al."

▶ Press the **Tab** key to indent the first line, as shown in Figure 4.15.

Notice that the indent indicators on the horizontal ruler show the first line indent at .5″ and the left paragraph margin at 0.

Now that we've experimented with a variety of paragraph formatting techniques, let's decide on one for all of the paragraphs in the document to give it a professional look. Let's use the paragraph formatting for Bob's paragraph, with single spacing rather than double.

▶ Move the mouse pointer to any position in Bob's paragraph, and click.

For the PC:

▶ Click the Paragraph Dialog Box icon.

▶ Select the line spacing as single.

▶ Click the **OK** button to apply the single spacing.

For the Mac:

▶ Click the Single Spacing line spacing button in the Formatting Palette.

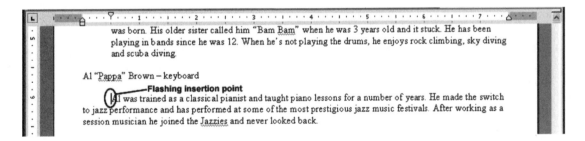

Figure 4.15 *Word displaying paragraph first line indent after tab.*

Format Painter

We know that we can copy text from one location to another. We can also copy formatting after it has been applied. Formatting includes enhancements such as font size, font color, bold, and so forth. Formatting also includes paragraph alignment, margins, and indents. Let's copy the formatting from Bob's paragraph to the others.

> ► Ensure that the flashing insertion point is located somewhere in Bob's paragraph. If not, click in Bob's paragraph to position the flashing insertion point there.
> ► On the PC, click the **Home** tab.
> ► Click the **Format Painter** button (PC) or **Format** button (Mac)

As you move the mouse pointer into the document window, notice that the pointer has changed to a brush.

> ► Drag through all of Ray's paragraph to apply the formatting to it.

Notice that the single space, indented first line, and right and left paragraph margin formatting has been applied to Ray's paragraph.

The formatting has been copied, but the mouse pointer has returned to normal. We still have two more paragraphs to format. Rather than clicking on the **Format Painter** button each time, we can double-click it to preserve the formatting to copy to multiple locations.

> ► Position the flashing insertion point in Bob's paragraph.
> ► Double-click the **Format Painter** button (PC) or **Format** button (Mac).

Again, notice as you move the mouse pointer that it has changed to a brush.

> ► Drag through all of Pat's paragraph to apply the formatting to it.
> ► Drag through all of Al's paragraph to apply the formatting to it.
> ► Press the **Esc** key to remove the formatting pointer and return the mouse pointer to normal.

Bulleted Lists

A list of items can be formatted with bullets or numbers. Let's create a bulleted list of the band members.

> ► Each paragraph is identified by the band member's name and position. Copy the band member's name and position to the top of the document, each on a separate line, as shown in Figure 4.16.

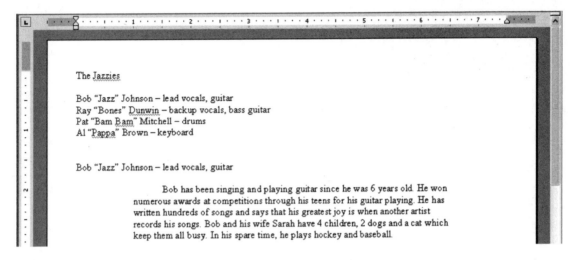

Figure 4.16 *Word list unformatted.*

Let's add bullets to the list of band members.

▶ Drag through the entire list of band members to select them.

▶ Click the **Bullets** button on the formatting toolbar as shown in Figures 4.17a and 4.17b.

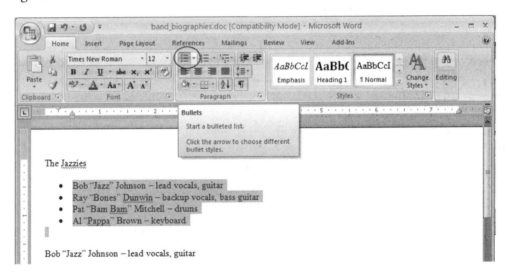

Figure 4.17a *Word list formatted with bullets for PC.*

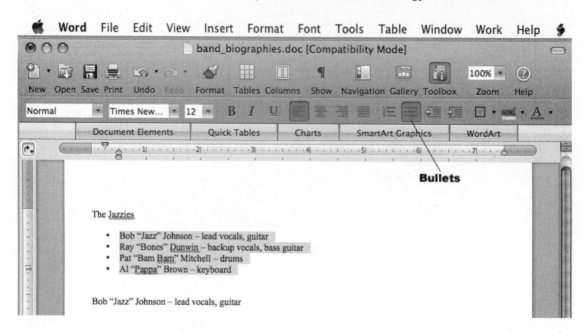

Figure 4.17b   *Word list formatted with bullets for Mac.*

Notice that each line now has a bullet at the left and there has been some paragraph alignment applied.

Let's take the descriptions of their roles and make bulleted items from those as well.

▶ Press the **Enter** key at the end of each of the band members' names and delete the hyphen for each new list item, as shown in Figure 4.18. Notice that each time you press the **Enter** key a new list item is formed and a new bullet appears.

The roles for each band member should be indented so that it is clear that these items belong to the individual band member. When we indent a bullet, the list item is moved to a new level and a different symbol is used to identify it.

▶ Position the flashing insertion point at the beginning of the "lead vocals, guitar" line. Notice that you cannot position the flashing insertion point to the left of the bullet. The flashing insertion point will be between the bullet and the first character in the line.

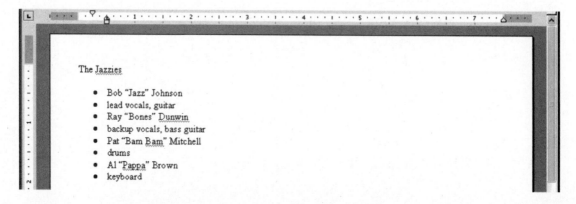

Figure 4.18   *Word bulleted list with more items.*

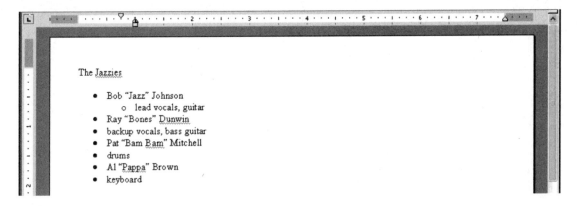

Figure 4.19 *Word bulleted list with indented item.*

▶ Press the **Tab** key to indent the list item. The indented item is shown in Figure 4.19.

▶ Similarly, use the **Tab** key to indent each of the descriptions for each band member.

The list for Bob and Ray include more than one item. Let's separate these into bullets too.

▶ Edit the list so that "lead vocals" and "guitar" are separate bullets. As before, you can position the mouse pointer at the beginning of the word "guitar" and press the **Enter** key to establish a new item.

▶ Edit the list such that "backup vocals" and "bass guitar" are separate bullets. Use the **Tab** key to indent if necessary.

The list should look something like that shown in Figure 4.20.

At the bottom of the page, let's add weekly concert information.

▶ Position the flashing insertion point at the end of the last paragraph in the document.

▶ Press the **Enter** key twice. Notice that the paragraph formatting from the previous paragraph has been continued. We'd like to start a new paragraph at the margin without indenting the first line.

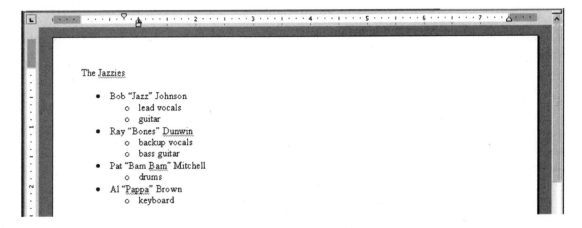

Figure 4.20 *Word completed bulleted list.*

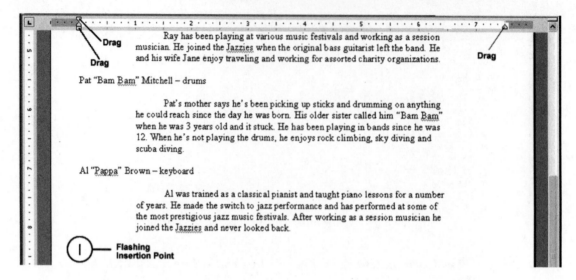

Figure 4.21   *Word horizontal ruler with left margin indicator and*
First Line pointer at left margin edge.

▶ Drag the left margin indicator and the First Line pointer back to the margin edge. This is shown in Figure 4.21.

▶ Drag the right margin indicator back to the right margin edge, as shown in Figure 4.21.

▶ Type: Weekly Concerts

▶ Click the **Center** button ☰ on the toolbar to center the title.

▶ Press the **Enter** key twice.

▶ Click the **Align Left** button ☰ on the toolbar to move the flashing insertion point to the left margin.

Tabs

At the beginning of this lab, we looked at the default tabs set every 0.5". All of these tabs are left tabs. When you tab, the text will left-align to the tab. There are a variety of other tabs available. We will look at manually setting a left tab and a right tab to see the difference.

One advantage of setting a tab is to be able to press the **Tab** key to move the flashing insertion point directly to the location you desire. With the default tabs, if you want to move the flashing insertion point to the 4" mark, you would have to hit the **Tab** key many times. Alternatively, you can manually set a tab at the 4" mark and hit the **Tab** key only once.

Let's set some left tabs. By default, the tab selection is the left tab. We can click the ruler bar to set tabs.

▶ Click the ruler bar at the 1.5" marker. Notice that a left tab has been added as shown in Figure 4.22.

▶ Click the ruler bar at the 3" marker. Notice that a left tab has been added at the 3" mark as shown in Figure 4.22.

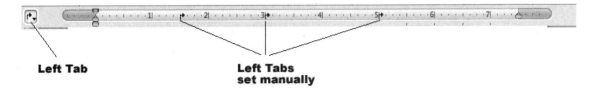

Left Tab

**Left Tabs
set manually**

Figure 4.22 *Word left tabs set on ruler.*

▶ Click the ruler bar at the 5" marker. Notice that a left tab has been added at the 5" mark as shown in Figure 4.22.

The default tabs which were previously set every .5" have now disappeared up to the 5″ mark. After the 5" mark, the default tabs are still available.

▶ Press the **Tab** key. Notice that the flashing insertion point jumps to the 1.5" marker.
▶ Type: Day
▶ Press the **Tab** key. Notice that the flashing insertion point jumps to the 3" marker.
▶ Type: Location
▶ Press the **Tab** key. Notice that the flashing insertion point jumps to the 5" marker.
▶ Type: Time
▶ Press the **Enter** key.

Your document should look something like that shown in Figure 4.23.

Let's add some concert information.

▶ Press the **Tab** key to move the flashing insertion point to the 1.5″ marker.
▶ Type: Monday
▶ Press the **Tab** key to move the flashing insertion point to the 3″ marker.
▶ Type: The Hilltop Tavern

The text for concert times is going to be a bit long. Instead of using a left tab at the 5″ mark, let's use a right tab at the 6″ mark. First we'll remove the left tab, and then we'll add the right tab.

▶ Drag the left tab at the 5″ mark down into the document window. This will remove it from the ruler.

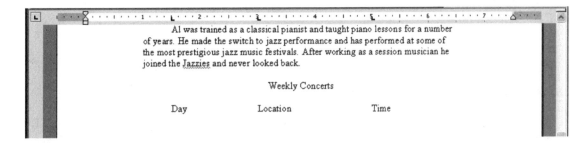

Figure 4.23 *Word tabs for weekly concert headings.*

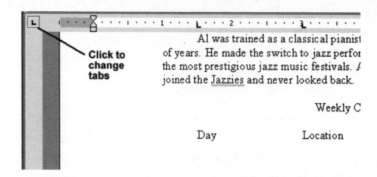

Figure 4.24a *Word change tab for PC.*

We will have to select the right tab symbol.

▶ Click the tab symbol to the left of the ruler, as shown in Figures 4.24a and 4.24b.

On the PC, when you click the tab symbol it will change to a different tab symbol. On the Mac, a drop-down menu will be revealed as shown in Figure 4.24b.

Figure 4.24b *Word change tab for Mac.*

▶ On the PC, click the tab symbol until it changes to a right tab symbol . If you miss it, don't worry. You can continue to click and it will cycle through again.

▶ On the Mac, select the menu item Right.

▶ Click the 6" mark to set a right-tab as shown in Figure 4.25.

▶ Press the **Tab** key to move the flashing insertion point to the 6" tab as shown in Figure 4.25.

▶ Type: 10:00 p.m.–11:30 p.m.

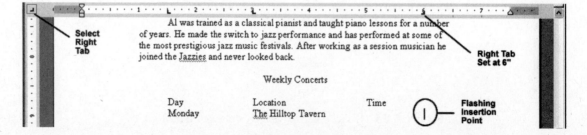

Figure 4.25a *Word right tab set for PC.*

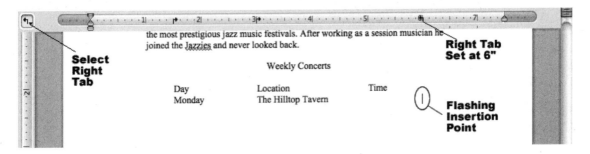

Figure 4.25b *Word right tab set for Mac.*

Notice that the text ends at the right tab. The right tab defines the right edge and text will be pushed to the left as you type.

▶ Press the **Enter** key.
▶ Press the **Tab** key to move the flashing insertion point to the 1.5" tab.
▶ Type: Thursday
▶ Press the **Tab** key to move the flashing insertion point to the 3" tab.
▶ Type: The Jazz Club
▶ Press the **Tab** key to move the flashing insertion point to the 6" tab.
▶ Type: 9:30 p.m.–11:00 p.m.

The document should look something like that shown in Figures 4.26a and 4.26b.

Clip Art

We can add images to our document to provide a little visual interest. Office installs a library of clip art images for this purpose.

Let's add an image between the title and the band members list.

▶ Position the flashing insertion point at the end of "The Jazzies" title.
▶ Press the **Enter** key twice.

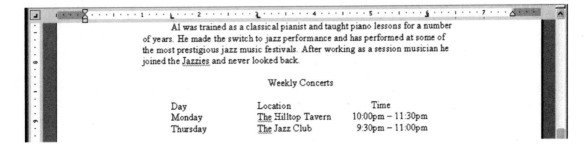

Figure 4.26a *Word weekly concert schedule for PC.*

the most prestigious jazz music festivals. After working as a session musician he
joined the Jazzies and never looked back.

Weekly Concerts

Day	Location	Time
Monday	The Hilltop Tavern	10:00pm – 11:30pm
Thursday	The Jazz Club	9:30pm – 11:00pm

Figure 4.26b *Word weekly concert schedule for Mac.*

▶ Click the **Insert** tab (PC) or Insert menu item (Mac).

▶ Click the **Clip Art** option, as shown in Figures 4.27a and 4.27b.

The **Clip Art** window (PC) or Clip Gallery (Mac) should open, as shown in Figures 4.27a and
4.27b. You can browse through categories using the drop-down arrow in the **Search In** box, or
you can type a keyword and search for clip art images related to the keyword. Let's search by
keyword.

▶ On the PC, in the **Search for:** box type: buildings. Click the **Go** button, as
shown in Figure 4.27a.

▶ On the Mac, click the Buildings category as shown in Figure 4.27b.

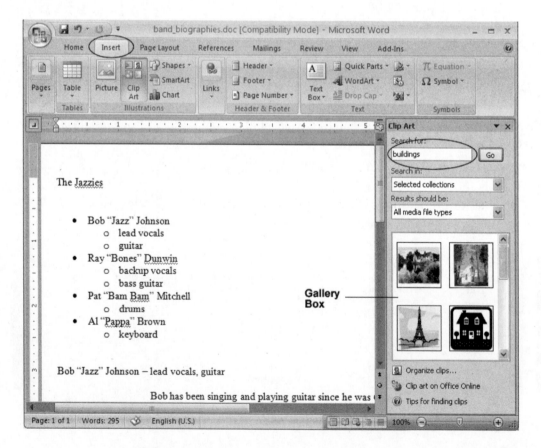

Figure 4.27a *Word Clip Art window for PC.*

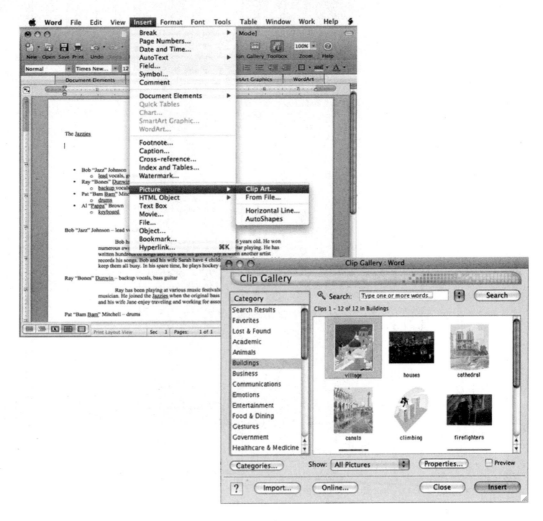

Figure 4.27b   *Word Clip Art window for Mac.*

You should see a selection of clip art images in the large gallery box. Depending on the version of Word you are using, and the images available on your computer, your actual selection of clip art may look different.

▶ Scroll through the gallery box and find a picture that you like.

On the PC:

▶ Hover your mouse over the clip art image you would like to insert. Notice that a drop-down arrow appears. If you click this arrow it will reveal a shortcut menu. Instead, we will click the picture, not the arrow.

▶ Click the clip art image you would like to insert, being careful not to click the drop-down arrow. Notice that the clip art image is automatically inserted at the flashing insertion point position.

▶ Close the **Clip Art** window by clicking on the close icon in the upper right corner, as usual.

On the Mac:

▶ Click the clip art image you would like to insert, as shown in Figure 4.27b.
▶ Click the Insert button as shown in Figure 4.27b.

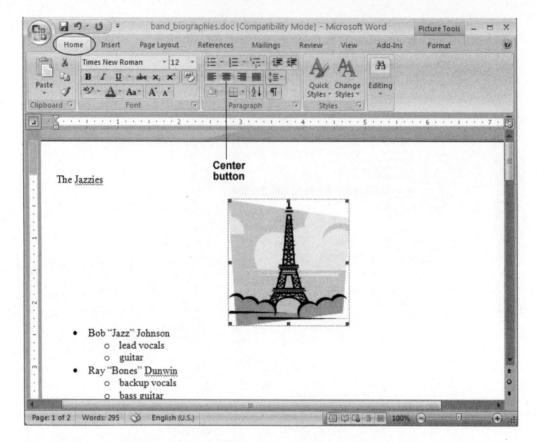

Figure 4.28a *Word Clip Art image centered for PC.*

Let's position the image so that it is centered.

> ► Click the clip art image in the document to select it.

When you select an image in the document, you should notice that picture tools are displayed on the toolbar.

> ► On the PC, click the **Home** tab and click the **Center** button on the toolbar to center the image as shown in Figure 4.28a.
> ► On the Mac, click the **Center** button on the formatting toolbar to center the image as shown in Figure 4.28b.

Notice that when it's selected, there are square handles at each corner and on each edge of the picture. You can drag the handles to size the image just as you would with a window.

If you need to delete the image, you can select it and press the **Delete** key, just as you would delete text characters.

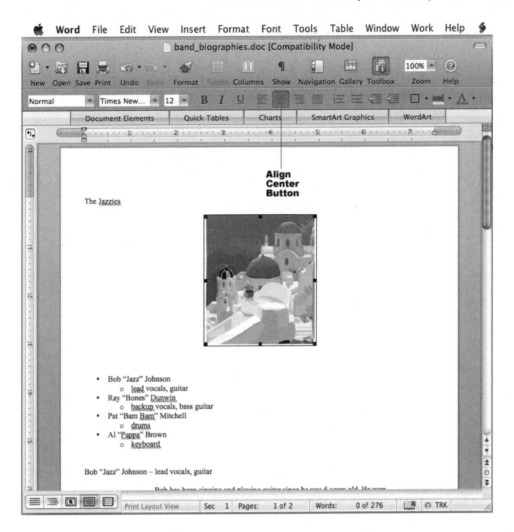

Figure 4.28b   *Word Clip Art image centered for Mac.*

Word Art

To add some more interest, let's replace the title "The Jazzies" with some word art.

▶ Delete the title "The Jazzies."

▶ Ensure that the flashing insertion point is at the beginning of the document.

▶ On the PC, click the **Insert** tab and Click the **Word Art** button as shown in Figure 4.29a.

▶ On the Mac, click the WordArt gallery tab as shown in Figure 4.29b.

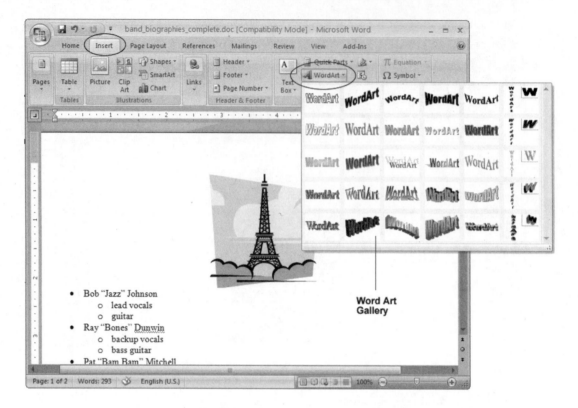

Figure 4.29a *Word WordArt Gallery for PC.*

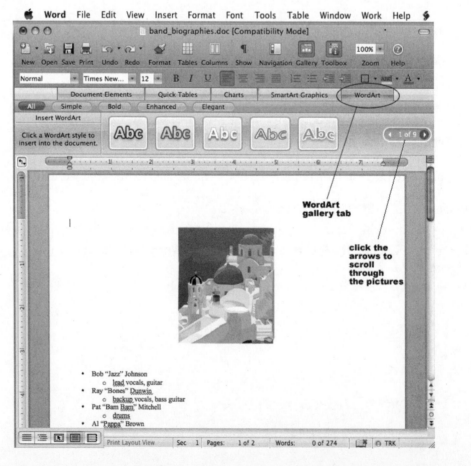

Figure 4.29b *Word WordArt Gallery for Mac.*

Figure 4.30a *WordArt Edit box with The Jazzies title for PC.*

The WordArt Gallery should appear as shown in Figures 4.29a and 4.29b.

As you can see, the gallery shows samples of WordArt styles. You can always change the style later if you decide you don't like the one you've chosen.

▶ Click one of the WordArt styles to select it.

▶ On the Mac, double-click on the text box that appears, as shown in Figure 4.30b.

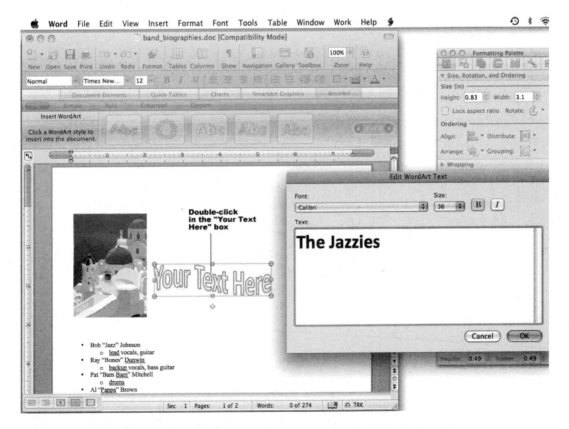

Figure 4.30b *WordArt Edit box with The Jazzies title for Mac.*

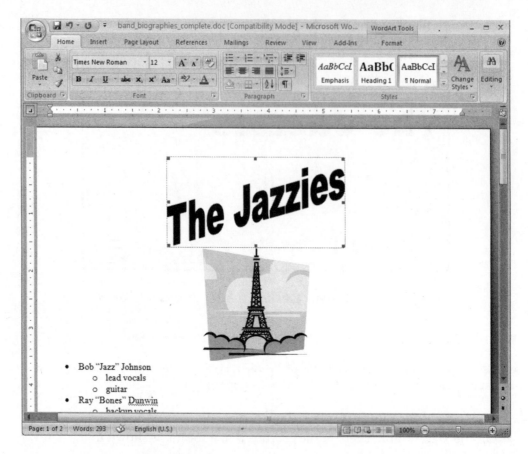

Figure 4.31a *Word WordArt centered for PC.*

The **WordArt Edit** box should appear. Notice that there are options for font and font size.

> ▶ In the **WordArt Edit** box type: The Jazzies, as shown in Figures 4.30a and 4.30b.
> ▶ Click the **OK** button to complete the WordArt.

The WordArt should appear in your document. Let's center it.

> ▶ Click the WordArt title to select it.

When you click the WordArt, the WordArt toolbar will also appear on the ribbon toolbar (PC) or on the Formatting Palette (Mac). It contains buttons for adjusting the color, depth, rotation, and access to the gallery to change the style.

> ▶ On the PC, click the **Home** tab and click the **Center** button on the toolbar to center the WordArt as shown in Figure 4.31a.
> ▶ On the Mac, drag the Word Art title above the image, as shown in Figure 4.31b.

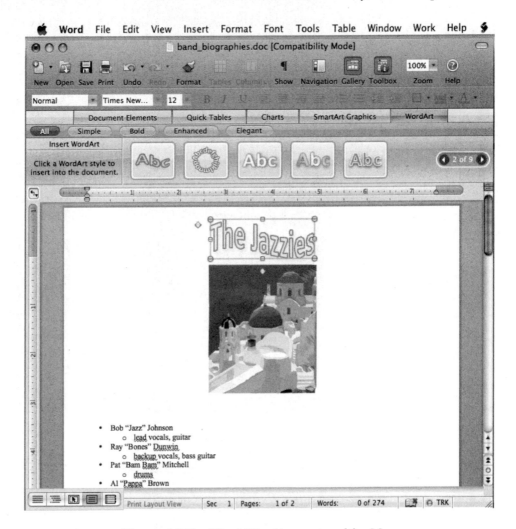

Figure 4.31b   *Word WordArt centered for Mac.*

This lab has provided a brief overview of page margins, paragraph margins, indentation, and tabs. This lab has also provided an overview of clip art and Word art.

Review

This has been a busy lab! We have covered the following topics:

- Set the ruler measurement to inches and display the ruler
- Page margins
    Top, bottom, left, and right
- Paragraph formatting
    Line spacing
    Margins
    First line indent
    Hanging indentation
- Understand the concepts of tabs and tab alignment
    Default tabs
    Left tabs and right tabs
- Create bulleted lists with indented bullets
- Insert clip art and set alignment
- Insert Word art

Figure 4.32 *Word Exercise 1.*

Exercises

1. Create the document shown in Figure 4.32. To save some typing time, the text is available in the file lab01_exercise_1_text.doc.

    a. Set the left and right page margins to 1"

    b. Center the WordArt for "The Jazzies" and "Concert"

    c. Find an appropriate clip art image and center it as shown

    d. Use a hanging indent as shown for the band members description paragraph

    e. Use a bulleted list for the items that are not allowed, with indenting as shown

    f. Use left tabs and right tabs as shown for the pricing list

    g. Use a first line indent and 1.5 line spacing for the last paragraph as shown

    h. Use 0.5" left and right paragraph margins for the last paragraph as shown

Spreadsheet Concepts Using Microsoft Excel

Objectives:

Upon successful completion of Lab 5, you will be able to

- Create and edit a simple spreadsheet document
- Describe the advantage of using formulas rather than entering values only
- Use copy, cut, and paste to copy and move data including formulas
- Use the built-in function sum
- View formulas
- Format data in cells including font, bold, underline, italic, and shading
- Print a spreadsheet and adjust the fit

Resources required:

- A computer running Microsoft Excel 2007 (PC) or Microsoft Excel 2008 (Mac)

Starter files:

- None

Prerequisite skills:

- General keyboarding skills; familiarity with editing keys such as Delete, Backspace, Shift, Caps Lock, and Arrow keys
- Ability to find files using Windows Explorer or Windows search feature
- Ability to open and save a file in a Windows application

NRC's Top Ten Skills, Concepts, and Capabilities:

- Skills
  Use a spreadsheet to model a simple process
  - Data entry
  - Formulas using relative cell references
  - Formatting
  - Printing
  - Simple built-in functions (average, sum)
- Concepts
  Modeling and abstraction
- Capabilities
  Engage in sustained reasoning
  Think abstractly about Information Technology—building generic electronic spreadsheet concepts

Lab Lesson

If you've ever had to manage a household budget, track your investments, or even manage a volunteer fundraiser, then you will see the advantages offered by an electronic spreadsheet program. A spreadsheet program can also be used for tasks that are not financial. It can be used to organize any kind of list, such as listing names and phone numbers, tracking a sports team's statistics, or managing the volunteer schedule at a nursery school. Information that would be organized into rows and columns can be managed easily using a spreadsheet program. We will use the spreadsheet program Excel to create a household budget spreadsheet.

▶ Open Excel.

On the PC, the Ribbon can be minimized to provide more room in the Excel window. Let's minimize the Ribbon and display it again. It may be minimized in your window by default.

▶ On the PC, right-click on the menu to display the shortcut menu as shown in Figure 5.1a.

▶ Click the menu item Minimize the Ribbon. If the Ribbon was visible before, it is now hidden. If the Ribbon was hidden, it is now visible.

▶ Ensure the Ribbon is visible, as shown in Figure 5.2. If it is hidden, use the above method to reveal it.

On the Mac, ensure the normal view is active, the Formula Bar is visible and the formatting toolbar is visible.

▶ On the Mac, click the menu items View, Normal, as shown in Figure 5.1b.

▶ On the Mac, click the menu items View, Toolbars, Formatting, as shown in Figure 5.1b.

▶ On the Mac, click the menu items View, Formula Bar, as shown in Figure 5.1b.

The Excel window contains a grid, toolbars, and sheet tabs as shown in Figures 5.2a and 5.2b.

The available worksheet area is quite large. The rectangular areas are called **cells**. There are 1,048,576 rows and 16,384 columns of cells available in each sheet. We will use only part of one sheet. Let's scroll to get a sense of the size of the work area.

▶ Click the left, right, up, and down scroll arrows on the right edge of the window as shown in Figures 5.2a and 5.2b.

As you click the down scroll arrow you will notice the row numbers increasing. As you click the right scroll arrow, you will notice the column letters scrolling. After the alphabet has expired, the "counting" begins again AA, AB, AC, . . . until the last column, XFD.

▶ On the PC, press and hold the **Ctrl** key while you tap the **Home** key to return to cell A1.

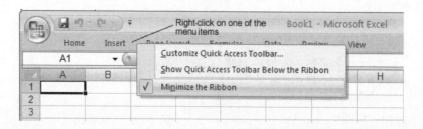

Figure 5.1a *Excel menu shortcut menu for PC.*

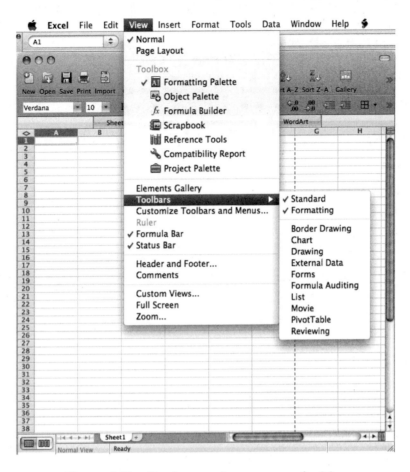

Figure 5.1b   *Excel menu shortcut menu for Mac.*

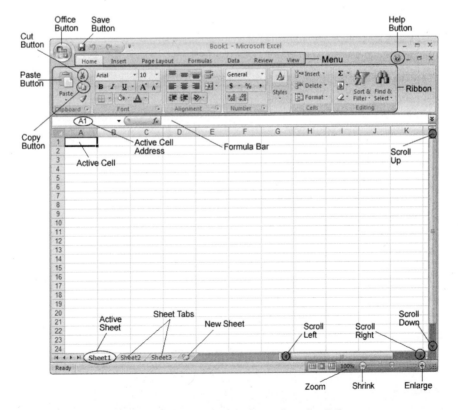

Figure 5.2a   *The Excel window for PC.*

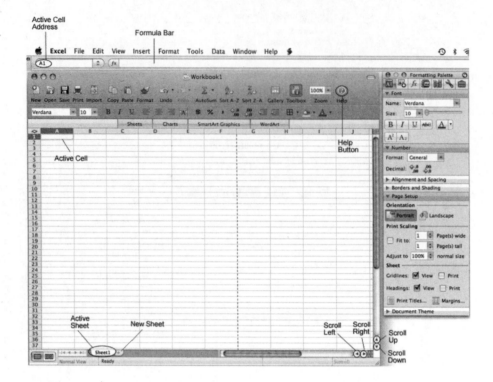

Figure 5.2b *The Excel window for Mac.*

Moving around the Worksheet

▶ Move the mouse pointer to cell D5.

▶ Click the **left mouse** button.

Notice that the cell is now outlined in bold. Only one cell will be outlined in bold. This indicates the active cell. You have activated cell D5 by clicking it.

The sheet tabs at the bottom of the window indicate different worksheets of the Excel workbook. Each of these sheets also contains 1,048,576 rows and 16,384 columns of cells. To activate a different sheet, click the appropriate tab. The Mac version shows only one sheet, but we will add more sheets later.

▶ On the PC, click the tab labeled Sheet2.

Now you have activated the Sheet2 worksheet.

▶ On the PC, click the Sheet1 tab to activate Sheet1 again.

Now, let's begin entering data. There are essentially three types of data: labels, values, and formulas. A label is text such as a title, the name of a month, or a street address. A value is a number and a formula is some kind of calculation.

Data Entry

▶ Activate cell A1.

▶ Type: Hello!

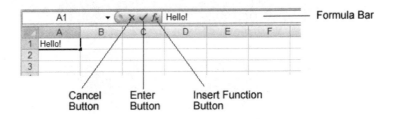

Figure 5.3a   *Excel formula bar for PC.*

While you type this label, several things are happening on the screen. You may notice that the label seems to appear in two places simultaneously. It appears in cell A1 and it also appears on the formula bar. Some symbols have also appeared on the formula bar as shown in Figures 5.3a and 5.3b.

▶ Click the **Cancel** button on the Formula Bar as shown in Figures 5.3a and 5.3b.

Notice that the input "Hello!" has disappeared. You can cancel any input before it has been entered by clicking the **Cancel** button.

▶ Type: Hello!
▶ Press the **Enter** key on the keyboard.

This button enters the data in the cell. Notice that the buttons on the Formula Bar have disappeared. On the PC version, you could have clicked the Enter button on the Formula Bar as shown in Figure 5.3. The **Insert Function** button is used to select a formula; we will examine this later.

Let's assume the cell entry is incorrect and we wish to erase it from the cell.

▶ Make sure that A1 is the active cell. If not, click cell A1 to activate it.
▶ Press the **Delete** key on the keyboard. Notice that the cell entry has been erased. There are other methods of deleting cell contents, but pressing the **Delete** key is quick and intuitive.

We can also make changes to the contents of a cell after it has been entered.

▶ Activate cell A1 if it is not already active.
▶ Type: Welcome to spreadsheet computing!
▶ Press the **Enter** key on the keyboard.

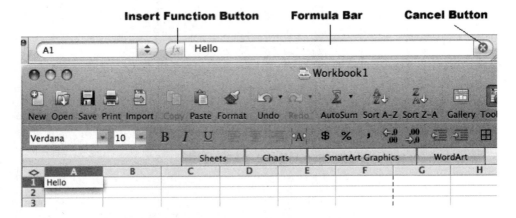

Figure 5.3b   *Excel formula bar for Mac.*

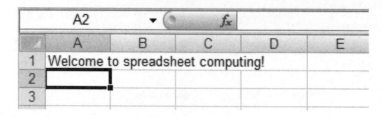

Figure 5.4 *Excel text entered.*

The text should be entered into the cell as shown in Figure 5.4.

You should notice a few things. First, since this label is longer than the width of the column, it scrolls onto adjacent blank cells. Column widths can be enlarged to accommodate data so cells B1, C1, and D1 could still contain data later and column A could be enlarged. Second, after pressing the **Enter** key, the active cell is now A2. After data is entered, the new active cell will usually be the cell below the entry.

Let's edit the contents of cell A1.

> ▶ Double-click cell A1. Notice that the flashing insertion point appears in cell A1. You can edit the contents of a cell directly in the cell or in the Formula Bar. Let's replace the words "spreadsheet computing" with "Microsoft Excel."
>
> ▶ Use your editing skills to delete the words "spreadsheet computing" and replace it with "Microsoft Excel."
>
> ▶ Press the **Enter** key to complete the cell entry.

Entering values is as easy as entering labels.

> ▶ Activate cell A2.
> ▶ Type: 3,456.78
> ▶ Press the **Enter** key

Notice that the comma separator has been accepted and the value is right-aligned in the cell.

> ▶ Activate cell A3 if it is not already active.
> ▶ Type: 123.456
> ▶ Press the **Enter** key.

Notice that the value has been entered in the cell. Notice also that the decimal places are different and not aligned. We will see later how formatting the cells can improve this situation.

Entering a Formula

The power of the spreadsheet application is the ability to perform calculations using formulas. Let's create a formula that adds the contents of cells A2 and A3.

> ▶ Activate cell A4 if it is not already active.
> ▶ Type: =A2+A3

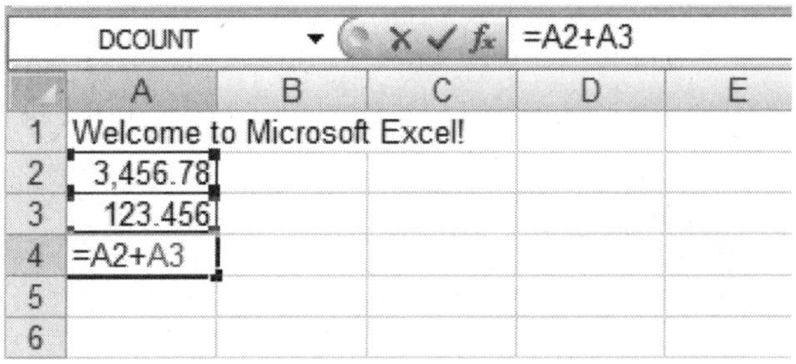

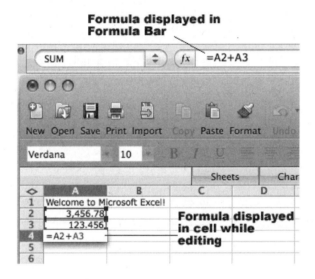

Figure 5.5a *Excel entering a formula for PC.*

Notice that the formula appears in the cell and in the Formula Bar as shown in Figures 5.5a and 5.5b. Also, the cells are color coded corresponding to the formula in cell A4.

Figure 5.5b *Excel entering a formula for Mac.*

▶ Press the **Enter** key.
▶ Activate cell A4.

Notice that the formula appears in the Formula Bar, but the result of the formula appears in cell A5, as shown in Figures 5.6a and 5.6b.

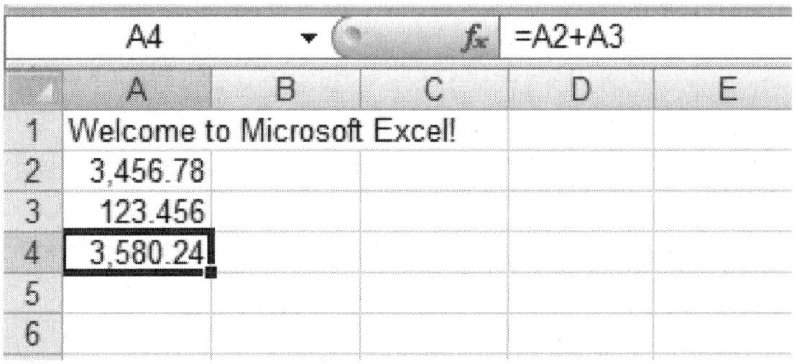

Figure 5.6a *Excel formula results for PC.*

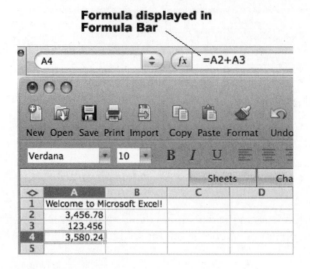

Figure 5.6b *Excel formula results for Mac.*

The power of a formula is in the cell references. Because the cell references are used in the formula, Excel updates the results when contents of these cells change.

- ▶ Activate cell A3.
- ▶ Type: 1,000
- ▶ Press the **Enter** key.

Notice that the results in cell A4 have now changed to reflect the new data. Excel formulas always begin with an equals = sign. In our example, =A2+A3, the plus sign is called an **operator**. Excel formulas can contain the following operators:

Operator	Description
^	(Caret symbol) Exponentiation
*	(Asterisk symbol) Multiplication
/	(Slash symbol) Division
+	(Plus sign) Addition
–	(Dash or minus sign) Subtraction

When we create a more complicated formula, we can use these operators and we can also use the parentheses ( ). Excel will follow the order of operations for mathematics when calculating formulas.

Let's start by entering some of the data into specific cells, as shown in Figure 5.7.

- ▶ Delete the contents of cells A1, A2, A3, and A4. You can select each cell and press the **Delete** key to delete the contents.
- ▶ Enter the data shown in Figure 5.7.

	A	B	C	D	E	F	G	H
1	Budget for Jane Doe							
2								
3		January	February	March	April	Year-to-Date		
4	Income	2578						
5								
6	Expenses							
7	Rent	950						
8	Car (gas)	120						
9	Car (insurance)				336			
10	Car (loan)	294						
11	Car (repairs)		628					
12	Food/hous	600						
13	Miscellane	325	170	228	294			
14								
15	Total Expenses							
16								
17	Net Surplus/Deficit							
18								
19								

Figure 5.7 *Excel sample data showing all cell content.*

Don't be concerned if some of the data appears to be "cut off" when you enter information in adjacent cells. We'll deal with column widths later. When you have completed entering all of the data, your spreadsheet should look something like that shown in Figure 5.8.

Let's take the opportunity now to save the file.

▶ Click the **Save** button and save the file as Sample.xlsx.

Save the file periodically as you work through this exercise.

▶ Activate cell A1 by using the **Ctrl-Home** combination (PC only) or clicking on cell A1.

	A	B	C	D	E	F	G	H
1	Budget for Jane Doe							
2								
3		January	February	March	April	Year-to-Date		
4	Income	2578						
5								
6	Expenses							
7	Rent	950						
8	Car (gas)	120						
9	Car (insurance)				336			
10	Car (loan)	294						
11	Car (repairs)		628					
12	Food/household	600						
13	Miscellaneous	325	170	228	294			
14								
15	Total Expenses							
16								
17	Net Surplus/Deficit							
18								
19								

Figure 5.8 *Excel sample data displays normal; some of the cell data appears cut off.*

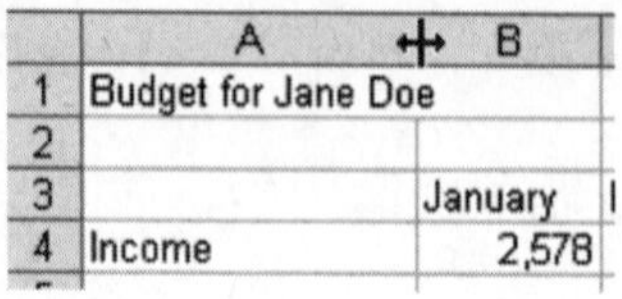

Figure 5.9 *Excel sizing a column.*

Changing the Column Width

Some of the titles in column A have been cut off because of information in cells in column B. This is not a problem since we can adjust the width of any column. Let's adjust the width of column A. The longest label in this column is "Net Surplus/Deficit." We'll adjust the width until the entire label is visible.

▶ Move the mouse pointer to the right border of the column A heading (the line between column A and B above cell A1) as shown in Figure 5.9. Notice that the pointer changes to a vertical line between a left and right arrow.

▶ Drag the border to the right until the longest label is visible.

Similarly, a column width can be decreased by dragging the line to the left. Using this method, any column width can be changed.

Moving Cell Contents

Cell contents can be easily copied or moved to other cells. Let's do some practicing!

▶ Activate cell B4. Let's move the income figure to cell C4.

▶ Move the pointer to the bottom edge of the active cell (any edge except the bottom right corner will do the trick).

You should see the pointer change from a cross icon to a large arrow with a move tool icon as shown in Figure 5.10 (PC) or a hand icon (Mac). Earlier versions of Excel will show a large arrow without the smaller move tool icon.

▶ Drag the pointer to cell C4 until you see a "shadow" appear on cell C4. Release the **left mouse** button. It's that easy! The income figure has been moved to cell C4. In earlier versions of Excel, you may see an outline for the cell instead of a shadow.

Using this method, you can move the contents of any cell to any other cell in the worksheet. An alternate method is to activate the cell to be moved and use a cut and paste method. Let's use a different method to move the income figure back to cell B4.

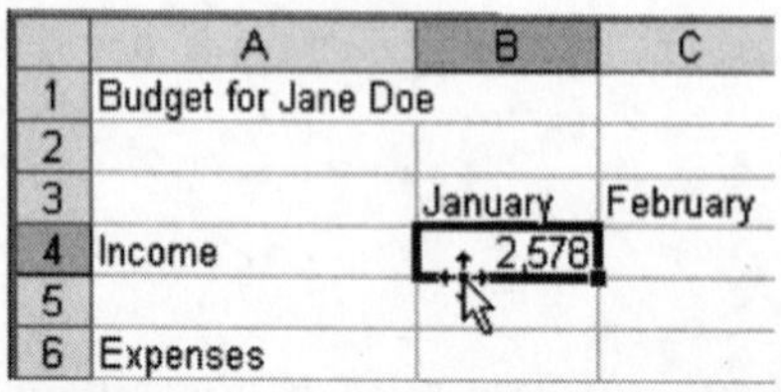

Figure 5.10 *Excel mouse pointer for moving a cell.*

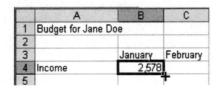

Figure 5.11   *Excel mouse pointer on the fill handle of an active cell.*

▶ Activate cell C4.
▶ Click the **menu options Edit, Cut**
▶ Click cell B4.
▶ Click the **menu options Edit, Paste.**

Copying Cell Contents

We can copy information from one cell to another as easily as we can move information from one cell to another. Let's copy the income figure in cell B4 to cells C4, D4, and E4.

▶ Activate cell B4.

Notice that the active cell is highlighted in bold and contains a box at the bottom right corner of the cell. This is called the **fill handle**.

▶ Move the mouse pointer to the fill handle. The pointer should change to a thin cross as shown in Figure 5.11.

▶ Drag the pointer to cell E4 and release the **left mouse** button.

Notice the dotted outline on the cells as you drag the mouse pointer, as shown in Figure 5.12.

You should notice that cells C4, D4, and E4 have been filled with the income figure! We can also use the copy and paste method to copy cell contents.

▶ Activate cell B7.
▶ Click the menu items Edit, Copy.

Notice that there is a flashing marquee around cell B7.

▶ Position the mouse pointer in the middle of cell C7 and drag it to cell E7 to select these cells. Release the **left mouse** button, as shown in Figure 5.13.
▶ Click the **menu items Edit, Paste** to paste a copy of the value from cell B7 into the selected cells.

	A	B	C	D	E	F	G
1	Budget for Jane Doe						
2							
3		January	February	March	April	Year-to-Date	
4	Income	2,578					
5					2,578		
6	Expenses						

Figure 5.12   *Excel mouse pointer dragging the fill handle.*

	A	B	C	D	E	F	G
1	Budget for Jane Doe						
2							
3		January	February	March	April	Year-to-Date	
4	Income	2,578	2,578	2,578	2,578		
5							
6	Expenses						
7	Rent	950					
8	Car (gas)	120					

Figure 5.13 *Excel cells selected.*

▶ Copy the Car (gas) figure in cell B8 to cells C8, D8, and E8 using any method you prefer.

▶ Copy the Car (loan) figure in cell B10 to cells C10, D10, and E10 using any method you prefer.

▶ Copy the Food/household figure in cell B12 to cells C12, D12, and E12 using any method you prefer.

Your document should look something like that shown in Figure 5.14.

Using the Undo and Redo Features

Now is a great time to introduce the Undo feature. This command will undo the effect of the most recent command.

▶ Click the **Undo** button ↶ on the upper left corner of the Excel window (PC) or standard toolbar (Mac).

Excel cannot undo all commands but it's ideal for commands such as editing, cut, copy, insert, delete, formatting and others. You can click the drop-down arrow on the **Undo** button to see the most recent tasks that can be "undone." Excel will allow you to click the **Undo** button repeatedly to progressively undo the most recent tasks, or you can choose from the list of tasks to undo a group of tasks. You will not be able to choose a single task in the middle of the list. When you select a task in the middle of the list, Excel will undo all of the tasks above the task selected.

Notice that the copied cells have been deleted.

	A	B	C	D	E	F	G	H
1	Budget for Jane Doe							
2								
3		January	February	March	April	Year-to-Date		
4	Income	2578	2578	2578	2578			
5								
6	Expenses							
7	Rent	950	950	950	950			
8	Car (gas)	120	120	120	120			
9	Car (insurance)				336			
10	Car (loan)	294	294	294	294			
11	Car (repairs)		628					
12	Food/household	600	600	600	600			
13	Miscellaneous	325	170	228	294			
14								
15	Total Expenses							
16								
17	Net Surplus/Deficit							
18								

Figure 5.14 *Excel cells containing budget figures.*

Once the Undo feature has been used, the Redo feature can be used to "redo" the most recently undone task.

▶ Click the **Redo** button ⟳ at the upper left corner of the Excel window (PC) or standard toolbar (Mac).

Notice that the copied cells have reappeared.

Entering Formulas

Most of the figures have been entered and it's time to enter the formulas. Let's start with the Total Expenses formula. We could enter a formula such as =B7+B8+B9+B10+B11+B12+B13, but this is long and cumbersome. When there is a group of cells to be included in a calculation that adds all of the data, we can use the SUM function. This will allow us to specify a group of cells by dragging to select the cells or typing a specific range.

▶ Activate cell B15.
▶ Type: =SUM(

Do not type any spaces in this formula. Be sure to type the left parenthesis because it is part of the function.

Select the group of cells from B7 to B13 by dragging through them. Notice that there is a marquee around the block of cells as shown in Figure 5.15.

▶ Press the **Enter** key to complete the formula.
▶ Activate cell B15 to see the formula in the formula bar.

Notice that Excel has placed a right parenthesis at the end of the function to end it. The formula should be =SUM(B7:B13). The end cells are specified, separated by a colon (:) to define the range of cells. The result of the formula appears in cell B15 but the actual formula appears on the formula bar.

▶ Copy the formula in cell B15 to the range C15:E15. You can use the dragging method or the copy and paste method.
▶ Activate each cell (C15, D15, E15) and look at the formula in the formula bar. The formula in cell C15 is =SUM(C7:C13).

Excel has changed the range in each cell accordingly. This is exactly the effect that we need at this point, so don't hesitate to copy formulas.

	A	B	C	D	E	F	G
1	Budget for Jane Doe						
2							
3		January	February	March	April	Year-to-Date	
4	Income	2,578	2,578	2,578	2,578		
5							
6	Expenses						
7	Rent	950	950	950	950		
8	Car (gas)	120	120	120	120		
9	Car (insurance)				336		
10	Car (loan)	294	294	294	294		
11	Car (repairs)		628				
12	Food/household	600	600	600	600		
13	Miscellaneous	325	170	228	294		
14							
15	Total Expenses	=sum(B7:B13					
16		SUM(**number1**, [number2], ...)					
17	Net Surplus/Deficit						
18							

Figure 5.15 *Excel Sum function.*

Now let's enter the formula for the Net Surplus/Deficit using a pointing method. We will subtract the Total Expenses figure from the Income figure.

▶ Activate cell B17.

▶ Type: =

▶ Click cell B4.

Notice the marquee around cell B4.

▶ Type: –

▶ Click cell B15.

Notice the marquee around cell B15, as shown in Figure 5.16.

▶ Press the **Enter** key to complete the formula.

The formula could have been manually entered as =B4-B15, however the cells can also be selected with the mouse as we have done.

▶ Copy the formula in cell B17 to the range C17:E17 using any method you prefer.

Let's create the Year-To-Date formulas.

▶ Activate cell F4.

▶ Type: =SUM(

▶ Select the range B4:E4 by dragging through this range to select those cells as shown in Figure 5.17.

▶ Press the **Enter** key to enter the formula in the cell.

▶ Copy this formula to the appropriate places in column F. You can use the **Edit, Copy** command in this case since the cells are not all adjacent. You can also use the drag and drop technique, and delete contents of the cells that contain "0." Figures 5.18 and 5.19 show the budget document as it is displayed and with the formulas.

	A	B	C	D	E	F	G
1	Budget for Jane Doe						
2							
3		January	February	March	April	Year-to-Date	
4	Income	2,578	2,578	2,578	2,578		
5							
6	Expenses						
7	Rent	950	950	950	950		
8	Car (gas)	120	120	120	120		
9	Car (insurance)				336		
10	Car (loan)	294	294	294	294		
11	Car (repairs)		628				
12	Food/household	600	600	600	600		
13	Miscellaneous	325	170	228	294		
14							
15	Total Expenses	2289	2762	2192	2594		
16							
17	Net Surplus/Deficit	=B4-B15					
18							

Figure 5.16 *Excel entering a formula using the pointing method.*

	A	B	C	D	E	F	G	H
1	Budget for Jane Doe							
2								
3		January	February	March	April	Year-to-Date		
4	Income	2,578	2,578	2,578	2,578	=SUM(B4:E4		
5						SUM(**number1**, [number2], …)		
6	Expenses							
7	Rent	950	950	950	950			
8	Car (gas)	120	120	120	120			
9	Car (insurance)				336			
10	Car (loan)	294	294	294	294			
11	Car (repairs)		628					
12	Food/household	600	600	600	600			
13	Miscellaneous	325	170	228	294			
14								
15	Total Expenses	2289	2762	2192	2594			
16								
17	Net Surplus/Deficit	289	-184	386	-16			

Figure 5.17 *Excel sum function across a row.*

Viewing Formulas—Menu

You can view the formulas as shown in Figure 5.19a.

▶ On the PC, click the Formulas tab, and click the Show Formulas button to display the formulas, as shown in Figure 5.19b. Click this button again to return to the normal view.

▶ On the Mac, click the menu items Excel, Preferences to display the Preferences window. In the Authoring section, click View and click the Show formulas checkbox to display the formulas, as shown in Figure 19b. Click the checkbox again to clear the checkmark and return to the normal view.

Viewing Formulas—Shortcut Key for the PC

▶ On the PC, press and hold the **Ctrl** key while you tap the ~ key.

The ~ key is at the upper-left position on your keyboard.

	A	B	C	D	E	F	G
1	Budget for Jane Doe						
2							
3		January	February	March	April	Year-to-Date	
4	Income	2578	2578	2578	2578	10312	
5							
6	Expenses						
7	Rent	950	950	950	950	3800	
8	Car (gas)	120	120	120	120	480	
9	Car (insurance)				336	336	
10	Car (loan)	294	294	294	294	1176	
11	Car (repairs)		628			628	
12	Food/household	600	600	600	600	2400	
13	Miscellaneous	325	170	228	294	1017	
14							
15	Total Expenses	2289	2762	2192	2594	9837	
16							
17	Net Surplus/Deficit	289	-184	386	-16	475	
18							
19							

Figure 5.18 *Excel budget document with all values.*

	A	B	C	D	E	F
1	Budget for Jane Doe					
2						
3		January	February	March	April	Year-to-Date
4	Income	2578	2578	2578	2578	=SUM(B4:E4)
5						
6	Expenses					
7	Rent	950	950	950	950	=SUM(B7:E7)
8	Car (gas)	120	120	120	120	=SUM(B8:E8)
9	Car (insurance)				336	=SUM(B9:E9)
10	Car (loan)	294	294	294	294	=SUM(B10:E10)
11	Car (repairs)		628			=SUM(B11:E11)
12	Food/household	600	600	600	600	=SUM(B12:E12)
13	Miscellaneous	325	170	228	294	=SUM(B13:E13)
14						
15	Total Expenses	=SUM(B7:B13)	=SUM(C7:C13)	=SUM(D7:D13)	=SUM(E7:E13)	=SUM(B15:E15)
16						
17	Net Surplus/Deficit	=B4-B15	=C4-C15	=D4-D15	=E4-E15	=SUM(B17:E17)
18						
19						

Figure 5.19a *Excel budget document formulas for PC.*

To return to the display view we will use the same key combination.

▶ On the PC, press and hold the **Ctrl** key while you tap the ~ key. Notice that the view has returned to the display view.

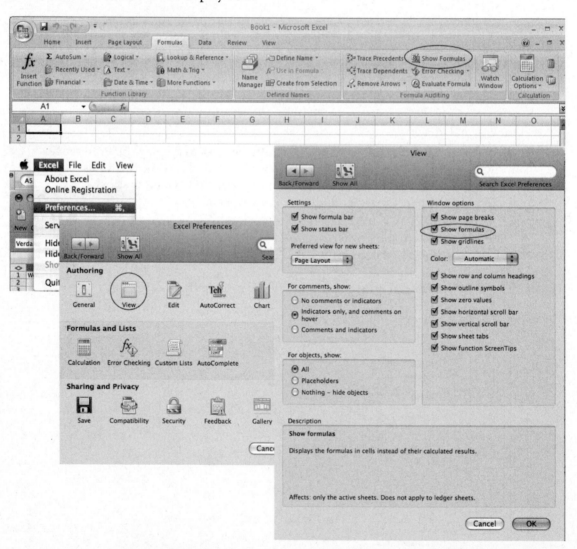

Figure 5.19b *Excel budget document formulas for Mac.*

Inserting and Deleting Rows and Columns

Excel allows us to insert rows and columns of cells into the worksheet and adjusts the formulas accordingly. Let's insert a row between the month headings and the income figures.

▶ Activate cell B4. This is the position of the new blank row and activating any cell in the row will work.

▶ On the PC, click the drop-down arrow beside or below the Insert button on the Ribbon as shown in Figure 5.20a. This reveals the Insert menu. Click the menu choice **Insert Sheet Rows** to add a row at the active cell position.

▶ On the Mac, click the menu choice Insert, Rows, as shown in Figure 5.20b.

Let's insert a column, and then delete it.

▶ Activate any cell in column F.

▶ On the PC, click the drop-down arrow beside the Insert button on the Ribbon as shown in Figure 5.20a. Click the menu choice **Insert Sheet Columns** to add a column at the active cell position.

▶ On the Mac, click the menu choice Insert, Columns as shown in Figure 5.20b.

Notice that a blank column has been inserted at the active cell position and any cell references have been adjusted.

Now that we've inserted a column, perhaps we decide that it really isn't necessary and now we want to delete it.

▶ Activate any cell in column F.

▶ On the PC, click the drop-down arrow beside or below the Delete button on the Ribbon. Click the menu item **Delete Sheet Columns** to delete the column.

▶ On the Mac, click the menu items Edit, Delete, as shown in Figure 5.20b. The **Delete** window will appear. Click the **Entire Column option**, as shown in Figure 5.20b. Click the **OK** button to delete the column.

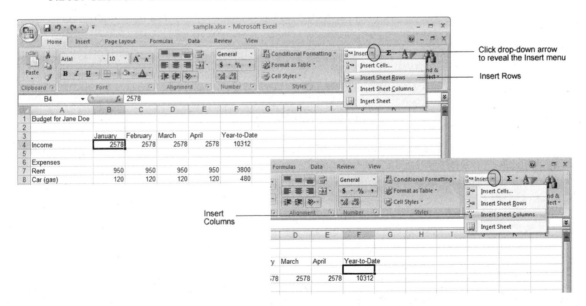

Figure 5.20a *Excel Insert Rows and Columns for PC.*

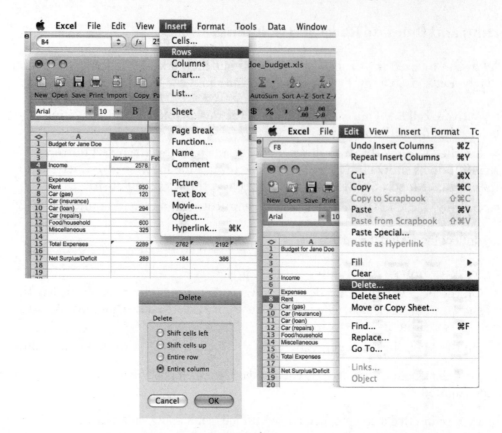

Figure 5.20b *Excel Insert Rows and Columns for Mac.*

Printing a Worksheet

You can print an Excel worksheet using the **Office** button and **Print** menu on the PC, or the **File, Print** menu on the Mac, as you would with any other application program. Worksheets can quickly become wide and long and will print on multiple pages, or can be fit to a single page. When the document is fit to a single page, the font size is reduced until the data fits on one page.

▶ On the PC, click the **Office** button and click the **Print** menu item. Click the **Print** option as shown in Figure 5.21a.

▶ On the Mac, click the **menu** options **File, Print**, as shown in Figure 5.21b.

The **Print** dialog box should appear as shown in Figures 5.21a and 5.21b.

Notice that the **Active sheet(s)** option is selected. As the workbook can have several sheets, there is an option to select only the active sheet, or the entire workbook.

▶ If you have a printer available, click the **OK** button to print the worksheet. If you do not have a printer available, click the **Cancel** button to cancel the print.

Changing Alignment in a Cell

To this point, we have been entering data, formulas, and adjusting the worksheet cells. Let's look at some formatting options to enhance the document.

Figure 5.21a *Excel Print dialog box for PC.*

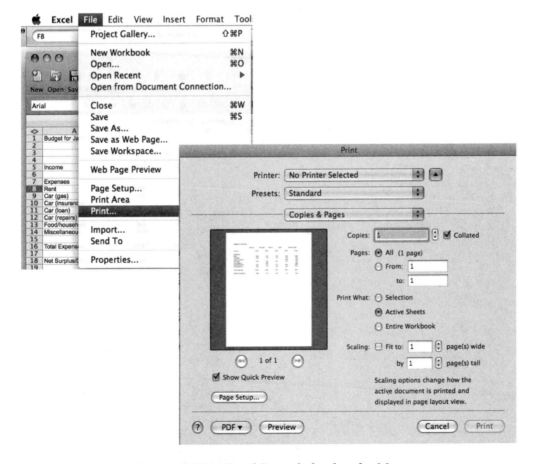

Figure 5.21b *Excel Print dialog box for Mac.*

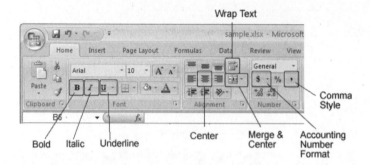

Figure 5.22a   *Excel Ribbon buttons for PC.*

By default, all of the labels are left-aligned within the cell and all of the values are right-aligned. Let's adjust the month labels so that they are centered in the cell.

▶ On the Mac, make sure that the Formatting Palette is displayed, as shown in Figure 5.22b. If it is not displayed, click the menu options View, Formatting Palette. Click on the headings to expand or collapse them as shown in Figure 5.22b.

▶ Select the cells containing the months by positioning the mouse pointer in the middle of cell B3 and dragging through to cell E3.

▶ Click the **Center** button ▤ on the Ribbon (PC) or Formatting Palette (Mac) as shown in Figures 5.22a and 5.22b.

Wrapping Text in a Cell

If the content of a cell is too long, we may prefer to wrap the text within the cell, rather than increase the column width. First, make sure that the title "Year-to-Date" is extending beyond column F and into column G. If column F is wide enough for the title, decrease the column width a bit.

▶ Activate cell F3.

▶ Click the **Wrap Text** button on the Ribbon (PC) or click the **Wrap Text** checkbox on the Formatting Palette (Mac) as shown in Figures 5.22a and 5.22b.

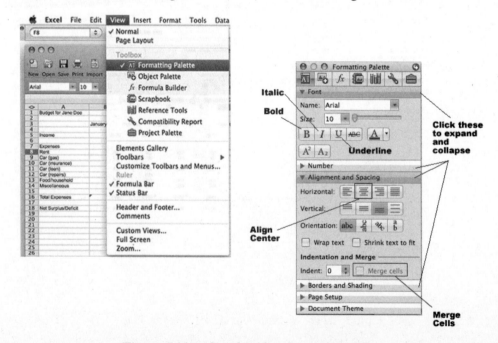

Figure 5.22b   *Excel Ribbon buttons for Mac.*

Notice that the Year-To-Date title is now wrapped within the cell. No new row has been added and the row height has been adjusted to accommodate the label.

Merge and Center

We can center a label across a group of columns easily.

▶ Activate cell A1. This cell contains the label "Budget for Jane Doe." It's important that the label to be centered is entered in the leftmost cell of the range.

▶ Select the range A1:F1 by dragging through the range.

▶ Click the **Merge & Center** button 🏛 on the Ribbon (PC) or click the **Merge** cells checkbox and click the **Align Center** button (Mac) as shown in Figures 5.22a and 5.22b.

Notice that the title has been centered across columns A through F. The cells A1:F1 have been merged. When you activate any of these cells the entire selection is activated, as shown in Figure 5.23.

Formatting Values

The values in the worksheet do not contain decimals or dollar signs. We can use formatting options to include these.

▶ Select the range B5:F5 by dragging through the range.

▶ On the PC, click the drop-down arrow beside the Accounting Number Format button $ on the Ribbon as shown in Figure 5.24a. Click the menu item **$English (U.S.)**.

▶ On the Mac, ensure the Number section is expanded on the Formatting Palette as shown in Figure 5.24b. Click the drop-down for the number format and select Accounting, as shown in Figure 5.24b.

Now look at the numbers in the worksheet. If numbers have disappeared and have been replaced with #, this indicates that the number of characters has exceeded the column width. If that occurs, it's necessary to increase the width of the columns. If there is more than one column affected, it may be easiest to increase the widths as a group.

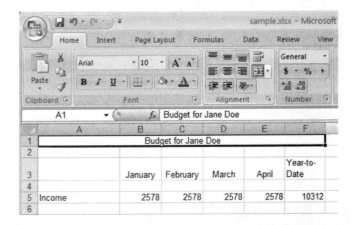

Figure 5.23 *Excel Merge and Center title.*

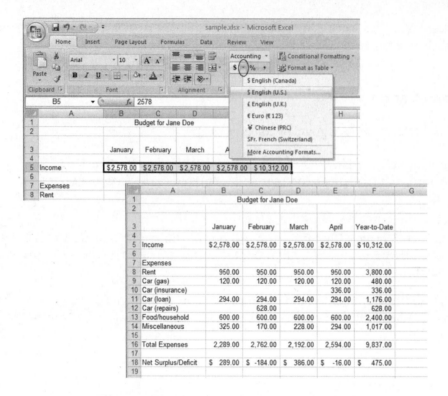

Figure 5.24a *Excel values formatted for PC.*

Figure 5.24b *Excel values formatted for Mac.*

Let's format some more values.

> ▶ Select the range B18:F18 by dragging through the range.
> ▶ On the PC, click the **Accounting Number Format** button $ on the Ribbon and select **$English (U.S.)**. On the Mac, click the drop-down for the number format and select Accounting.
> ▶ Select the range B8:F16 by dragging through the range. Start dragging at one of the corner positions and continue to the opposite corner to select all of the cells in the range.
> ▶ On the PC, click the , (comma) button , on the formatting toolbar. On the Mac, click the drop-down for the number format and select **Number** as shown in Figure 5.24b.

Notice that all of the numbers greater than three digits now have comma separators and all of the numbers have two decimal places, as shown in Figures 5.24a and 5.24b.

Bold, Underline, Italic, and Font Changes

Let's display all titles in bold so that they stand out.

> ▶ Select the range A5:A18 by dragging through it.
> ▶ Click the **Bold** button **B** on the Ribbon (PC) or on the Formatting Palette (Mac) as shown in Figures 5.22a and 5.22b.

Notice that the titles in column A are now bold. The bold formatting increases the width of the characters slightly and you may have to increase the width of column A to view the Net Surplus/Deficit title.

> ▶ Using whichever method you prefer, display all of the other titles in bold as well. Note that to bold the "Budget for Jane Doe" title, you will select the merged cell A1:F4.

Let's underline the title of the worksheet.

> ▶ Activate cell A1.
> ▶ Click the **Underline** button **U** on the Ribbon (PC) or on the Formatting Palette (Mac) as shown in Figures 5.22a and 5.22b.

Italic print is a slanted print. Let's change the titles to italic print.

> ▶ Select the range A1:F3 by dragging through it.
> ▶ Click the **Italic** button *I* on the Ribbon (PC) or the Formatting Palette (Mac) as shown in Figures 5.22a and 5.22b.

Notice that all of the contents of the cells are slanted to the right. The title at the top of the worksheet is also underlined.

Let's adjust the font for the worksheet title in cell A1. Here are a few quick definitions:

Font is a character set. That is, a font is the set of characters including the alphabet, numbers, and all special characters. A font generally has a name such as Courier, Times, Times New Roman, and so forth.

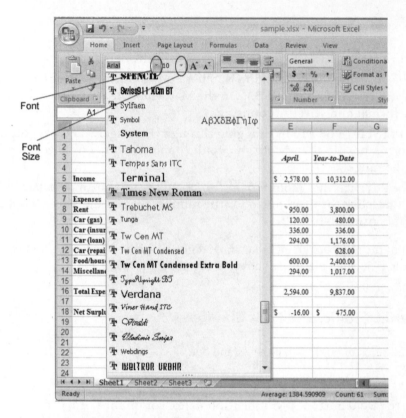

Figure 5.25a *Excel Font and Font Size indicators for PC.*

Font Style is the manner in which the font is displayed. The font may be bold, underlined, or italicized.

Size is measured in points. A point is 1/72". A good readable text is 10 or 12 point and a headline text might be 14 or 20 point.

▶ Select cells A1:F18 by dragging through them.

▶ Click the drop-down box for the Font as shown in Figures 5.25a and 5.25b.

Notice that the font list is displayed using the font that is named.

▶ Scroll through the list to get an idea of the fonts that are available. As you scroll through the list you may see the text change font in the worksheet.

▶ Select the Times New Roman font by clicking the name in the **Font** box.

▶ Change the font size to 18 by clicking the Font Size drop-down arrow and selecting 18 from the listing. Notice that the font size has increased and the row height has increased to accommodate the characters.

▶ If the numbers are replaced with # symbols, increase the column width. The # symbol indicates the column width is too narrow to display all of the digits.

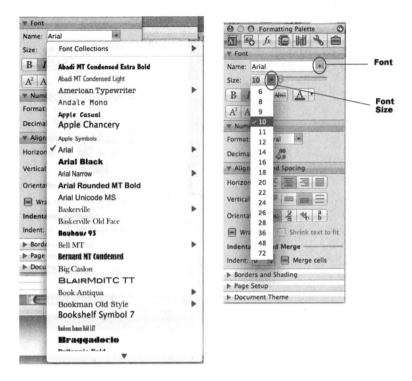

Figure 5.25b *Excel Font and Font Size indicators for Mac.*

Let's change the color of the text in the title.

▶ Make sure cell A1 is selected.

▶ Click the Font Color drop-down arrow as shown in Figures 5.26a and 5.26b. Notice that a color palette is displayed.

▶ Click one of the color swatches to change the color of the title.

When you are setting font color in a financial worksheet you should be aware that when values (numbers) are colored red, this is interpreted as negative or loss.

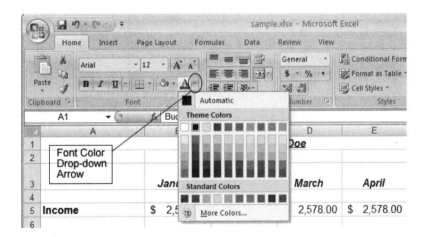

Figure 5.26a *Excel Font Color drop-down arrow for PC.*

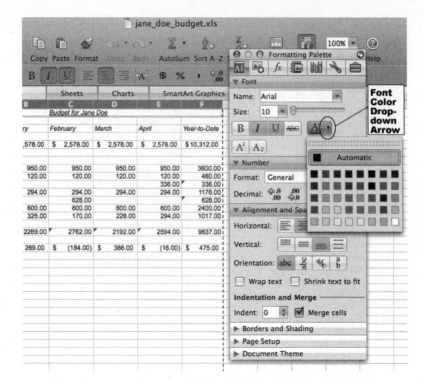

Figure 5.26b *Excel Font Color drop-down arrow for Mac.*

We can also add shading to any cell. Let's shade the Net Surplus/Deficit figures.

▶ Select the range A18:F18 by dragging through it.
▶ Click the Fill Color drop-down arrow as shown in Figures 5.27a and 5.27b.
▶ Click one of the very light colors to select the shading.

Your worksheet should look something like that shown in Figure 5.28.

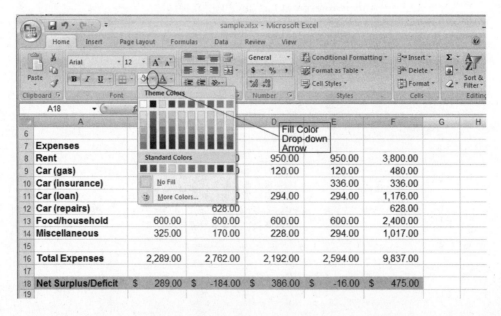

Figure 5.27a *Excel Fill Color drop-down arrow for PC.*

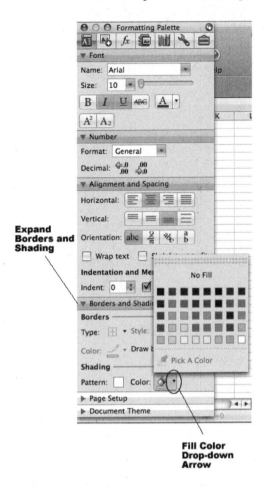

Figure 5.27b   *Excel Fill Color drop-down arrow for Mac.*

Review

This has been a busy lab! We have covered the following topics:

- Electronic spreadsheet concepts
  - Parts of the window
  - Cell references
- Entering data in a cell
- Editing and deleting data in a cell
- Using cut/copy/paste and drag and drop techniques to copy and move cell contents
- Relative cell formulas
  - Copying cell formulas and references adjust accordingly
  - Sum built-in function
- Formatting enhancements
  - Alignment within the cell
  - Merge and center across cells
  - Bold, italic, and underline
  - Fonts and font sizes
- Printing worksheets

	A	B	C	D	E	F	G
1			Budget for Jane Doe				
2							
3		January	February	March	April	Year-to-Date	
4							
5	Income	$ 2,578.00	$ 2,578.00	$ 2,578.00	$ 2,578.00	$ 10,312.00	
6							
7	Expenses						
8	Rent	950.00	950.00	950.00	950.00	3,800.00	
9	Car (gas)	120.00	120.00	120.00	120.00	480.00	
10	Car (insurance)				336.00	336.00	
11	Car (loan)	294.00	294.00	294.00	294.00	1,176.00	
12	Car (repairs)		628.00			628.00	
13	Food/household	600.00	600.00	600.00	600.00	2,400.00	
14	Miscellaneous	325.00	170.00	228.00	294.00	1,017.00	
15							
16	Total Expenses	2,289.00	2,762.00	2,192.00	2,594.00	9,837.00	
17							
18	Net Surplus/Deficit	$ 289.00	$ -184.00	$ 386.00	$ -16.00	$ 475.00	
19							

Figure 5.28 *Excel completed worksheet.*

Exercises

1. Enter the data shown in Figure 5.29.

> ► The budget sheet will have figures for January, February, and March. Copy the cell containing "January" to the two cells to the right by dragging on the bottom right corner of the cell. This enters "February" and "March" in the following two cells. This technique also works for the days of the week. (This technique only works when using the drag and drop method for copying cell contents; it does not work when using copy and paste.)

> ► The values for Income, Mortgage, and Car Loan remain unchanged for the three-month period. Copy these values into the appropriate cells for February and March.

> ► Enter the values for the remaining expenses as follows:

Car Insurance:	325.00 paid in February only
Car gas/maintenance:	120.00 for January and February, 80.00 for March
Food:	300.00 for January, 250 for February and March
Clothes:	300.00 for February only
Entertainment:	−250.00 for January, 100.00 for February and March

> ► Increase cell widths where appropriate in order to display the contents.

> ► Use the SUM function to create a formula for the total expenses.

> ► Create a formula for Net Surplus (Deficit), which will result in the Total Income − Total Expenses

> ► Create a column to the right of March for Year-to-Date calculations.

> ► Use the SUM function to calculate the total of each of the rows. You can use the **AutoSum** button Σ ▾ on the Ribbon (PC) or Standard Toolbar (Mac) to automatically enter the Sum function. After you click the **AutoSum** button, you can drag to adjust the range of cells to be included in the sum.

> ► Save this spreadsheet as Exercise1.xlsx.

	A	B	C
1	Budget for Alfred Doe		
2			
3		January	
4	Income	2458	
5			
6	Expenses		
7	Mortgage	1147	
8	Car Loan	268	
9	Car Insurance		
10	Car gas/maintenance		
11	Food		
12	Clothes		
13	Entertainment		
14	Total Expenses		
15			
16	Net Surplus/Deficit		
17			

Figure 5.29   *Excel Exercise 1.*

2.   Apply the following formatting enhancements to the Exercise1.xlsx worksheet.

  ▶ Underline the title "Budget for Alfred Doe" and center it across all columns of the budget sheet.

  ▶ Use the font Tahoma, size 16 for the title "Budget for Alfred Doe."

  ▶ Bold all of the titles in column A.

  ▶ Use bold and italic formatting for all of the month names.

  ▶ Center the month names in each cell.

  ▶ Wrap the Year-to-Date title in the cell.

  ▶ Select all cells that contain values and use the **Increase Decimal** button 🔲 on the Ribbon (PC) or Formatting Palette (Mac) to increase all cells with values to two decimal places.

  ▶ Use the Currency formatting for the Income figures.

  ▶ Apply a light shading to the Net Surplus/Deficit row.

Spreadsheet Concepts: Creating Charts in Microsoft Excel

Objectives:

Upon successful completion of Lab 6, you will be able to

- Create a simple chart on a separate chart sheet and embed it in the worksheet
- Create a pie chart using one series of data
- Understand the difference between plotting series by rows and by columns
- Identify and format chart elements including series, legend, titles, and chart area
- Add and delete a series from a chart
- Understand the linked relationship between the data and the chart
- Understand that some chart types are more appropriate for some types of data

Resources required:

- A computer running Microsoft Excel 2007 for PC or Microsoft Excel 2008 for Mac

Starter files:

- None

Prerequisite skills:

- General keyboarding skills
- Comfortable editing an Excel worksheet or another electronic spreadsheet application
- Ability to find files using Windows Explorer or Windows search feature
- Ability to open and save a file in a Windows application

NRC's Top Ten Skills, Concepts, and Capabilities:

- Skills
  Use a spreadsheet to model a simple process—household budget expenses
  - Create simple charts including line, bar, column, and pie
  - Identify and format chart elements
- Concepts
  Modeling and abstraction
- Capabilities
  Engage in sustained reasoning
  Think abstractly about Information Technology—building generic electronic spreadsheet concepts

	A	B	C	D	E
1	Stock Performance				
2	Highest Trading price/share				
3					
4		April	May	June	
5	Resort Hotels	35.5	37.9	42.6	
6	Sporty Autos	54	53.5	56	
7	Toys for You	21	17	14	
8	Furniture Manufacturir	29	31	32	
9					

Figure 6.1 *Excel chart data.*

Lab Lesson

Frequently we find ourselves using data in some sort of table form and would like to "see" how the data changes overall. In this case, a chart can make all the difference in how the data is presented. There is a wide variety of charts available and some are more suited to different types of data than others, but they all add a terrific visual effect to any presentation material!

Creating a Simple Column Chart

In order to create a chart, we must start with an active sheet containing data.

► Open a new workbook, activate the first sheet and enter the data shown in Figure 6.1. Formatting such as bold and alignment is not important.

► Save the file as stock.xlsx.

Remember to save your file periodically as you work through this lab. When you save a file, all sheets, including the chart sheet, will be saved in the Excel workbook file.

For our first chart, we will create a column chart, which will be placed on a separate worksheet in the workbook.

► Select the range A4:D8 by dragging through it to select it. It saves time if you include a row of titles and a column of titles when selecting the range for charting before selecting the chart type.

► On the PC, click the **Insert** menu option to display the Charts options in the ribbon as shown in Figure 6.2a. On the Mac, click the **Charts** tab to display the Charts gallery as shown in Figure 6.2b.

There is a wide variety of chart types to choose from. As we will see, once we have defined all of the appropriate ranges and titles, changing the chart type is as easy as selecting a new type from this screen. For now, let's create a basic column chart. The major chart types appear in the ribbon toolbar.

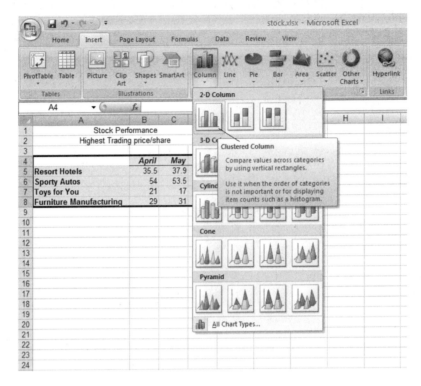

Figure 6.2a   *Excel Column chart gallery for PC.*

Let's create a 2-D Column chart.

▶ On the PC, click the Column button as shown in Figure 6.2a.

▶ Click the 2-D Clustered Column button as shown in Figures 6.2a and 6.2b.

The chart will be created and placed in the worksheet as shown in Figure 6.3.

You can move and size the chart.

▶ Position the mouse pointer in an empty part of the chart and drag the chart to a location where it is not covering the data.

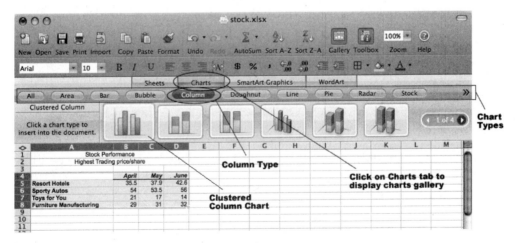

Figure 6.2b   *Excel Column chart gallery for Mac.*

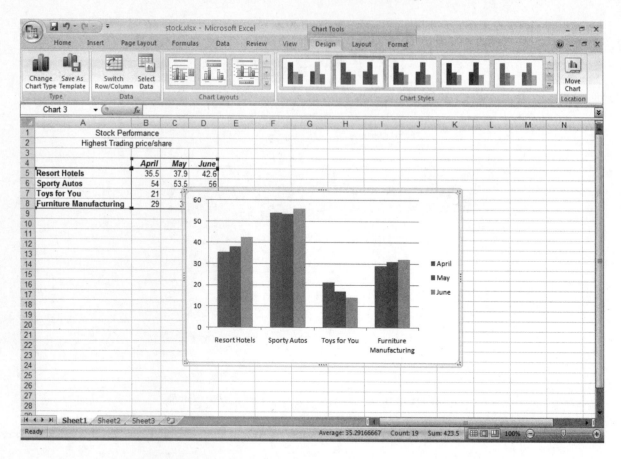

Figure 6.3 *Excel 2-D Chart embedded in the worksheet.*

▶ Position the mouse pointer on the sizing handles (indicated by three dots) on the chart edges or corners until it changes to a double arrow.

▶ Drag the mouse pointer to enlarge or shrink the chart slightly.

Notice that the columns are grouped by stock and each month value is represented by a different color. Sometimes it's useful to switch the grouping. The current chart is plotted by column (months) such that each column of data is a different color.

Suppose we wish to plot the chart such that each stock is a different color. We can do this by switching the row and column data.

▶ Click the **Switch Row/Column** button (PC) or **Row button** (Mac) as shown in Figures 6.4a and 6.4b.

For this data, it makes more sense to plot the months in series as we had originally.

▶ Click the **Switch Row/Column** button (PC) or **Column button** (Mac) to plot the chart with the months in series.

We can change the colors and styles of the columns using the Chart Styles gallery. Let's select a different style.

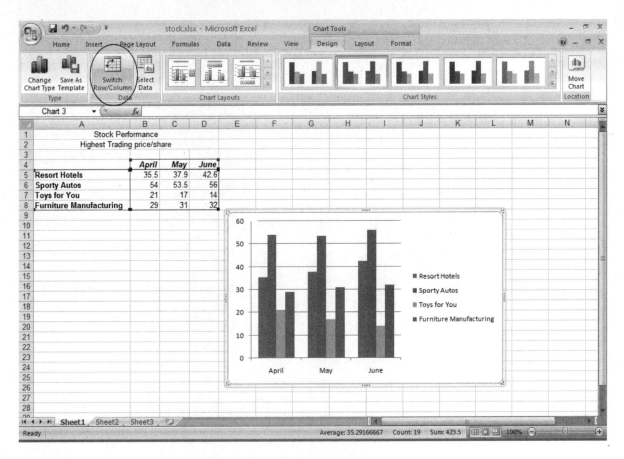

Figure 6.4a   *Excel Chart after Switch Row/Column for PC.*

▶ Click the **Scroll up** and **Scroll down** buttons in the Chart Styles as shown in Figures 6.5a and 6.5b.

▶ Click one of the styles to apply it to the chart as shown in Figures 6.5a and 6.5b.

Let's add some titles and other features to the chart.

On the PC:

▶ Click the **Layout** menu option and click the **Chart Title** button as shown in Figure 6.6a.

▶ Click the option **Above Chart** as shown in Figure 6.6a. The Chart Title will appear and the chart will be resized.

▶ Drag through the Chart Title and type: Stock Performance. This is shown in Figure 6.6a.

On the Mac:

▶ Click the drop-down Title on the Formatting Palette to select Chart Title.

▶ In the text box below type: Stock Performance

This is shown in Figure 6.6b.

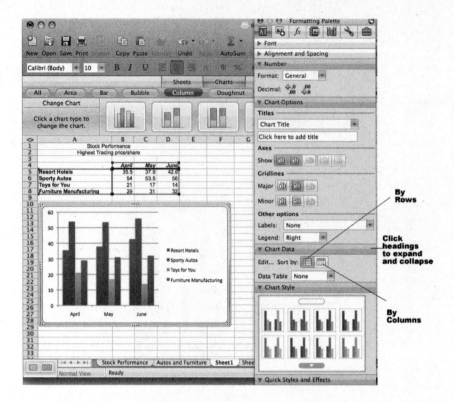

Figure 6.4b *Excel Chart after Switch Row/Column for Mac.*

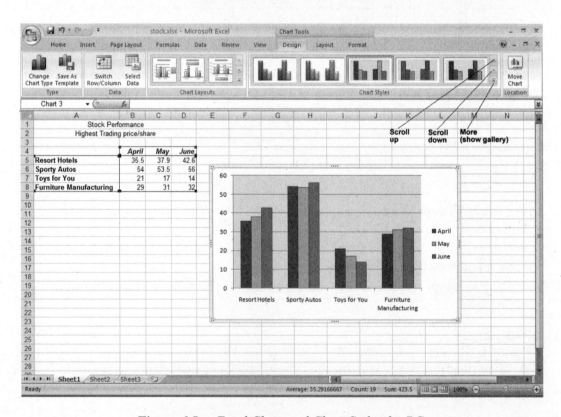

Figure 6.5a *Excel Chart and Chart Styles for PC.*

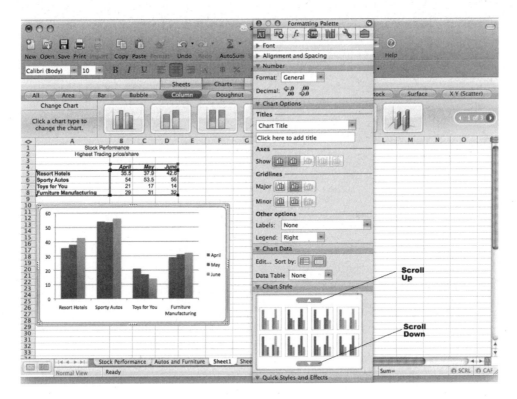

Figure 6.5b   *Excel Chart and Chart Styles for Mac.*

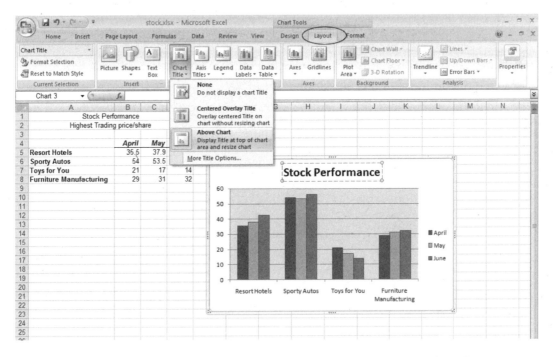

Figure 6.6a   *Excel Layout options with Chart Title selection for PC.*

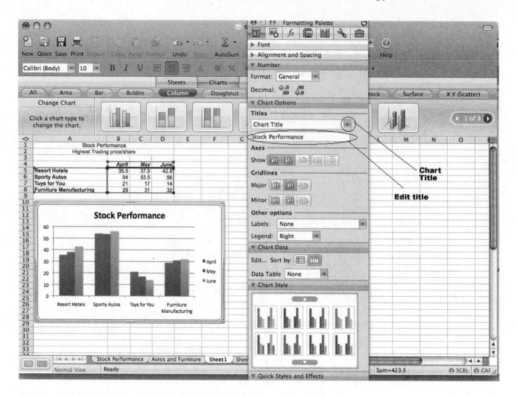

Figure 6.6b *Excel Layout options with Chart Title selection for Mac.*

Let's add a title at the bottom of the chart to identify the names as stocks.

On the PC:

▶ Click the **Axis Titles** button as shown in Figure 6.7a.
▶ Click the option, **Primary Horizontal Axis Title**.
▶ Click the option **Title Below Axis** as shown in Figure 6.7a.

The x-axis Chart Title will appear and the chart will be resized.

▶ Drag through the x-axis title and type: Stock. This is shown in Figure 6.7a.

On the Mac:

▶ Click the drop-down Title on the Formatting Palette to select Horizontal (Category) Axis.
▶ In the text box below type: Stock

This is shown in Figure 6.7b.

Let's reposition the legend, moving it to the bottom, below the chart.

▶ On the PC, click the **Legend** button, and click the option **Show Legend at Bottom** as shown in Figure 6.8a.
▶ On the Mac, click the **Legend position drop-down** and select the option **Bottom**, as shown in Figure 6.8b.

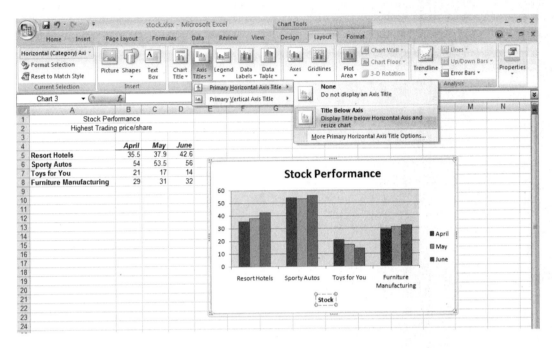

Figure 6.7a   *Excel Chart with horizontal axis title for PC.*

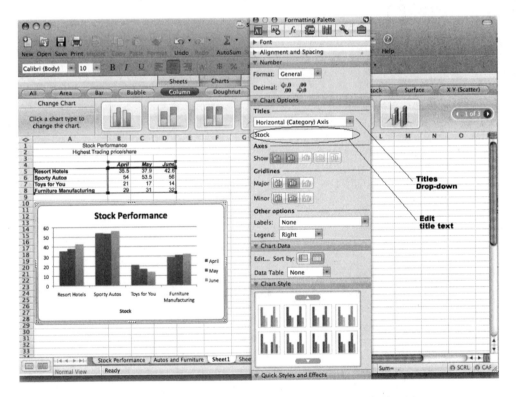

Figure 6.7b   *Excel Chart with horizontal axis title for Mac.*

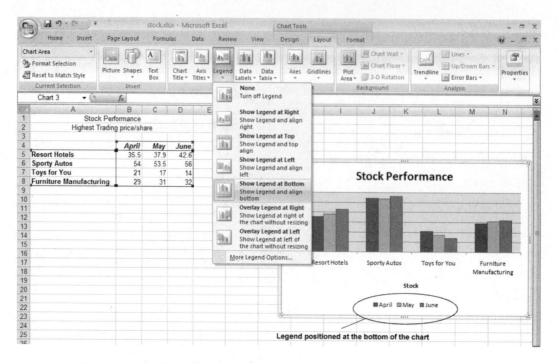

Figure 6.8a *Excel Chart with legend positioned at the bottom for PC.*

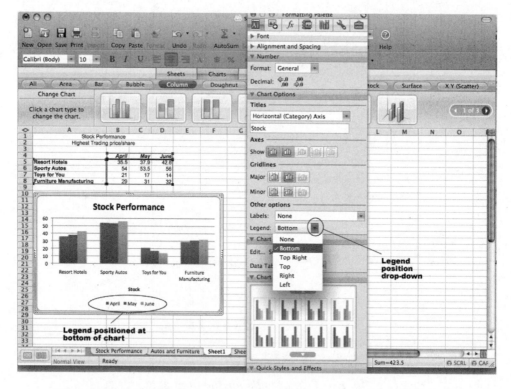

Figure 6.8b *Excel Chart with legend positioned at the bottom for Mac.*

Notice that the legend is now positioned below the chart.

Let's change the location of the chart to place it on its own sheet.

> ▶ On the PC, click the **Design** menu option and click the **Move Chart Location** button as shown in Figure 6.9a.
> ▶ On the PC, click the menu options Chart, Move Chart as shown in Figure 6.9b.

The **Chart Location** dialog box will appear as shown in Figures 6.9a and 6.9b.

> ▶ Click the **New Sheet** button, as shown in Figures 6.9a and 6.9b.
> ▶ Click the **OK** button.

The chart will appear on a separate sheet in the workbook called Chart1, as shown in Figure 6.10.

Since the chart is stored on a sheet, let's change the name of the sheet to reflect its contents.

> ▶ Move the mouse pointer to the **Chart1** tab and double-click.
> ▶ Press the **Delete** key to erase the current name of the sheet.
> ▶ Type: Stock Performance
> ▶ Press the **Enter** key to enter the name in the **Chart** tab.
> ▶ Click once on an empty part of the chart to activate the chart.

There are many parts of a chart. To determine the name of a particular part of the chart, position your mouse pointer on top of the part you wish to identify, and rest the mouse pointer for a moment. The chart item will appear in a pop-up label.

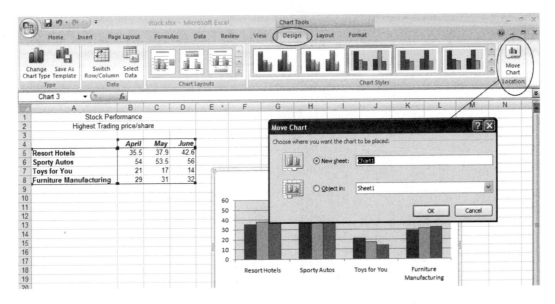

Figure 6.9a *Excel Chart Location button and dialog box for PC.*

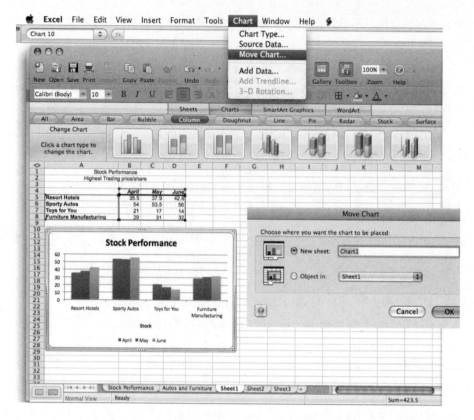

Figure 6.9b *Excel Chart Location button and dialog box for Mac.*

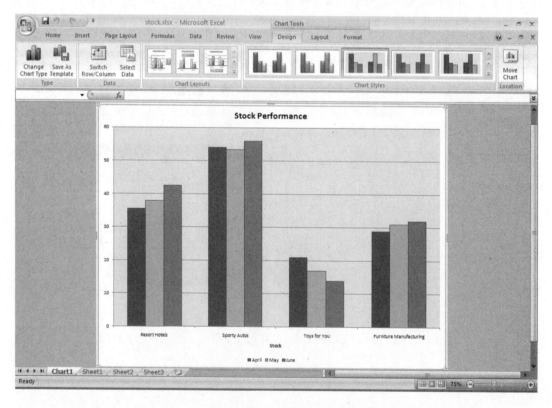

Figure 6.10 *Excel completed column chart.*

Charts are linked to the table of data in the worksheet, by default.

▶ Click the **Sheet 1** tab and change the figure for Resort Hotels for April, to 100.
▶ Click the **Stock Performance** tab and observe how the chart has changed.
▶ Click the **Sheet1** tab and return the figure for Resort Hotels for April, to 35.5.

When the numbers in the table change, the charts that were created from the data also change.

Changing the Chart Type

Let's change the chart type.

▶ On the PC, click the **Design** menu option and click the **Change Chart Type** button to reveal the chart types gallery as shown in Figure 6.11a.
▶ On the Mac, notice that the chart types are displayed in the gallery as shown in Figure 6.11b.

Once chart settings have been created, changing the chart type is only a few clicks away. Experiment a little here!

▶ Click one of the **Chart Type** buttons and click the **OK** button (PC) to see how the look of your chart changes.

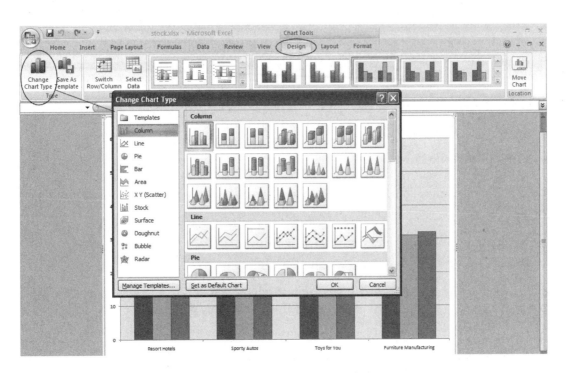

Figure 6.11a   *Excel Change Chart Type gallery for PC.*

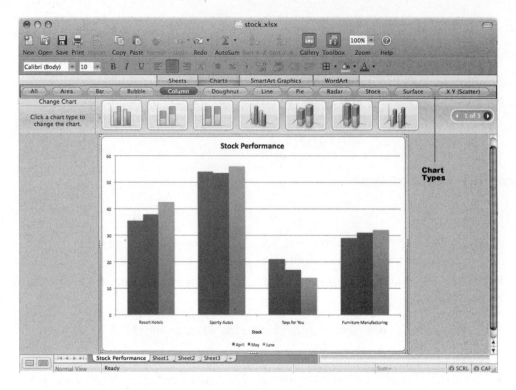

Figure 6.11b *Excel Change Chart Type gallery for Mac.*

Notice that the same data ranges and chart titles are used when creating different chart types. Also, note that not all chart types are suitable for the current data ranges selected. As we will see later, the pie charts require only one data range.

▶ Use the **Change Chart Type** button (PC) or select the Column Chart type from the gallery (Mac) to select the chart type as we had displayed originally.

Selecting Nonadjacent Series

Let's create another chart in which we will choose nonadjacent blocks of data. We will still need to specify the block of data that contains the labels.

▶ Click on the **Sheet 1** tab to display the values.

▶ Select the range A4:D4 by dragging through it.

We have included a blank cell (A4) in this range because Excel expects that the x-axis series will begin with a blank cell. If this cell is not included, then this row will be interpreted as a series and the chart will not look as expected.

▶ Press and hold the **Ctrl** key (PC) or **command** key (Mac) while you drag through the range A6:D6. Release the **mouse** button first, and then release the **Ctrl** key (PC) or **command** key (Mac). The selected range is shown in Figure 6.12.

▶ Press and hold the **Ctrl** key (PC) or **command** key (Mac) while you drag through the range A8:D8. Release the **mouse** button first, and then release the **Ctrl** key (PC) or **command** key (Mac). The selected range is shown in Figure 6.12.

	A	B	C	D	E
1	Stock Performance				
2	Highest Trading price/share				
3					
4		April	May	June	
5	Resort Hotels	35.5	37.9	42.6	
6	Sporty Autos	54	53.5	56	
7	Toys for You	21	17	14	
8	Furniture Manufacturing	29	31	32	
9					

Figure 6.12   *Excel nonadjacent ranges selected.*

You should notice that three ranges have been selected. Now we are ready to create a chart.

> ▶ On the PC, press the **F11 function** key to use the shortcut key combination to create a default chart on a separate sheet.
> ▶ On the Mac, click the **Clustered Column Chart** type in the gallery and change the location to a new sheet using the menu options **Chart, Move Chart.**

Excel created the chart based on the nonadjacent ranges selected. The chart should be displayed on a separate sheet, Chart2.

> ▶ Double-click on the **chart sheet** tab and rename it: Autos and Furniture
> ▶ Press the **Enter** key to complete the sheet name.

Simple Chart Modifications

Now is a perfect time to discuss some simple chart modifications. Let's make some changes to this new Autos and Furniture chart. First, let's change the type of chart.

> ▶ Click an empty area on the chart to select the chart.

Adding Data Labels

Sometimes charts are difficult to read, and it may be important to know the exact value for each data point. Let's add some data labels.

> ▶ On the PC, click the **Layout** menu option, click the **Data Labels** button, and click the **Outside End** menu option as shown in Figure 6.13a.
> ▶ On the Mac, click the **Labels drop-down** and select **Value** as indicated in Figure 6.13b.

Data labels will appear above the bars in a column chart, near the points on a line chart, or around the pieces of pie in a pie chart. That is, data labels usually appear close to the plotted points on a chart.

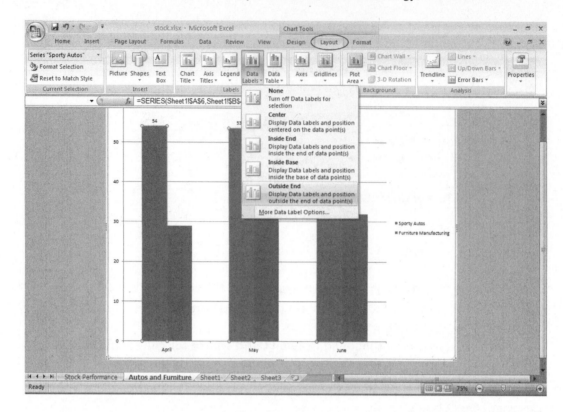

Figure 6.13a *Excel Chart Options dialog box showing Data Labels tab for PC.*

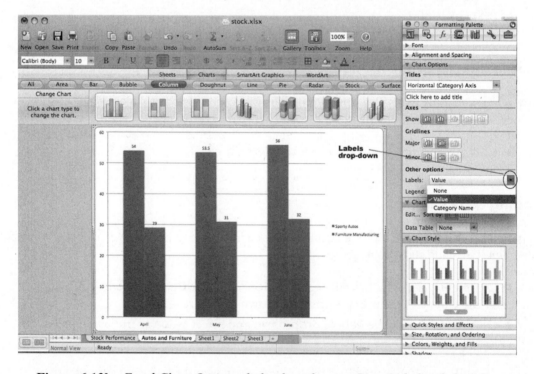

Figure 6.13b *Excel Chart Options dialog box showing Data Labels tab for Mac.*

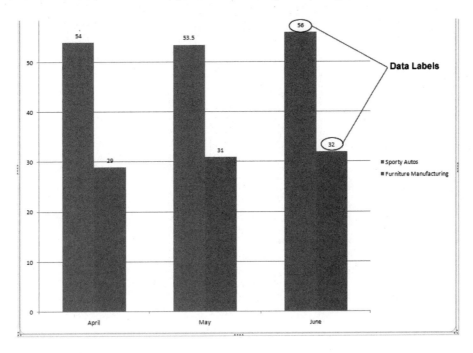

Figure 6.14   *Excel column chart with data labels.*

In the column chart, we selected the Outside End position for the data labels (PC) and they appear above the columns as shown in Figure 6.14.

Formatting Chart Elements

Although we are focusing on a column chart, the skills outlined here can also be used for any other chart type. Let's look at the various elements in this column chart and use the formatting option to customize the chart. The Design, Layout, and Formatting options will show tools in the Ribbon toolbar that are applicable to the type of chart currently selected.

The chart area is the blank area that surrounds the chart. We can specify the color and other aspects.

▶ Click in the large empty area to activate the Chart Area as shown in Figure 6.15.

▶ On the PC, click the **Format** menu option, and click in the **Shape Fill** button as shown in Figure 6.16a.

▶ On the Mac, click the heading **Colors, Weights and Fills** on the Formatting Palette if it is not already expanded, and click on the **Fill Color** drop-down as shown in Figure 6.16b.

▶ Click a color from the Color Palette to color the entire chart area.

In addition to selecting a simple color, we can also apply a gradient and texture. Let's experiment some more, adding a gradient to the Sporty Autos columns.

▶ Position the mouse pointer on one of the Sporty Autos columns and click to select the series.

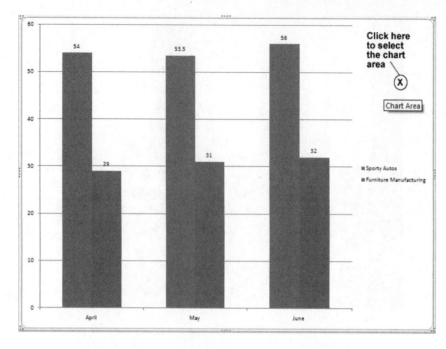

Figure 6.15 *Excel Chart selecting Chart Area.*

Notice that handles appear on the corners of each of the columns indicating that the columns are selected.

▶ On the PC, click the **Shape Fill** button as shown in Figure 6.17.

▶ On the PC, click the **Gradient** menu option as shown in Figure 6.17.

▶ Click one of the gradient variations to apply it to the selected series.

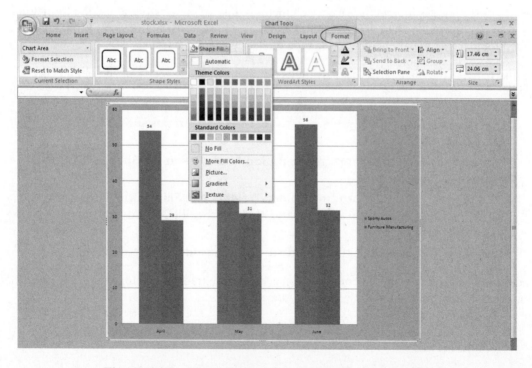

Figure 6.16a *Excel Format Chart Area fill color for PC.*

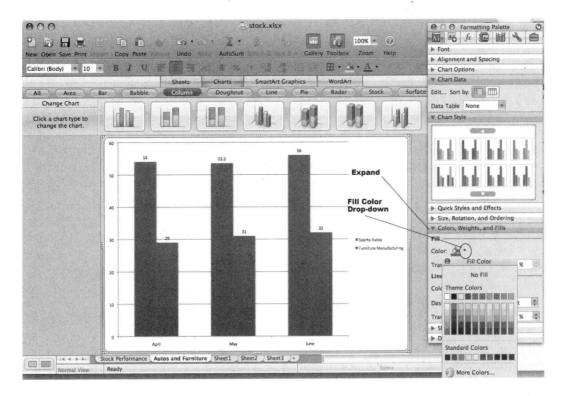

Figure 6.16b   *Excel Format Chart Area fill color for Mac.*

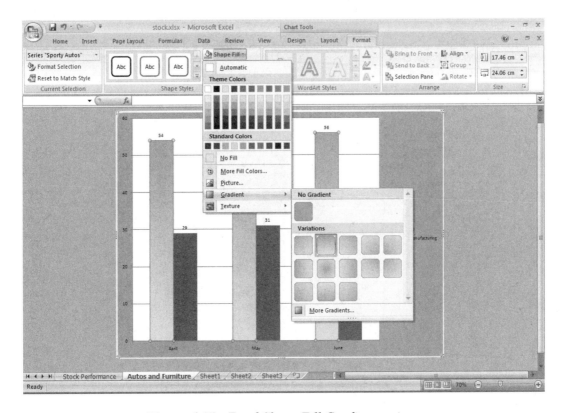

Figure 6.17   *Excel Shape Fill Gradient options.*

Chart Types

Sometimes the most difficult decision is choosing the appropriate chart type for the data. We have focused on a 2D Column chart because our table data lends itself well to this type of chart. Most data can be represented well in a column, bar, line, or area chart. Three-dimensional charts tend to be a bit more difficult to read, but a 3D column or area chart is quite readable. A ribbon chart may be more difficult to read and suitable for impact rather than readability. A pie chart is a special case in which only one series is plotted. The XY chart is suitable for data when there is a dependency such as time versus distance (km/hr, for instance). Radar charts are used in medical applications, and a stock chart type may be suitable for some financial and engineering applications.

Pie Chart

Let's create a pie chart which shows the sales price for each stock for the month of June.

> ► Click the **Sheet1** tab to display the data.
> ► Select the ranges A4:A8 and D4:D8.

Recall that you can drag through the first range, and then press and hold the **Ctrl** key (PC) or **command** key (Mac) while you drag through the second range.

> ► On the PC, click the **Insert** menu command and select the **2-D Pie** Chart type as shown in Figure 6.18a.
> ► On the Mac, select the **2D Pie Chart type** as shown in Figure 6.18b.

Let's choose a Chart Layout to add appropriate titles and data labels.

> ► Click the **Design** menu option (PC) as shown in Figure 6.19 or click one of the chart styles on the Formatting Palette (Mac).

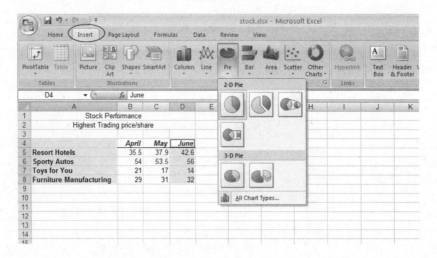

Figure 6.18a   *Excel Pie Chart type for PC.*

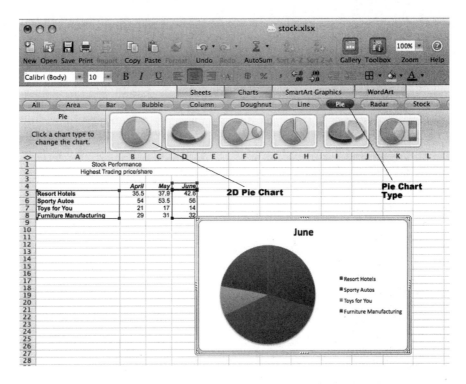

Figure 6.18b *Excel Pie Chart type for Mac.*

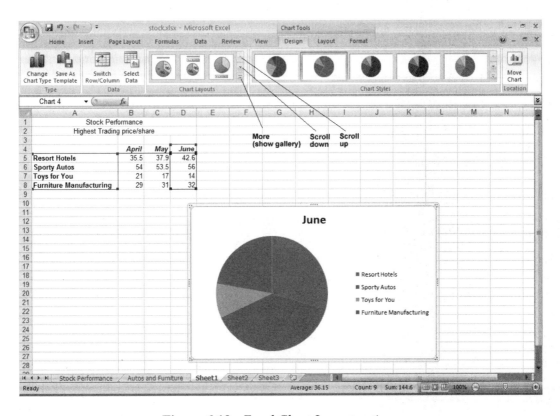

Figure 6.19 *Excel Chart Layout options.*

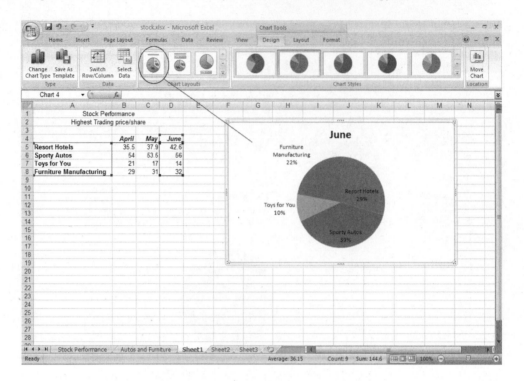

Figure 6.20a *Excel Pie Chart Layout 1 option for PC.*

You may use the scroll buttons to browse through the available layout selections.

> ▶ On the PC, click Layout 1 as shown in Figure 6.20a.

> ▶ On the Mac, click the drop-down for Labels and select **Category Name and Percent** and click the Legend drop-down and select **None** as shown in Figure 6.20b.

Notice that the legend has disappeared and the pie slices are identified with the stock name and percentage.

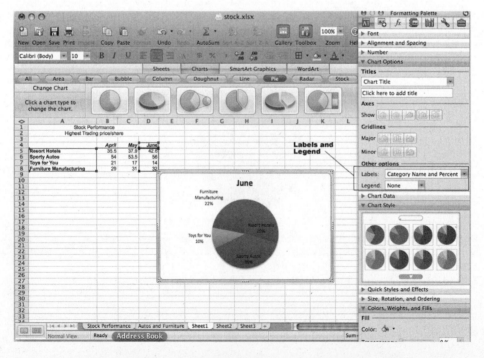

Figure 6.20b *Excel Pie Chart Layout 1 option for Mac.*

Review

This has been a busy lab! We have covered the following topics:

- Create a column chart on a separate worksheet
    Format chart elements including a series and chart area
    Plot the series by rows and by columns
- Add and modify chart options including series, legend, titles, and chart area
- Add and delete a series from a chart
- Understand that when the data in the worksheet changes, the corresponding charts also change
- Create a pie chart using one series of data
- Understand that some types of charts are more appropriate for some types of data

Exercises

Use the stock.xlsx Sheet1 data and try to recreate the following charts. Don't try to copy them exactly, but try to replicate the general look.

1. Line Chart. *Hint:* Switch Row/Column (PC) or choose column or row (Mac) in order to plot the stocks as lines.

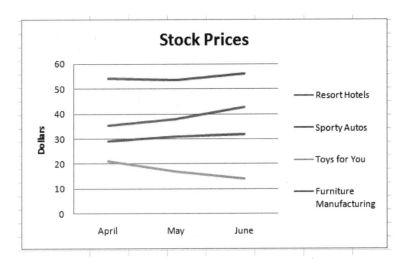

Figure 6.21   *Line Chart.*

2. Pie Chart. *Hint:* Select the cells containing the stock names and April values. Use the Layout options to add the percentages (PC) or select Labels (Mac).

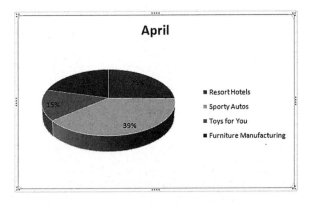

Figure 6.22   *Pie Chart.*

3. 3D Column Chart. *Hint:* Use the Layout options to add the data labels (PC) or select Labels (Mac).

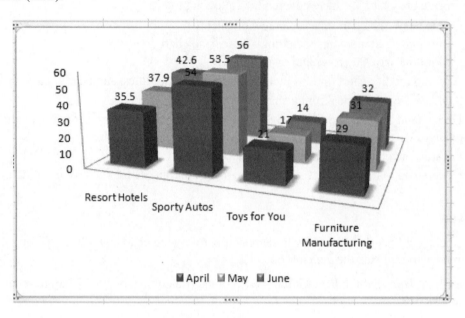

Figure 6.23 *3D Column Chart.*

Debugging Concepts
Using Microsoft Excel

Objectives:

Upon successful completion of Lab 7, you will be able to

- Define the terms troubleshooting and debugging
- Describe the steps required to analyze and find a solution for an everyday problem or computer problem
- Use the following troubleshooting and debugging steps to analyze and find a solution for a simple everyday or computer problem
    1. Identify the problem
    2. Describe the expected behavior
    3. Consider how the system works
    4. Guess the possible causes
    5. Eliminate the obvious causes
    6. Expand the scope

Resources required:

- A computer running any version of Excel

Starter files:

- budget.xls
- budget_exercise.xls

Prerequisite skills:

- General keyboarding skills
- Comfortable editing an Excel worksheet or another electronic spreadsheet application
- Ability to find files using Windows Explorer or Windows search feature
- Ability to open and save a file in a Windows application

NRC's Top Ten Skills, Concepts, and Capabilities:

- Skills
    Use a spreadsheet to model a simple process
    - Starter files, which contain errors will be provided
    - Debugging and fixing the errors
    - Focus on debugging techniques

- Concepts
    - Limitations of Information Technology
    - Modeling and abstraction
- Capabilities
    - Find problems in a faulty use of IT
    - Test a solution

Lab Lesson

In our everyday lives we encounter problems and try to solve them. We may have to come up with a solution to a problem, or we may have to troubleshoot something that has been working for a while and is suddenly broken. Troubleshooting involves examining a situation and trying to figure out what went wrong and how to fix it. For instance, perhaps your flashlight isn't working. You replace the batteries and then it works perfectly. In Information Technology, troubleshooting is referred to as **debugging**. A computer program or computer system may have a bug. A **bug** is an error or some kind of failure that prevents the computer system from working properly. Debugging is the process of finding and eliminating the bug, thereby fixing the problem.

Everyday Troubleshooting

Let's look at some everyday problems and the steps we might use to troubleshoot them. We'll look again at the flashlight example and outline the troubleshooting steps in detail.

- **Identify the problem.** When you move the flashlight switch to the on position, the light bulb does not illuminate.
- **Describe the expected behavior.** When the flashlight switch is moved to the on position, the light bulb should illuminate.
- **Consider how the system works.** A flashlight is a simple device consisting of a case with a switch, a light bulb, and batteries. When the switch is moved to the on position the batteries supply electricity to the light bulb and the light bulb illuminates.
- **Guess the possible causes.** The most obvious causes are dead batteries or a burned light bulb. Of those two causes, the most common cause is dead batteries.
- **Eliminate the obvious causes.** You replace the dead batteries and test the flashlight. It works! Problem solved.

If changing the batteries had not solved the problem the next step would have been to change the light bulb, which was the next likely cause of the problem. This was a very simple example of troubleshooting or debugging an everyday problem. If the problem had been more complex a few more troubleshooting steps could have been taken. It may require further investigation, including research and asking for expert advice.

Let's look at a slightly more complicated problem. The desk lamp plugs into a wall socket, and when you turn the switch on, the light does not illuminate. Fill in the blanks to try to solve the problem. Do not skip ahead even though the possible causes may seem obvious. The process is important.

1.   Identify the problem. Write the problem in your own words.

2.   Describe the expected behavior. How should the desk lamp function?

3.   Consider how the system works. Describe how the desk lamp works as a system. Include in your description the source of the electricity, the on/off switch, and the light bulb.

4.   Guess the possible causes. Describe at least three possible causes for the problem.

5.   Eliminate the obvious causes. Rank the order of the solutions you would try.

Now, let's say you eliminated the obvious causes, and the desk lamp still doesn't work. Further investigation is required. You would have to widen the scope of your investigation. Rather than concentrating on the desk lamp, what are other possible causes? The problem could be the lamp, or the problem could be with the electrical source. Answer the following questions.

1. How would you determine if the problem was with the lamp?

2. How would you determine if the problem was with the electrical source?

This is how the scope of investigation broadens. Once the obvious causes have been eliminated, we must look for other causes with the knowledge we have of the system. We know that the lamp requires electricity from the wall socket. We could try plugging the lamp into a wall socket that we know is working. If the lamp works, then we know the problem is with the electrical source. Similarly, we could plug another lamp or other electrical device that we know is working into the wall socket. If the device does not work, we know that the problem is with the electrical source. If the device works, we know the problem is with the lamp itself.

Sometimes the problem cannot be fixed easily and we require a workaround. In the case of the desk lamp, if the problem turns out to be the wall socket, further investigation is required. Again, using troubleshooting techniques, perhaps you check the fuse box and all fuses seem to be functioning. You may decide to call an electrician, but in the meantime, the workaround is to plug the lamp into a different wall socket.

Now, let's look at another problem. You have a small freezer that contains boxes of frozen food. The freezer lid has a light that illuminates when you open the door. The freezer plugs into a wall socket. You've been at work all day, and when you come home you discover that all of the contents in your freezer have begun to thaw. Complete the troubleshooting steps.

1.   Identify the problem.

2.   Describe the expected behavior.

3.   Consider how the system works (simplify—do not research how a freezer works).

4.   Guess the possible causes.

5.   Eliminate the obvious causes.

6.   Expand the scope. What would you do for a workaround if eliminating the obvious causes does not fix the problem? What would you do next to try to fix the problem?

	A	B	C	D	E	F	G
1		*Budget for John Doe*					
2							
3		January	February	March	April	Year-to-Date	
4							
5	Income	$ 2,475.00	$ 2,475.00	$ 2,475.00	$ 2,475.00	$ 9,900.00	
6							
7	Expenses						
8	Rent	950.00	950.00	950.00	950.00	3,800.00	
9	Car (gas)	120.00	120.00	120.00	120.00	480.00	
10	Car (insurance)				336.00	336.00	
11	Car (loan)	294.00	294.00	294.00	294.00	1,176.00	
12	Car (repairs)		628.00			628.00	
13	Food/household	600.00	600.00	600.00	600.00	2,400.00	
14	Miscellaneous	325.00	170.00	228.00	294.00	1,017.00	
15							
16	Total Expenses	1,964.00	2,592.00	1,964.00	2,300.00	8,820.00	
17							
18	Net Surplus/Deficit	$ 511.00	-$ 117.00	$ 511.00	$ 175.00	$ 1,080.00	
19							

Figure 7.1   *Excel budget.xls.*

Debugging Computer Problems

Troubleshooting computer problems is referred to as debugging. The same techniques used for troubleshooting everyday issues can also be used for debugging computer problems. Let's look at a problem with an Excel spreadsheet.

Your friend, John Doe, gives you his budget spreadsheet.

▶ Open the file, budget.xls, as shown in Figure 7.1.

John tells you that he hates math. He meticulously entered the Miscellaneous expenses so he's absolutely sure those figures are correct. He copies the other expenses from one month to the next, and he's sure all expenses were correct for January. He tells you that the only change to his expenses is that his rent was increased to $982.00 in April. He also tells you that he has $31 in his bank account, not $1,080.00. Let's go through the troubleshooting steps to debug the spreadsheet.

1. **Identify the problem.** The final Year-to-Date figure is incorrect, indicating that there is at least one problem with the spreadsheet calculations or data.

2. **Describe the expected behavior.** The final Year-to-Date figure should be $31.

3. **Consider how the system works.** The values are entered by hand. The calculations for Year-to-Date should result in the sum of the figures in each row. The Total Expenses calculations should result in the sum of the expenses for each column. The Net Surplus/Deficit row should result in the Income minus the Total Expenses for each month. The Year-to-Date Net Surplus/Deficit figure should be the Year-to-Date Income minus the Year-to-Date Total Expenses. This can be calculated as well by adding all of the Net Surplus/Deficit figures for the four-month period.

	A	B	C	D	E	F
1			*Budget for John Doe*			
2						
3		January	February	March	April	Year-to-Date
4						
5	Income	2475	2475	2475	2475	=SUM(B5:E5)
6						
7	Expenses					
8	Rent	950	950	950	982	=SUM(B8:E8)
9	Car (gas)	120	120	120	120	=SUM(B9:E9)
10	Car (insurance)				336	=SUM(B10:E10)
11	Car (loan)	294	294	294	294	=SUM(B11:E11)
12	Car (repairs)		628			=SUM(B12:E12)
13	Food/household	600	600	600	600	=SUM(B13:E13)
14	Miscellaneous	325	170	228	294	=SUM(B14:E14)
15						
16	Total Expenses	=SUM(B8:B13)	=SUM(C8:C13)	=SUM(D8:D13)	=SUM(E8:E13)	=SUM(B16:E16)
17						
18	Net Surplus/Deficit	=B5-B16	=C5-C16	=D5-D16	=E5-E16	=F5-F16
19						

Figure 7.2 *Excel budget.xls with formulas displayed.*

4. **Guess the possible causes.** Well, John was adamant that the Miscellaneous expenses were correct so that's not likely a cause of the problem. He did say that he hates math, so the cause of the problem could be in the formulas. He also mentioned that the Rent was increased in April, so that figure should be checked as well.

5. **Eliminate the obvious causes.** The obvious causes are data entry errors, and errors in formulas. He was sure that the Miscellaneous expenses were correct. As he copies the expenses from one month to the next and January expenses were correct, the only possible data entry error could be the rent increase in April.

► Look at the Rent figure for April. John said that the Rent increased to $982.00. Make the correction on his spreadsheet.

So, you've fixed one of the problems, but the final Year-to-Date figure is still not correct. Let's look at the formulas.

► Use the **Ctrl + ~** key combination (PC) or the menu commands Excel, Preferences, View, Formulas (Mac) to reveal the formulas, as shown in Figure 7.2.

When you activate the cells that contain formulas, the cells referred to in the formulas are outlined. Let's use this method to determine whether the formulas are correct. The Year-to-Date formulas should add all values in the row. The Total Expenses formulas should add all of the expenses. The Net Surplus/Deficit formulas should indicate the Income minus the Total Expenses.

► Click on each of the cells in column F and determine whether the formulas are correct (they are correct!). Notice that the cells referred to in the formulas are outlined each time you activate a cell containing a formula.

► Click on cell B16, the Total Expenses formula for January.

Figure 7.3 shows the cells outlined when cell B16 is activated.

What do you notice about the formula?

If you said that the Miscellaneous figure should be included in the formula you are correct! John has missed a figure in his SUM formula.

► Look at each of the formulas for Total Expenses for each month. What do you notice?

	A	B	C	D	E	F
1			*Budget for John Doe*			
2						
3		January	February	March	April	Year-to-Date
4						
5	Income	2475	2475	2475	2475	=SUM(B5:E5)
6						
7	Expenses					
8	Rent	950	950	950	982	=SUM(B8:E8)
9	Car (gas)	120	120	120	120	=SUM(B9:E9)
10	Car (insurance)				336	=SUM(B10:E10)
11	Car (loan)	294	294	294	294	=SUM(B11:E11)
12	Car (repairs)		628			=SUM(B12:E12)
13	Food/household	600	600	600	600	=SUM(B13:E13)
14	Miscellaneous	325	170	228	294	=SUM(B14:E14)
15						
16	Total Expenses	=SUM(B8:B13)	=SUM(C8:C13)	=SUM(D8:D13)	=SUM(E8:E13)	=SUM(B16:E16)
17						
18	Net Surplus/Deficit	=B5-B16	=C5-C16	=D5-D16	=E5-E16	=F5-F16
19						

Figure 7.3 *Excel budget.xls with Total Expenses cell for January activated.*

Again, if you noticed that each formula is missing the Miscellaneous Expense, you are correct!

▶ Use the **Ctrl + ~** key combination (PC) or the menu commands Excel, Preferences, View (Mac) to return the display to values.

▶ Correct the formula for the January Total Expenses to sum all expenses, including the Miscellaneous expense.

▶ Copy the newly corrected formula to the other month columns.

The results are shown in Figure 7.4.

Notice the Year-to-Date figure for Net Surplus/Deficit. It's $31.00! Problem solved.

	A	B	C	D	E	F	G
1			*Budget for John Doe*				
2							
3		January	February	March	April	Year-to-Date	
4							
5	Income	$2,475.00	$2,475.00	$2,475.00	$2,475.00	$ 9,900.00	
6							
7	Expenses						
8	Rent	950.00	950.00	950.00	982.00	3,832.00	
9	Car (gas)	120.00	120.00	120.00	120.00	480.00	
10	Car (insurance)				336.00	336.00	
11	Car (loan)	294.00	294.00	294.00	294.00	1,176.00	
12	Car (repairs)		628.00			628.00	
13	Food/household	600.00	600.00	600.00	600.00	2,400.00	
14	Miscellaneous	325.00	170.00	228.00	294.00	1,017.00	
15							
16	Total Expenses	2,289.00	2,762.00	2,192.00	2,626.00	9,869.00	
17							
18	Net Surplus/Deficit	$ 186.00	-$ 287.00	$ 283.00	-$ 151.00	$ 31.00	

Figure 7.4 *Excel budget.xls with correct Total Expenses formulas.*

If fixing the formulas had not solved the problem, what would you have investigated next to broaden the scope? Certainly, the other formulas could be verified. The individual values which John entered could also be verified. Even though John insisted that his values were correct, that would be the next likely cause for error in this example. As it turns out, John was correct and his values had been entered correctly.

Let's look at another example related to computing and hardware. The printer you've been using for months has suddenly stopped working. You are working on a Word document and click the **Print** button. Normally the printer would begin printing, but the printer doesn't even make a sound. Let's look at the debugging steps we might use to fix the problem.

1. **Identify the problem.** You attempt to print a Word document and it does not print.

2. **Describe the expected behavior.** You click the **Print** button in Word, and the printer makes a noise as it prepares to print, and then it prints the document.

3. **Consider how the system works.** The printer has an electrical plug that is connected to a power bar. The printer also has a data cable connected to the computer. In addition, the computer has software that identifies this printer as the default printer and uses a printer driver to communicate with the printer. The printer itself is an inkjet printer and contains an ink cartridge that travels back and forth inside the casing and expels ink onto the paper.

4. **Guess the possible causes.** Since the printer is not making any noises, the cause is not likely the printer cartridge. The possible causes are related to power. Perhaps the printer is not turned on or not plugged into the power bar.

5. **Eliminate the obvious causes.** You check the on/off switch and determine that the printer is turned on. Next, you check the plug and determine that it is plugged into the power bar. You check the plug for the power bar and determine that it is plugged into the wall. You notice a switch on the power bar and see that it has been turned off. You turn the switch to the on position and hear the startup noise from the printer. You click the print icon in Word and the document prints.

If investigating the power source had not fixed the problem, how would you have expanded your debugging? You could have tried plugging the printer into another wall outlet to determine if the problem was the power source. The problem could also have been a mechanical problem related to the on/off switch. If further investigation revealed that the cause was a mechanical problem with the printer, you may have had to call a technician or buy a new printer.

Review

This has been a busy lab! We have covered the following topics:
- Everyday troubleshooting to analyze and solve problems
- Debugging computer problems
- Six steps for troubleshooting and debugging
    1. Identify the problem
    2. Describe the expected behavior
    3. Consider how the system works
    4. Guess the possible causes
    5. Eliminate the obvious causes
    6. Expand the scope

Exercises

1. List the six troubleshooting steps and the specific details for each of the following problem scenarios. Explain how you would approach Step 6 to expand the scope of the investigation and possible workarounds.

   a. Each day at 8:00 a.m. your friend Jim picks you up and drives you to work. Today, it is 8:15 a.m. and Jim has not arrived.

   b. You pick up the television remote control and press the power button, but the television does not turn on.

2. Your friend John's budget file has somehow been corrupted again! Open the budget_exercise.xls file and fix the errors. The Year-to-Date Net Surplus/Deficit figure should be $31 as before.

Database Concepts Using Microsoft Excel

Objectives:

Upon successful completion of Lab 8, you will be able to

- Identify the records and fields in a table or list of items
- Use Excel to find specific items in a list
- Use Excel to sort a list over several fields, including a subfield sort
- Use the Excel AutoFilter feature to filter a list using specific criteria

Resources required:

- A computer running any recent version of Excel

Starter file:

- students.xls

Prerequisite skills:

- General keyboarding skills
- Comfortable editing an Excel worksheet or another electronic spreadsheet application
- Ability to find files using Windows Explorer or Windows search feature
- Ability to open and save a file in a Windows application

NRC's Top Ten Skills, Concepts, and Capabilities:

- Skills
  Use a database to access information
  - Use Excel to store lists of information
  - Identify fields and records
  - Sort fields
  - Use search and AutoFilter to filter records
- Concepts
  Structuring information
- Capabilities
  Manage complexity
  Navigate a collection

Lab Lesson

There seem to be lists everywhere you turn. We have lists of friends, lists of expenses, lists of things to do, lists of items in our homes, and even lists of lists. A business might have lists of employees, lists of products, lists of purchases, lists of projects, and many more. We can maintain lists using a pencil and paper, sticky notes, or memory. Or we may find ourselves looking up information rather than maintaining lists. As lists grow, however, none of these methods is very efficient. We need to find ways to manage our lists so that we can find items. A manual method might include an index card for each item and a box to contain them, or in the case of contacts, a Rolodex. These days information is more likely to be stored electronically. Personal contacts can be stored using Microsoft Outlook or a personal information manager. Other lists can be stored using a spreadsheet package or a database package. A **database** is simply one or more lists of items.

Once a list grows, finding specific items becomes more challenging. You may also wish to sort the list in different ways, search for items that meet certain criteria, and view statistics. There are several computer applications designed to work with databases and perform these tasks. If the list is fairly small, a spreadsheet package such as Excel will do the trick. As the list becomes larger, with thousands or even millions of items, a database package such as Microsoft Access is required.

Database Terminology

To illustrate some of the basic database terminology and tasks, let's look at an example of student records stored in an Excel file.

▶ Open the students.xls file.

This file contains information about students who have completed courses in CS1, Math, and Psychology, as shown in Figure 8.1. The data contained in a column is all the same type of data; this is called a **field**. The data contained in a **row** is all related to a particular student, in this case. The column headings are called **field names**. The data in a row contains different types of data about a single entity, and is called a **record**. This database contains one table consisting of 8 fields and 193 records. Large databases can contain many tables, but we will concentrate on a database using only one table.

Data Types

As we look through the table of information we can see that there are different types of data. The Last Name, First Name, and Gender fields contain text. Text data can include numbers, letters, and special characters like spaces and punctuation. For example, telephone numbers and street addresses are also stored in text fields.

The grades for CS1, Math, and Psychology are numbers. As numeric fields, we can perform math functions such as calculating the average grade.

The Student ID field is also a numeric field. It's not likely that we will be performing math functions on this field and sometimes numbers such as student number, employee number or credit card numbers are stored as text.

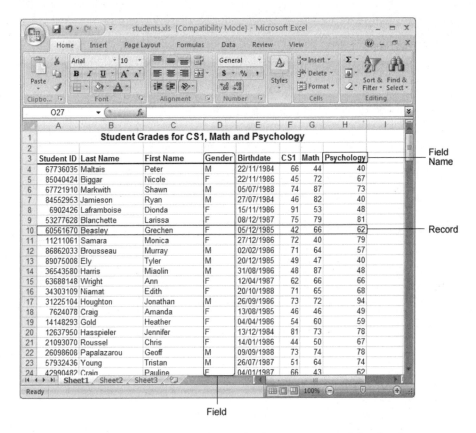

Figure 8.1   *Excel with students.xls showing parts of the database.*

The Birthdate field is a date field. We may do some date arithmetic with this field such as determining age. Dates are not stored as text because we cannot use date arithmetic on text. Other examples of date fields might include invoice issue date, retirement date, course completion date, and so forth. Date arithmetic might include calculating the number of years to retirement or the number of months an invoice is past due.

Sorting

One of the first things we tend to do with a table is to sort the records. We can sort a table on any field, and sort on additional fields within that if necessary. Let's sort our list alphabetically by Last Name.

> ▶ Activate any cell in the Last Name field.
> ▶ On the PC, click the **Sort & Filter** button and click the menu option **Sort A to Z** as shown in Figure 8.2a.
> ▶ On the Mac, click the the **Sort A-Z button** (Mac) as shown in Figure 8.2b.

Excel automatically detects the cells containing the entire table and sorts the list on the column of the active cell. The Last Name field should be sorted in ascending order as shown in Figures 8.2a and 8.2b.

Scroll through the list to verify that the Last Name field is sorted in ascending order. Ascending order sorts the data from smallest to largest. Descending order sorts the list from largest to smallest. Let's sort the CS1 grade field in descending order.

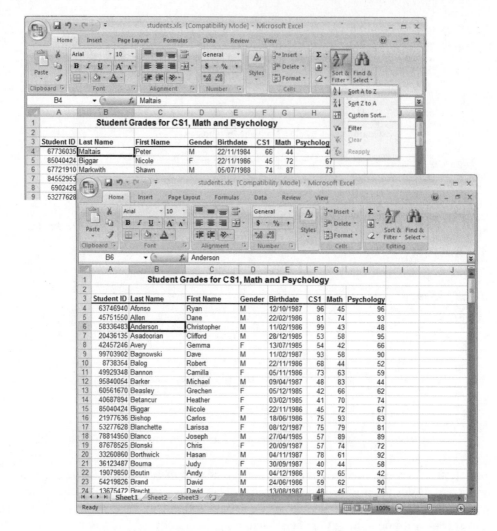

Figure 8.2a   *Excel students.xls with Last Name field sorted in ascending order for PC.*

▶ Activate any cell in the CS1 field.

▶ On the PC, click the **Sort & Filter** button and click the menu option **Sort Largest to Smallest** as shown in Figure 8.3.

▶ On the Mac, click the Sort Z-A button as shown in Figure 8.3b.

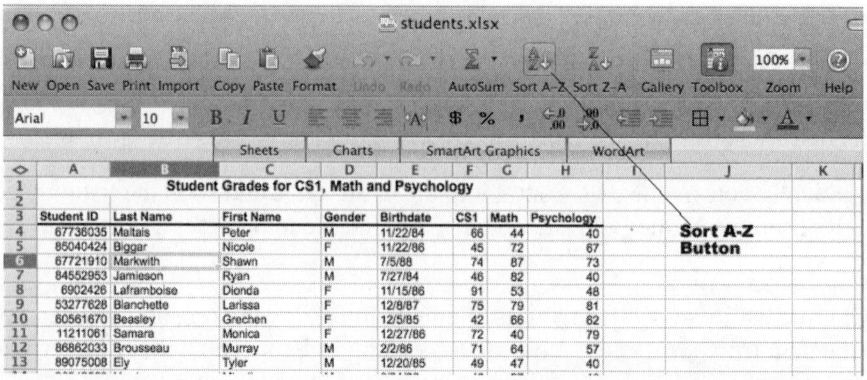

Figure 8.2b   *Excel students.xls with Last Name field sorted in ascending order for Mac.*

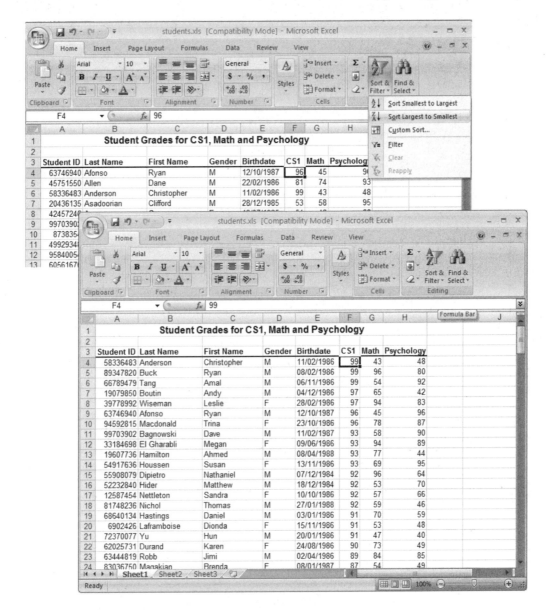

Figure 8.3a *Excel students.xls with CS1 field sorted in descending order (largest to smallest) for PC.*

Again, Excel detects the cells that contain the table and sorts the list on the column containing the active cell. The CS1 field should be sorted in descending order as shown in Figures 8.3a and 8.3b.

We've sorted a text field (Last Name) and a numeric field (CS1). We can also sort a date field. Let's sort the Birthdate field in ascending order.

▶ Activate any cell in the Birthdate field.

▶ On the PC, click the **Sort & Filter** button and click the menu option **Sort Newest to Oldest** as shown in Figure 8.4a.

▶ On the Mac, click the **Sort Z-A button** as shown in Figure 8.4b.

Again, Excel has detected the cells that contain the table and sorted all records on the Birthdate field from newest to oldest, as shown in Figures 8.4a and 8.4b.

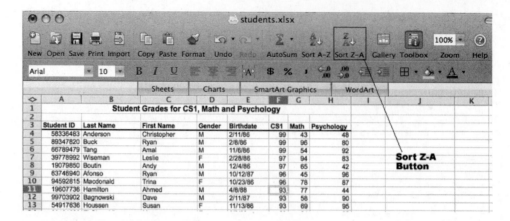

Figure 8.3b *Excel students.xls with CS1 field sorted in descending order (largest to smallest) for Mac.*

The table is now sorted by Birthdate from newest to oldest. Since we stored the birthdates as date information, the sort performs perfectly. If we had stored the birthdates as text, this would not be an easy maneuver. For instance, if we had stored the dates in a form such as "April 22, 1984" without converting to a date, then the field would be sorted alphabetically, with April at the top of the list. Understanding data types is important for completing tasks such as sorting, searching, and filtering.

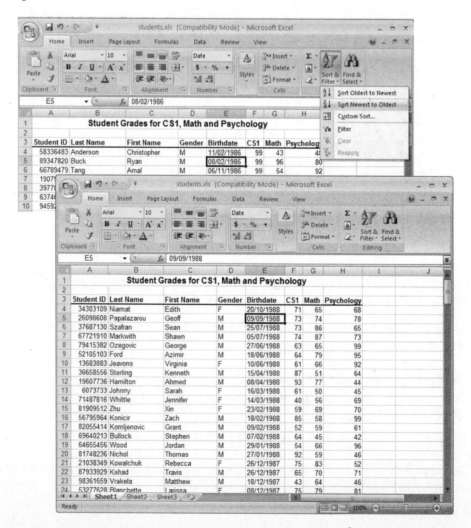

Figure 8.4a *Excel students.xls with Birthdate field sorted by Birthdate for PC.*

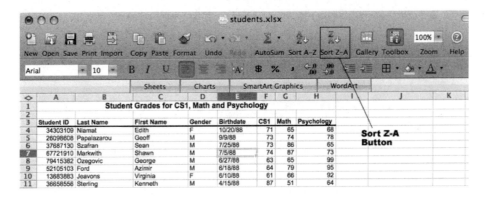

Figure 8.4b   *Excel students.xls with Birthdate field sorted by Birthdate for Mac.*

We can also perform sorts within sorts. For instance, we may wish to sort the list on the Last Name field and discover that several students have the same last name. For students with the same last name, we may wish to sort additionally on the First Name field. To do this, we will be using the menu commands. Let's give this a try.

▶ Activate any cell in the table. You do not have to activate a cell in the sort column in order to use this method.

On the PC:

▶ Click the **Sort & Filter** button.
▶ Click the menu option **Custom Sort**.

The Sort dialog box appears as shown in Figure 8.5a.

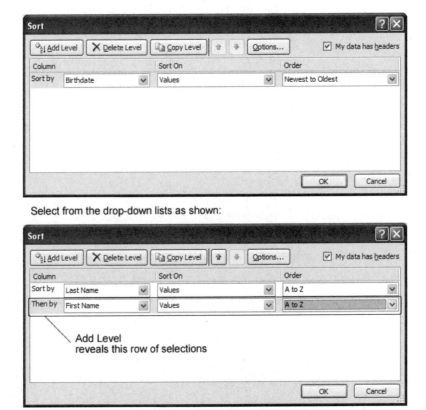

Select from the drop-down lists as shown:

Figure 8.5a   *Excel Sort dialog box for PC.*

Figure 8.5b *Excel Sort dialog box for Mac.*

We will sort by Last Name, then by First Name. In order to do this, we will need to add another level of sort options.

▶ Click the **Add Level** button.

▶ Click the drop-down arrows to select the options to sort by Last Name, from A to Z in the first level as shown in Figure 8.5a.

▶ Click the drop-down arrows to select the options to sort by First Name, from A to Z in the second level as shown in Figure 8.5a.

On the Mac:

▶ Click the menu commands **Data, Sort** as shown in Figure 8.5b.

▶ Click the **Sort by** drop-down and select Last Name, as shown in Figure 8.5b.

▶ Click the **Ascending radio button** as shown in Figure 8.5b.

▶ Click the **Then by** drop-down and select First Name, as shown in Figure 8.5b.

▶ Click the **Ascending radio button** for the First Name sort, as shown in Figure 8.5b.

As you clicked the drop-down arrow, you probably noticed that the list contained the field name headings. Excel detected the table and used the first row of cells as the field names. Notice that the **Sort dialog** box contains a checkbox (PC) or radio button (Mac) specifying that the data range has Headers. The Headers are the field names.

▶ Click the **OK** button to perform the sort.

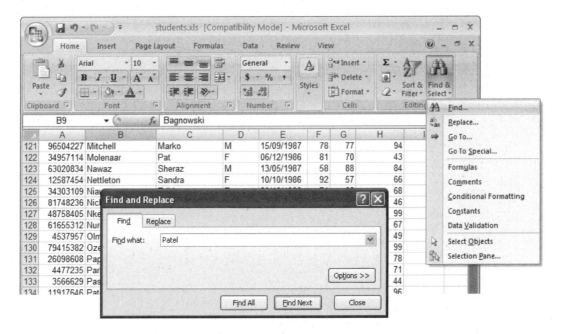

Figure 8.6a *Excel Find and Replace dialog box for PC.*

▶ Scroll through the list and notice that there are several records that contain the same Last Name, such as "Catbog" and "Patel." Notice that for those last names, the first names are also sorted in ascending order.

Searching for Records

Now that the list is sorted, one method we can use to search for records is to sort a field and simply scroll through the list until we find what we're looking for. This method may be fine for a small list, but as the list grows to hundreds or thousands of records, this method is inefficient and just takes too long! Another simple method we can use is the Find feature. The Find feature will activate a cell that contains the search criteria. Let's use this method to find the records for students whose last name is Patel.

▶ On the PC, click the **Find & Select** button and click the **Find** menu command as shown in Figure 8.6a.

▶ On the Mac, click the **Edit, Find** menu commands, as shown in Figure 8.6b.

The **Find and Replace** dialog box will appear as shown in Figures 8.6a and 8.6b.

▶ In the **Find what:** box, type: Patel, as shown in Figures 8.6a and 8.6b.

▶ Click the **Find Next** button. The first cell containing the last name "Patel" will be activated.

▶ Click the **Find Next** button again. The next cell containing the last name "Patel" will be activated.

As you click the **Find Next** button Excel activates the next cell that contains the search information. After the last cell, Excel activates the first cell again. In this case, there are only two instances of "Patel" and Excel will activate one, then the other, as you click the **Find Next** button several times.

▶ Click the **Close** button to close the **Find and Replace** dialog box.

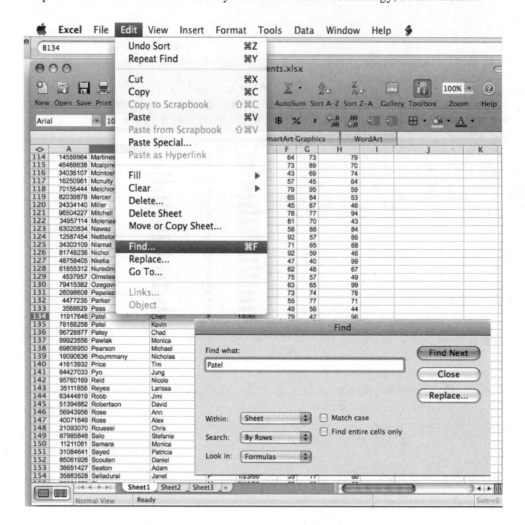

Figure 8.6b   *Excel Find and Replace dialog box for Mac.*

The Find feature is ideal when searching for a record that contains information that is not common in the list. For instance, if we were to search for "an" we would quickly find that "an" appears within many first and last names in the list. The Find feature is not suitable for numeric searches such as "all students whose CS1 grade is 80 or higher." It is also not suitable for range searches such as "all students whose last name begins with the letter S" or "all students born in 1985." For those searches, we will use the AutoFilter and Advanced Filter methods.

AutoFilter

The AutoFilter will find records that match certain criteria, and hide records that do not match the criteria. This is called **filtering** the list. Let's filter the list to display male students only.

   ▶ Activate any cell in the table.

   ▶ On the PC, click the **Sort & Filter** button and the menu option **Filter** as shown in Figure 8.7a

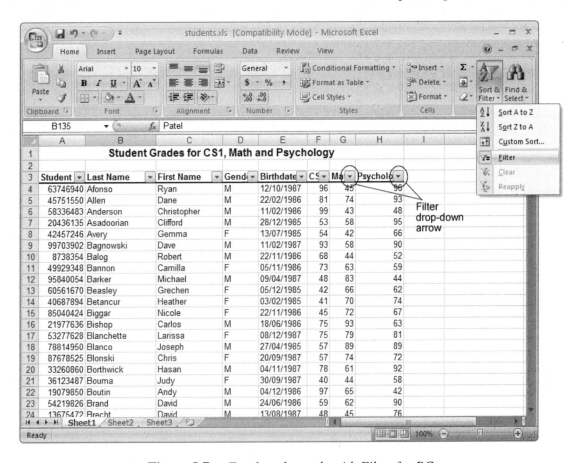

Figure 8.7a   *Excel students.xls with Filter for PC.*

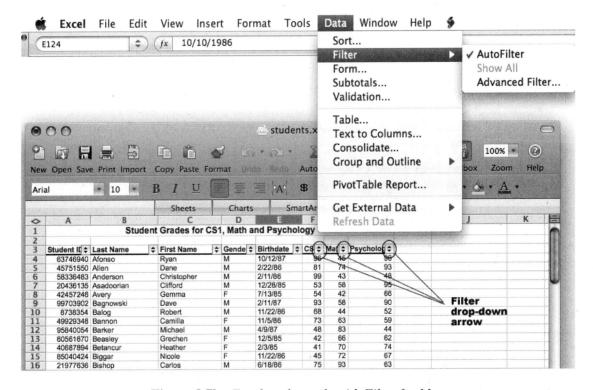

Figure 8.7b   *Excel students.xls with Filter for Mac.*

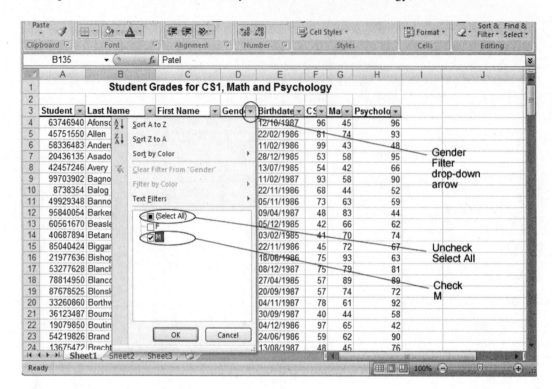

Figure 8.8a *Excel students.xls displaying Gender Filter options for PC.*

▶ On the Mac, click the menu commands Data, Filter, Autofilter as shown in Figure 8.7b.

▶ Scroll to the top of the table so that the field names are visible, as shown in Figures 8.7a and 8.7b.

Notice that Excel has added filter drop-down arrows in each cell containing a field name. Let's use the filter arrow to display only the records that contain an "M" in the Gender field.

▶ Click the filter arrow in the Gender field, as shown in Figures 8.8a and 8.8b.

▶ On the PC, click the **Select All** checkbox to remove the check mark and click the checkbox for the selection **M**, as shown in Figure 8.8a. Click the **OK** button to filter the records.

▶ On the Mac, click the menu option **M** as shown in Figure 8.8b. The menu will close and the records will be filtered immediately.

Notice that all records displayed contain "M" in the Gender field, as shown in Figure 8.9. Also notice the row numbers. The numbers skip as the records that contain "F" in the Gender field have been hidden. They are not lost or deleted, and will be displayed when we display all records. Notice that the row numbers seem to skip as the hidden records are not displayed.

Since the list was sorted in ascending order by last name, the filtered list displays records for male students, sorted by last name.

Let's add more criteria to the filter. Let's filter for all male students whose math grade is 80 or greater. We can add criteria by selecting another field and using the AutoFilter drop-down menu to add criteria. The filtered records will satisfy all criteria specified in all fields.

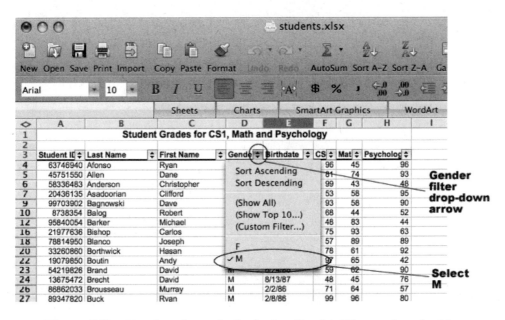

Figure 8.8b   *Excel students.xls displaying Gender Filter options for Mac.*

	Student	Last Name	First Name	Gend	Birthdate	CS	Ma	Psycholo		
4	63746940	Afonso	Ryan	M	12/10/1987	96	45	96		
5	45751550	Allen	Dane	M	22/02/1986	81	74	93		
6	58336483	Anderson	Christopher	M	11/02/1986	99	43	48		
7	20436135	Asadoorian	Clifford	M	28/12/1985	53	58	95		
9	99703902	Bagnowski	Dave	M	11/02/1987	93	58	90		
10	8738354	Balog	Robert	M	22/11/1986	68	44	52		
12	95840054	Barker	Michael	M	09/04/1987	48	83	44		
16	21977636	Bishop	Carlos	M	18/06/1986	75	93	63		
18	78814950	Blanco	Joseph	M	27/04/1985	57	89	89		
20	33260860	Borthwick	Hasan	M	04/11/1987	78	61	92		
22	19079850	Boutin	Andy	M	04/12/1986	97	65	42		
23	54219826	Brand	David	M	24/06/1986	59	62	90		
24	13675472	Brecht	David	M	13/08/1987	48	45	76		
26	86862033	Brousseau	Murray	M	02/02/1986	71	64	57		
27	89347820	Buck	Ryan	M	08/02/1986	99	96	80		
28	69640213	Bullock	Stephen	M	07/02/1984	64	45	42		
30	79068183	Carter	Jordan	M	13/07/1985	73	53	71		
32	5660799	Catbog	James	M	18/05/1985	72	47	87		
33	59070610	Catbog	Ryan	M	04/08/1985	56	91	57		
34	90916953	Chen	Gregory	M	02/05/1987	82	56	63		
36	92947340	Consoli	Tim	M	26/10/1986	63	50	62		

Ready   107 of 193 records found

Figure 8.9   *Excel students.xls displaying "M" in the Gender field.*

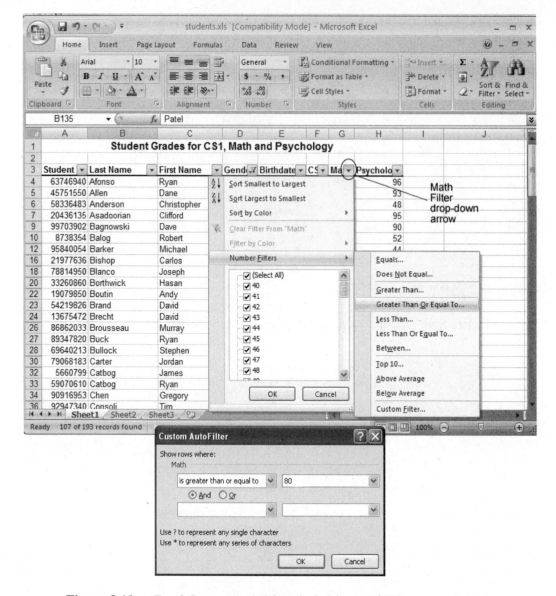

Figure 8.10a *Excel Custom AutoFilter dialog box and Filter menu for PC.*

▶ Click the Filter drop-down arrow for the Math grade field, as shown in Figures 8.10a and 8.10b.

▶ On the PC, click the menu options **Number Filters** and **Greater Than Or Equal To**, as shown in Figure 8.10a.

▶ On the Mac, click the menu option, **(Custom Filter . . .)** as shown in Figure 8.10b.

The **Custom AutoFilter** dialog box will appear, as shown in Figure 8.10. We will add the criteria shown in Figures 8.10a and 8.10b.

▶ Click the upper right box and type: 80, as shown in Figures 8.10a and 8.10b.

▶ Ensure that the option "is greater than or equal to" is displayed. If it is not displayed, click the drop-down arrow in the upper left box to select it.

▶ Click the **OK** button to filter the list.

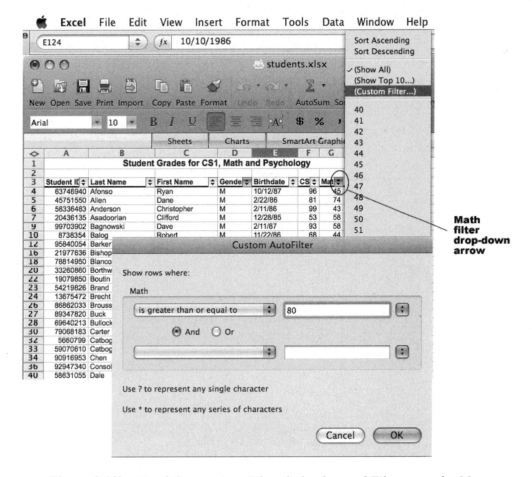

Figure 8.10b   *Excel Custom AutoFilter dialog box and Filter menu for Mac.*

Notice that the list has been further filtered to display only the records that have a Math grade of 80 or greater. Let's filter the list to display the records that also have a CS1 grade of 80 or greater.

▶ Click the Filter drop-down arrow for the CS1 grade field, as shown in Figures 8.11a and 8.11b.

▶ On the PC, click the menu options **Number Fields** and **Greater Than Or Equal To**, as shown in Figure 8.11a.

▶ On the Mac, click the menu option, **(Custom Filter . . .)** as shown in Figure 8.11b.

▶ Add the criteria to the **Custom AutoFilter** dialog box as we did with the Math grade, as shown in Figures 8.11a and 8.11b.

▶ Click the **OK** button to filter the list.

Figures 8.11a and 8.11b also show the list of records that satisfy the criteria of "M" in the Gender field, CS1 grade greater than or equal to 80, and Math grade greater than or equal to 80. Again, notice that all other rows are hidden, as indicated by the row numbers.

Let's display all records, progressively.

▶ Click the Filter drop-down arrow for Gender.

▶ On the PC, click the **Select All** checkbox and click the **OK** button.

▶ On the Mac, click the option **(Show All).**

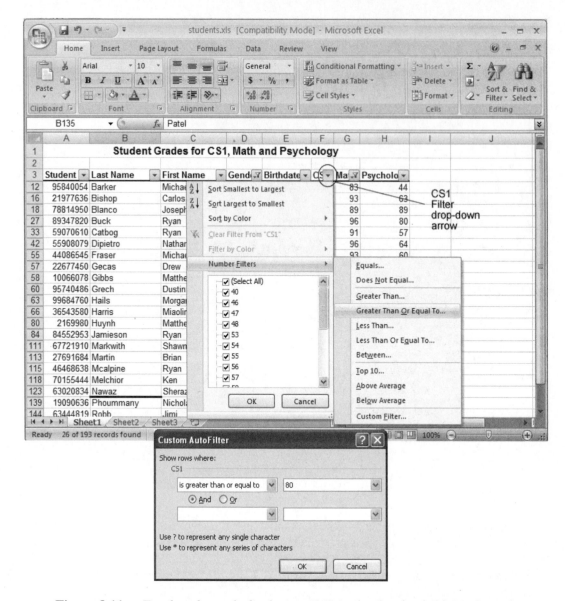

Figure 8.11a *Excel students.xls displaying "M" in the Gender field, Math grade field >=80 and CS1 grade field >=80 for PC.*

Now the list is filtered to display records for all students (both genders) with CS1 and Math grades of 80 or greater.

> ► Click the Filter drop-down arrow for Math.
> ► On the PC, click the **Select All** checkbox and click the **OK** button.
> ► On the Mac, click the option **(Show All)**.

Now the list is filtered to display records for all students with CS1 grades of 80 or greater.

> ► Click the Filter drop-down arrow for CS1.
> ► On the PC, click the **Select All** checkbox and click the **OK** button.
> ► On the Mac, click the option **(Show All)**.

Now the list shows all records for all fields and is no longer filtered.

The Filter drop-down menu also contains options for sorting.

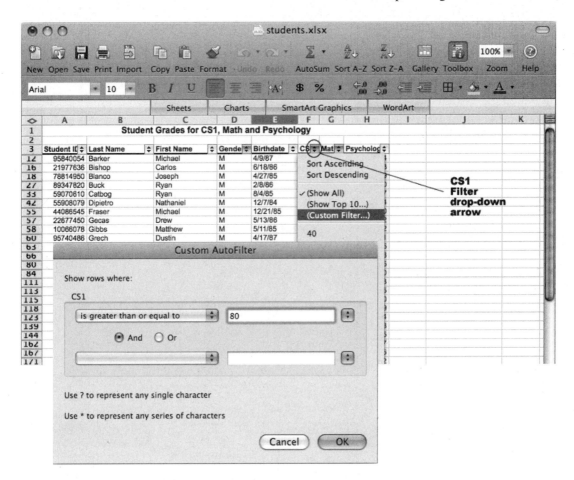

Figure 8.11b *Excel students.xls displaying "M" in the Gender field, Math grade field >=80 and CS1 grade field >=80 for Mac.*

As you would expect, we can filter records on numeric fields using criteria for "less than," "greater than," and "equals." We can also search for records that have numeric data between two values as well. Let's filter for all records for students born in 1985. In this case, we will specify records that have a Birthdate between January 1, 1985 and December 31, 1985. We can achieve the same results if we use "less than January 1, 1986" rather than "less than or equal to December 31, 1985."

▶ Click the Filter drop-down arrow for Birthdate.

▶ On the PC, click the menu options **Date Filters** and **Between** as shown in Figure 8.12a.

▶ On the Mac, click the menu option **(Custom Filter . . .)** as shown in Figure 8.12b.

▶ Enter the criteria as shown in Figures 8.12a and 8.12b to specify greater than or equal to 01/01/1985 and less than 01/01/1986.

Notice that the "And" radio button is selected. The "And" selection ensures that the criteria is "greater or equal to 01/01/1985 And less than 01/01/1986."

▶ Click the **OK** button to filter the list.

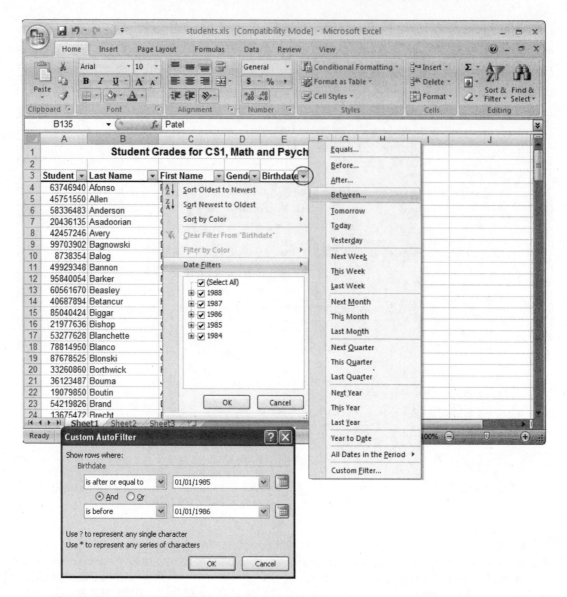

Figure 8.12a *Excel students.xls Custom AutoFilter for the Birthdate field for PC.*

Notice that all Birthdates in the filtered list contain the year 1985, as shown in Figure 8.13.

Let's display all of the records again.

► Click the Filter drop-down arrow for Birthdate.

► On the PC, click the **Select All** checkbox and click the **OK** button.

► On the Mac, click the option **(Show All)**.

Sometimes we wish to filter a text field based on only part of the text. For instance, we may wish to filter the list to display only the records where the last name begins with the letter H. Other examples might include displaying all records for street address on Main Street, or account ID containing CA.

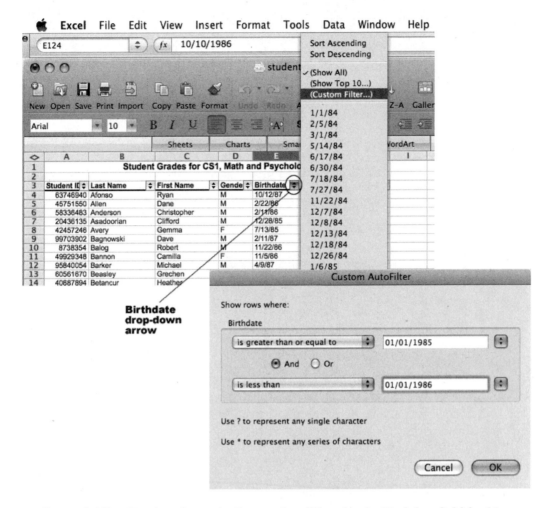

Figure 8.12b   *Excel students.xls Custom AutoFilter for the Birthdate field for Mac.*

Let's filter the list to display records where the Last Name begins with the letter H.

> ▶ Click the Filter drop-down arrow for Last Name.
> ▶ On the PC, click the menu options **Text Filters** and **Begins With**, as shown in Figure 8.14a.
> ▶ On the Mac, click the menu option **(Custom Filter . . .)**.

The Custom AutoFilter dialog box will appear as shown in Figures 8.14a and 8.14b.

> ▶ Click the upper right box and type: **H**, as shown in Figures 8.14a and 8.14b.
> ▶ Click the **OK** button to filter the records.

Notice that the Last Name field now contains records where the last name begins with H.

Let's remove the Filter and display all records.

> ▶ On the PC, click the **Sort & Filter** button and click the Filter option to remove the Filter drop-down arrows from the field name cells.
> ▶ On the Mac, click the menu options **Date, Filter, AutoFilter** to remove the Filter drop-down arrows from the field names.

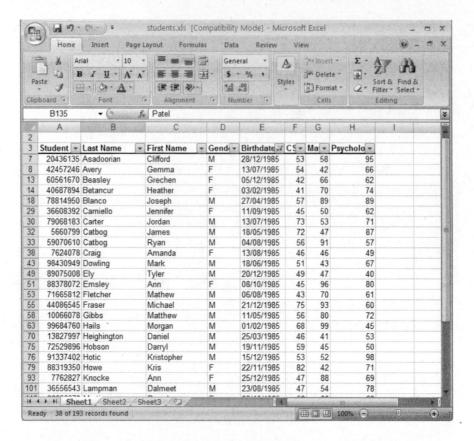

Figure 8.13   *Excel students.xls records filtered by Birthdate in 1985.*

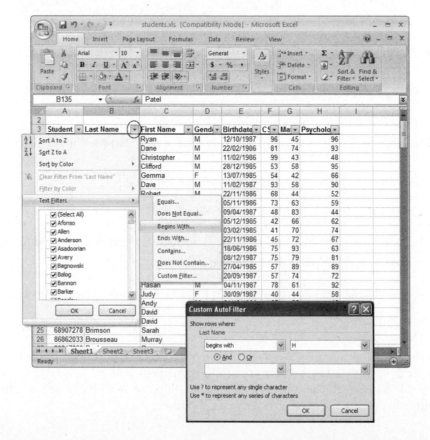

Figure 8.14a   *Excel students.xls Last Name beginning with the letter H for PC.*

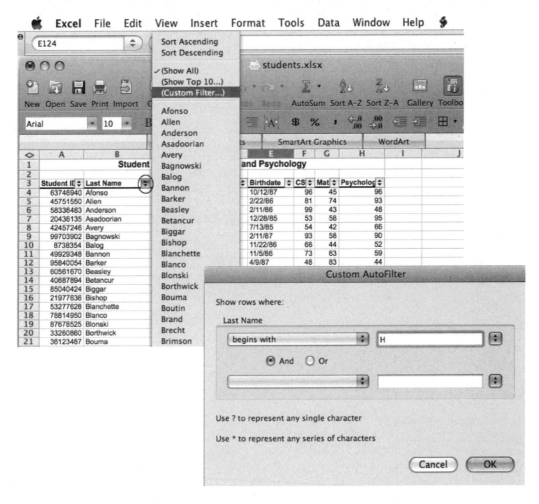

Figure 8.14b   *Excel students.xls Last Name beginning with the letter H for Mac.*

Review

This has been a busy lab! We have covered the following topics:

- Database terminology: table, record, field, field heading, filter, and criteria
- Simple data types including text, numeric, and date
- Sorting records in a table using Excel's sort buttons
    Sorting records in a table using multiple fields
- Using the Find feature to find specific data
- Using the Filter feature to filter records using specific text and numeric range criteria

Exercises

Use the students.xls file to complete the following exercises.

1. Sort the records so that the Psychology grade is in order from highest to lowest, with the highest grade at the top. For records that have the same Psychology grade, sort the records by Last Name alphabetically.

2. Sort the records so that the Student IDs are listed with the highest numbers at the top of the list, to the lowest at the bottom.

3.   Sort the records by Birthdate so that the youngest student is at the top of the list and the eldest student is at the bottom of the list.

4.   Use the Filter feature to filter the list as follows:

    a.   All female students who achieved a grade of 50 or less in CS1 and Psychology.

    b.   All students born in 1987 who also have a grade of 70 or more in Math.

    c.   All students whose last name begins with the letter "S" who also have a Psychology grade between 80 and 89 (including 80 and 89).

Database Concepts
Using Microsoft Access

Objectives:

Upon successful completion of Lab 9, you will be able to

- Understand fundamental concepts including database, table, record, field, field name, and primary key
- Understand the uses of simple data types including text, number, and date
- Create a table in Access using Design view
- Add records to a table using Datasheet view
- Find data using the Find feature
- Delete a record from a table
- Sort a table on one field

Resources required:

- A computer running Access 2007 (not available for the Mac at the time this lab was published)

Starter files:

- None

Prerequisite skills:

- General keyboarding skills
- Comfortable editing an Excel worksheet or another electronic spreadsheet application
- Ability to find files using Windows Explorer or Windows search feature
- Ability to open and save a file in a Windows application

NRC's Top Ten Skills, Concepts, and Capabilities:

- Skills
    Use a database to access information
    - Use Access to store information in tables
    - Data types
    - Organizing data into tables

- Concepts
    - Structuring information
- Capabilities
    - Manage complexity
    - Navigate a collection

Lab Lesson

We deal with lists and tables of information every day. Often the lists are small and easy to manage. We might have a list of tasks to do today, a grocery list, or a few phone numbers of friends. When the number of items in a list grows it's no longer practical to write them on paper or work with them from memory. We can use word processing software, but that's really no better than writing the items on paper. If the list is fairly small, spreadsheet software can work quite well. However, once the list grows to hundreds or thousands of items, it should be managed using database software.

Database software, such as Access, is designed to be able to manage large lists with millions of entries. Lists are organized as tables of information. A database can consist of a single table or many tables of information. A sample of a table of information is shown in Figure 9.1.

As shown in Figure 9.1, a field is a column of information. All of the information in a field is the same type of information. For instance, all of the birthdates are dates. Fields in the table shown in Figure 9.1 include Student ID, Last Name, First Name, Gender, Birthdate, CS1, Math, and Psychology. Each field is identified by its field name.

A record is a row of information. Each record contains information about a particular entity. In this case, each record contains information about an individual student. Each student record includes a Student ID, Last Name, First Name, and so forth.

A database could contain many tables. The table in Figure 9.1 contains student grade records for three courses, CS1, Math, and Psychology. The database could also contain another table of student contact information, another table with faculty information, another table with course information, and so forth. In this lab, we will create a simple table, manage the records in the table, and use some techniques to find records as well.

Figure 9.1 *Access table showing student data.*

Figure 9.2 *Access Blank Database option.*

Creating a Database Table

Let's create a table of student records using Access.

> ▶ Open Access.

The Access 2007 window should display a **Blank Database** button as shown in Figure 9.2.

> ▶ If the Access window does not display the **Blank Database** button, click the **Office** button and click the menu item **New** as shown in Figure 9.3.
> ▶ Click the **Blank Database** button, as shown in Figure 9.2.

Access will display a text box for the name of the database file. This may seem odd, but as soon as you start to create a table, Access will save the table structure and the data you enter.

> ▶ In the **File Name** box type: students, as shown in Figure 9.3.

Figure 9.3 *Office button and New menu option.*

By default, the database will be saved in the **Documents** folder.

▶ Click the **Create** button to create the blank database.

Access will display an empty table, as shown in Figure 9.4.

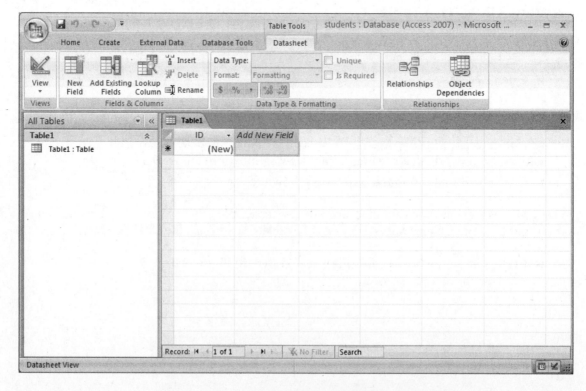

Figure 9.4 *Access window with empty table.*

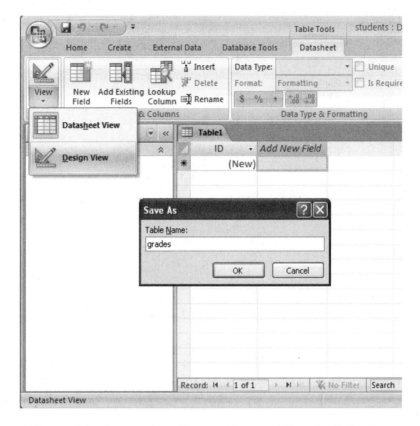

Figure 9.5   *Access View, Design View, and Save As dialog box.*

There are several options available for creating a table. We will create our table in design view in order to define each field.

▶ Click the **View** button and click the option **Design View**, as shown in Figure 9.5.

The **Save As** dialog box will appear as shown in Figure 9.5.

▶ In the **Save As** dialog box type: grades
▶ Click the **OK** button to save the table.

The **Design View** should be displayed and the flashing insertion point should be positioned in the first Field Name input area.

▶ Type: Student ID, as shown in Figure 9.6.
▶ Click on the drop-down arrow for the Data Type options as shown in Figure 9.6.

A drop-down menu will be revealed, as shown in Figure 9.6.

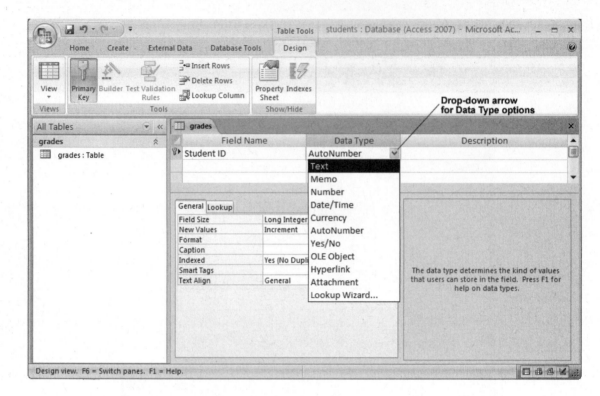

Figure 9.6 *Access Table using Design View creating Student ID field.*

Data Types

We will store the Student ID as a text field. As Figure 9.6 shows, there are a variety of data types available. Other database programs may have some of these data types and some additional data types, but the general concept is the same. A field will contain items that are all of the same type of data. For instance, a field of first names will contain text items and a field of birthdates will contain items that are all dates. Access supports the following data types.

Text: Use this data type for data that contains alphabetic characters or a combination of letters, numbers, and special characters. Examples include last name, street address, and phone number. It can also be used for data that contains only numbers, such as a credit card number or employee number when the number will not be used in mathematical calculations. The text data type stores up to 255 characters.

Memo: Use this data type for lengthy text data when the text data type is not suitable. The memo data type is suitable for a comment or description field and stores up to 63,999 characters.

Number: Use this data type for values that will be used for mathematical calculations.

Date/Time: Use this data type for dates and times.

Currency: Use this data type for values that represent money. The currency data type will prevent rounding errors of fractions of a cent.

AutoNumber: Use this data type to create index numbers for your records. The data in this field will automatically be inserted.

Yes/No: Use this data type when the data has only two possible values. The values could be yes/no, true/false or on/off.

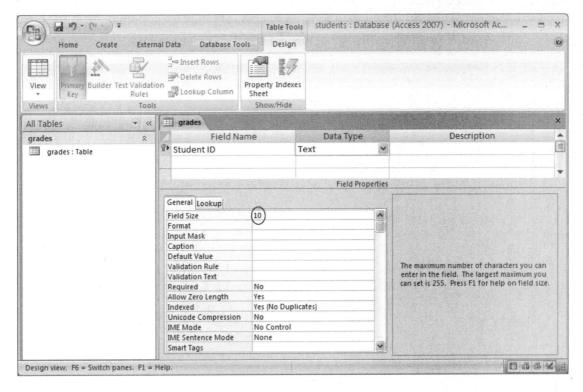

Figure 9.7 *Access table using Design View showing Student ID field with field size 10.*

We will keep these data types in mind when defining the fields. Let's define the Student ID field as a text field since we will not be using this data in mathematical calculations.

▶ Ensure that the text data type is selected as shown in Figure 9.6.

The default field size is 255 characters. We will change the field size to 10. Choosing the smallest appropriate field size will save storage space for the table. This also restricts the data entry to 10 characters, which minimizes data entry errors. The user will not be able to enter more than 10 characters.

▶ Click the **Field Size** box and change the value to 10, as shown in Figure 9.7.

Entering a description for the field is optional. If the field name describes the contents of the field clearly, it is not necessary to add further description.

Let's create fields for the students' names. We will separate the last name from the first name so that we can sort on either name and the separation is clear.

▶ Click the next **Field Name** box and type: Last Name, as shown in Figure 9.8.
▶ Click the **Data Type** box and click the Text option from the drop-down box, as shown in Figure 9.8.
▶ Click the **Field Size** box and edit the size as 20, as shown in Figure 9.8.

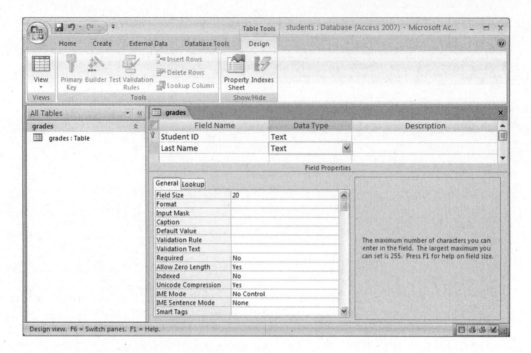

Figure 9.8 *Access table using Design View showing the Last Name field.*

Let's create the First Name field.

▶ Click the next **Field Name** box and type: First Name, as shown in Figure 9.9.

▶ Click the **Data Type** box and click the Text option from the drop-down box, as shown in Figure 9.9.

▶ Click the **Field Size** box and edit the size as 20, as shown in Figure 9.9.

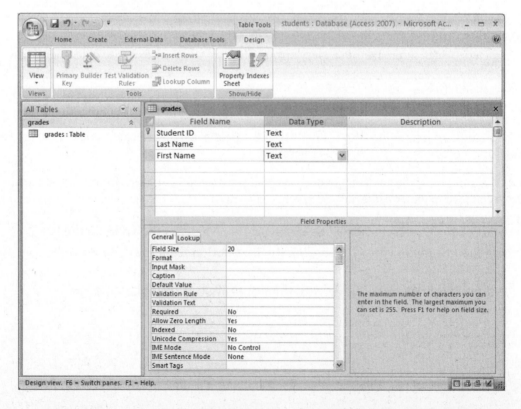

Figure 9.9 *Access table using Design View showing the First Name field.*

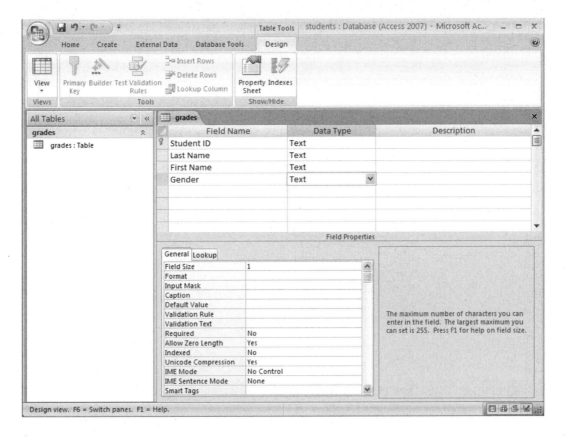

Figure 9.10   *Access table using Design View showing the Gender field.*

Let's add the Gender field.

▶ Click the next **Field Name** box and type: Gender, as shown in Figure 9.10.

▶ Click the **Data Type** box and click the Text option from the drop-down box, as shown in Figure 9.10.

In the case of Gender, we could have also used the Yes/No type and chosen True/False. Gender is often stored as True/False where Female is set as False and Male is set as True. Setting Female as False is easy to remember because Female and False both begin with the letter F.

▶ Click the **Field Size** box and edit the size as 1, as shown in Figure 9.10.

Let's create a field for birthdates.

▶ Click the next **Field Name** box and type: Birthdate, as shown in Figure 9.11.

▶ Click the **Data Type** box and click the **Date/Time** option from the drop-down box, as shown in Figure 9.11.

We do not need to set a field size since the Date/Time field has a preset size.

Let's create a numeric field for the grade for the History course.

▶ Click the next **Field Name** box and type: History Grade, as shown in Figure 9.12.

▶ Click the **Data Type** box and click the **Number** option from the drop-down box, as shown in Figure 9.12.

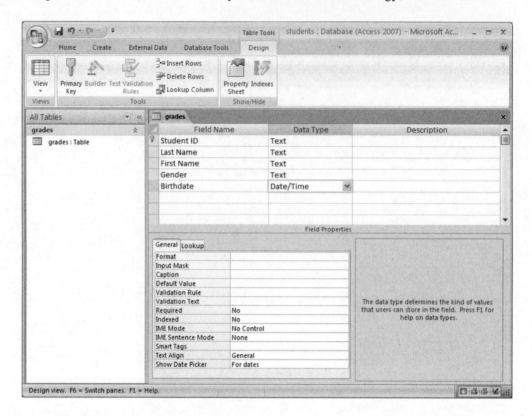

Figure 9.11 *Access table using Design View showing the Birthdate field.*

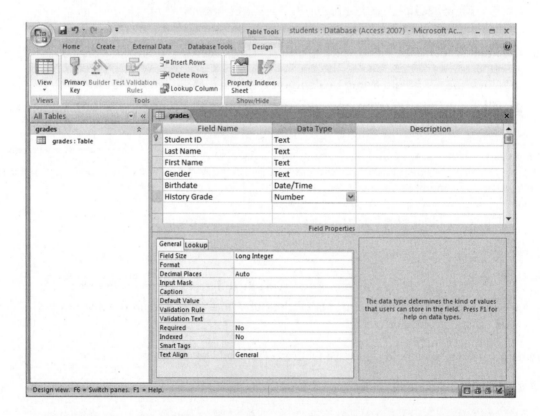

Figure 9.12 *Access table using Design View showing the History Grade field.*

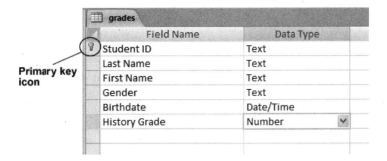

Figure 9.13   *Access grades table showing primary key icon.*

We do not need to set a field size for a numeric field.

You may have noticed the key symbol to the left of the Student ID field name, as shown in Figure 9.13.

A **primary key** is a field that contains unique data so that there are no duplications. This field can be used to identify each record. In the case of the grades table, the Student ID field contains data items that would be unique. No two students would have the same Student ID. It is not necessary for a table to have a primary key. The primary key is used to link a table to other tables and is beyond the scope of this lab. For completeness, let's use the Student ID as the primary key for this table. As it happens, we entered the Student ID as the first field in the table and it was assumed to be the primary key.

▶ Scroll up to the Student ID field so that it is visible in the field name listing, if it is not already visible.

▶ Click the **Primary Key** button on the Ribbon toolbar to remove the primary key selection as shown in Figure 9.14.

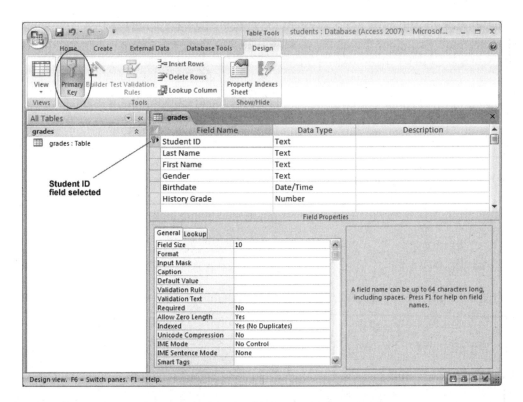

Figure 9.14   *Access setting the primary key.*

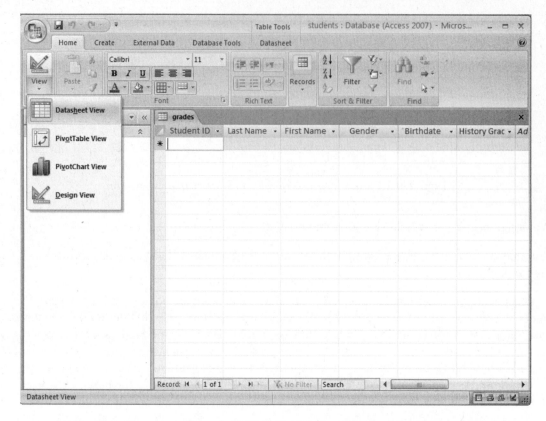

Figure 9.15 *Access View button with Datasheet View option highlighted.*

Notice that the primary key icon to the left of the Student ID field has disappeared.

> ► Click the **Primary Key** button to select the Student ID as the primary key again. You should see a key symbol appear to the left of the Student ID field name.
>
> ► Click the **Save** button to save the table.

Now that we've created the structure of the table, we can add records. To do this, we will switch from Design View to Datasheet View.

> ► Click the **View** button and select the Datasheet View menu option, as shown in Figure 9.15.
>
> ► Click the **Datasheet View** menu option, as shown in Figure 9.16.

The grades table will be displayed, as shown in Figure 9.15.

Inserting Records

Entering data now is as easy as entering data into cells of a spreadsheet. The hard work was setting up the table!

Let's enter some sample data, as shown in Figure 9.16.

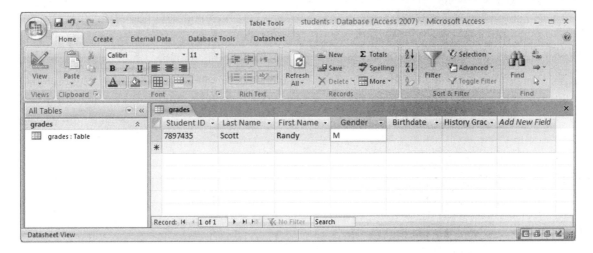

Figure 9.16 *Access data for the first record of the grades table.*

▶ Click each cell and enter the data, as shown in Figure 9.16. You can use the same basic editing skills as you would use to enter cell data in Excel or another spreadsheet package. After you enter the data for a cell, you can press the **Enter** key or the **Tab** key to move to the next cell.

When it comes to entering dates, Access is smart about it. It does not allow you to enter invalid dates. For instance, you cannot enter a month greater than 12 or a day greater than the month will allow. Let's try entering an invalid date and see what happens.

▶ Click on the Birthdate cell for the first record.

Access is expecting dates of the format mm/dd/yyyy or dd/mm/yyyy depending on the configuration of your computer, where dd is the 2 digit date, mm is the 2 digit month, and yyyy is the 4 digit year.

▶ Type: 20/40/1980
▶ Press the **Enter** key.

Access will display an alert message indicating that there is an error in the date as shown in Figure 9.17. There sure is! The date entered represents the 20th day of the 40th month of 1980.

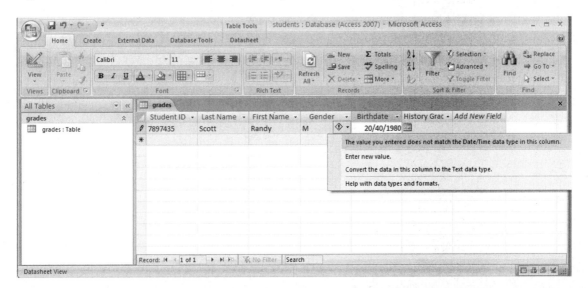

Figure 9.17 *Access date field with error.*

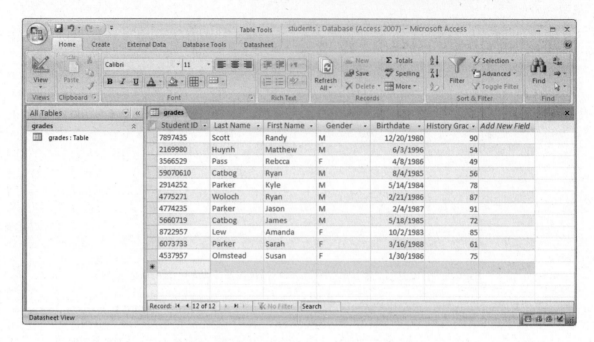

Figure 9.18 *Access grades table with data.*

▶ Edit the Birthdate data to: 12/20/1980
▶ Press the **Enter** key.

Now Access does not display an error message and the History Grade cell is activated. If your system configuration requires dd/mm/yyyy, Access will correct the date.

Enter data for more records as shown in Figure 9.18.

Finding a Record

Although this table is small, let's use the Find feature to find a record. Let's find the record for Amanda Lew, searching on her first name.

▶ Click the **Find** button on the Ribbon toolbar. The **Find and Replace** dialog box will appear, similar to that shown in Figure 9.19.
▶ Click in the **Find What** box to activate it.
▶ Type: Amanda, as shown in Figure 9.20.
▶ Click the **Look In** drop-down menu.
▶ Select the **grades:Table** option, as shown in Figure 9.20.

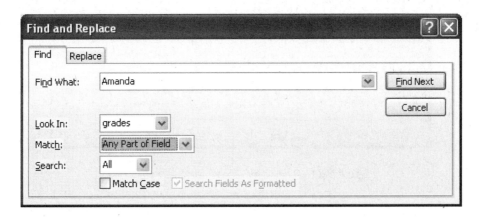

Figure 9.19 *Access Find and Replace dialog box with information to find the record for Amanda Lew.*

Selecting the **grades:Table** option allows Access to search each piece of data in the grades table.

▶ Click the **Match** drop-down menu.
▶ Select the **Any Part of Field** option, as shown in Figure 9.20.

Although we are searching for the whole word "Amanda," we could type only part of the word and use the **Match** option for **Any Part of Field** to find the data as well.

▶ Click the **Find Next** button.
▶ Close the **Find and Replace** dialog box.

You should notice that the record containing Amanda as the First Name has been selected and the first name is highlighted. You can edit data by clicking on the data and using your editing skills to make changes.

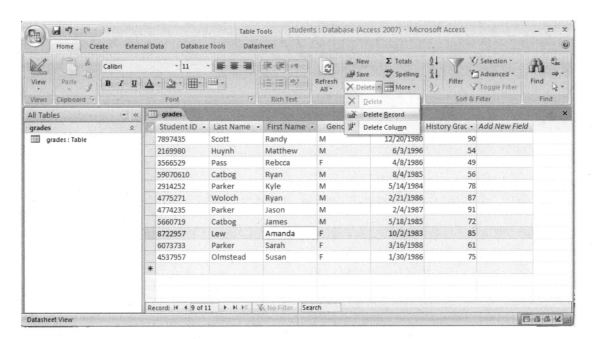

Figure 9.20 *Access delete drop-down menu.*

Figure 9.21 *Access delete record warning box.*

Deleting Records

Let's delete the record for Amanda Lew. Essentially this means we will delete a row of data. You can click on any field in a record to select the record, and then delete it.

▶ Make sure that the record for Amanda Lew is selected.

▶ Click the **Delete** button drop-down arrow on the Ribbon toolbar as shown in Figure 9.20.

Access will display a warning box as shown in Figure 9.21.

▶ Click the menu option **Delete Record**

Since we are sure that we want to delete this record, we will click the **Yes** button. If you had selected a record by mistake and do not wish to delete it, you would click the **No** button.

▶ Click the **Yes** button to delete the record for Amanda Lew. You should notice that the record for Amanda Lew is deleted.

Sorting Records

We can perform some simple sorting on any field in the table. Let's sort the table on the Last Name field.

▶ Click the Last Name field heading to select the entire field, as shown in Figure 9.22.

▶ Click the drop-down arrow on the Last Name field heading to display the shortcut menu, as shown in Figure 9.22.

▶ Select the **Sort A to Z** menu option, as shown in Figure 9.22.

Using this method, you can sort the table on any field.

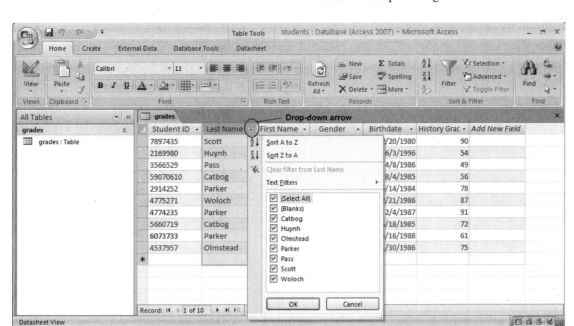

Figure 9.22 *Access grades table sorted on Last Name field.*

Review

This has been a busy lab! We have covered the following topics:

- Concepts including database, table, record, field, field name, and primary key
- Data types, including text, number, and date
- Creating a table in Design view
- Adding records to a table using Datasheet view
- Finding data using the Find feature
- Deleting a record from a table
- Sorting a table on one field

Exercises

Use the students file created in this lab to perform the following tasks.

1. Add the records shown in Figure 9.23 to the grades table.

2. Find the record for Susan Olmstead by searching for data containing "olm".

3. Sort the Birthdate field in ascending order.

4. Sort the History Grade field in descending order.

Student ID	Last Name	First Name	Gender	Birthdate	History Grade
998623	D'Angelo	Lori	F	4/18/1984	63
992714	Richardson	Jeremy	M	9/18/1982	86
982741	Hampton	Sandra	F	2/2/1983	92

Figure 9.23 *Records to add to the students grades table.*

5.   Create a new table called Faculty with the following fields.

    a.   First Name: text field of 20 characters

    b.   Last Name: text field of 20 characters

    c.   Telephone: text field of 15 characters

    d.   Gender: text field of 1 character

    e.   Birthdate: date/time field

Make sure there is no primary key selected, deleting the primary key icon from any fields that may have been set. It is not necessary to always have a primary key field.

6.   Add a record for yourself in the Faculty table.

7.   Add three of your friends as records in the Faculty table.

Advanced Database Concepts Using Microsoft Access

Objectives:

Upon successful completion of Lab 10, you will be able to

- Understand database terminology, including database, table, record, field, and field name
- Understand data integrity issues and the importance of storing only one copy of data items
- Create a query using the Design view and multiple tables
- Create a query using multiple criteria
- Add tables to a query
- Create a relationship between tables in a query
- Generate a report from a query

Resources required:

- A computer running Access 2007 (not available for the Mac at the time this lab was published)

Starter file:

- academic_records.accdb

Prerequisite skills:

- General keyboarding skills
- Ability to find files using Windows Explorer or Windows search feature
- Ability to open and save a file in a Windows application
- Basic Access editing skills, including adding, deleting, and editing records and creating a table in design view

NRC's Top Ten Skills, Concepts, and Capabilities:

- Skills
    Use a database to access information
    - Use Access to find information stored in tables
    - Create relationships, queries, and reports
- Concepts
    Structuring information

- Capabilities
    Manage complexity
    Think abstractly about Information Technology
    Navigate a collection

Lab Lesson

Each day we find ourselves using lists of information. Sometimes the lists are small, such as a list of things to do today, a grocery list, or a list of songs on a CD. Sometimes the lists are larger, such as a list of friends or business associates, products in a catalog, or a telephone directory.

As we work with lists we find that we need to find information, create smaller lists from the larger lists based on some criteria, and update information.

Database Terminology

Database software, such as Access, is designed to be able to manage large lists with millions of entries. Lists are organized as tables of information. A database can consist of a single table, or many tables of information. A sample of a table of information is shown in Figure 10.1.

As shown in Figure 10.1, a row of data is called a **Record**. Data items in a row all refer to the same entity. In Figure 10.1, a record contains data pertaining to a student. A column of data is called a **Field** and is identified by the Field Name heading. A field contains the same type of data. For instance, in Figure 10.1 the Last Name is a field containing text data, the Birthdate field contains date/time data, and the Math field contains numeric data.

A database can contain many tables. The table in Figure 10.1 contains student grade records for three courses: CS1, Math, and Psychology. The database can also contain another table of student contact information, another table with faculty information, another table with course information, and so forth.

Once data is stored in tables we will want to do things such as edit record data, print lists of records that satisfy certain criteria, or generate reports containing statistics about records in certain categories or summaries of fields. A search for records that meet certain criteria is done using a query. A query can establish relationships between tables and can result in lists of data that combine fields from many tables.

Student ID	Last Name	First Name	Gender	Birthdate	CS1	Math	Psychology
2169980	Huynh	Matthew	M	6/3/1986	54	83	55
2914252	Simpson	Kyle	M	5/14/1984	78	55	61
3566629	Pass	Rebecca	F	4/8/1986	49	58	44
4477235	Parker	Jason	M	2/4/1987	55	77	71
4537957	Olmstead	Susan	F	1/30/1986	75	57	49
4775271	Woloch	Ryan	M	2/21/1986	87	68	52
5660799	Catbog	James	M	5/18/1985	72	47	87
6073733	Johnny	Sarah	F	3/16/1988	61	50	45
6902426	Laframboise	Dionda	F	11/15/1986	91	53	48
7308405	Guo	Rachel	F	6/30/1984	53	62	56
7624078	Craig	Amanda	F	8/13/1985	46	46	49
7762827	Knocke	Ann	F	12/25/1985	47	88	69

Record: of 193

Figure 10.1 *Access table showing student data.*

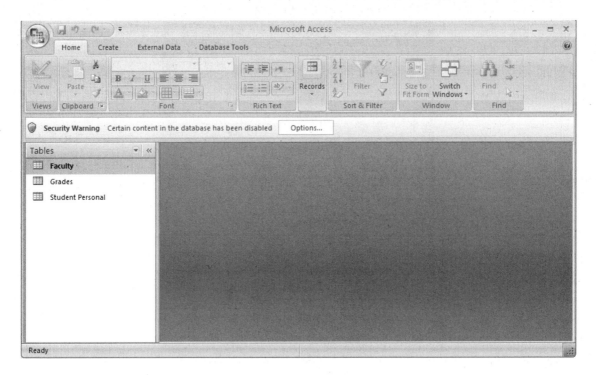

Figure 10.2   *Access 2003 Tables window.*

This lab will focus on creating queries, relationships, and reports for a database containing some simple tables. It is assumed that the student completing this lab is comfortable with Access tables and has an understanding of table structure, editing records data, and data types.

Data Integrity

One of the things we have to be wary of is duplicating data in many tables. For instance, there may be separate tables for the students' personal information and for grades. If there are multiple copies of data the danger is that when there is a change, one or more of the copies might be missed and thus some data will be inaccurate. Let's look at how this situation might be avoided with a unique identifier for each record.

▶ Open Access 2007.

▶ Open the academic_records.accdb database file.

There are three tables in this database: Faculty, Grades, and Student Personal. Let's look at the tables and see how they fit together.

▶ Double-click the Faculty table name to open it, as shown in Figure 10.2.

The Faculty table will appear, as shown in Figure 10.3.

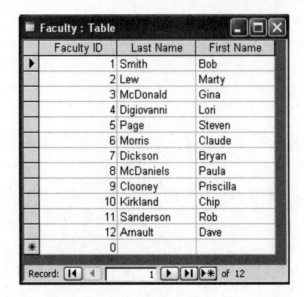

Figure 10.3 *Faculty table in the academic_records.accdb database.*

The Faculty table contains a Faculty ID, Last Name, and First Name, as shown in Figure 10.3.

The Faculty ID is a unique identifier. Let's look at the structure of the table.

► Click the drop-down arrow for the **View** button, as shown in Figure 10.4.
► Click the **Design View** option as shown in Figure 10.4.

The design view of the Faculty table should display, as shown in Figure 10.4.

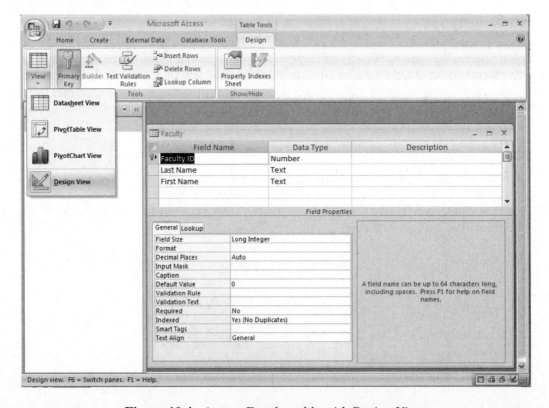

Figure 10.4 *Access Faculty table with Design View.*

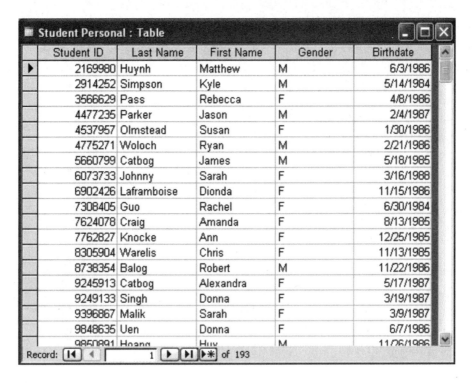

	Student ID	Last Name	First Name	Gender	Birthdate
▶	2169980	Huynh	Matthew	M	6/3/1986
	2914252	Simpson	Kyle	M	5/14/1984
	3566629	Pass	Rebecca	F	4/8/1986
	4477235	Parker	Jason	M	2/4/1987
	4537957	Olmstead	Susan	F	1/30/1986
	4775271	Woloch	Ryan	M	2/21/1986
	5660799	Catbog	James	M	5/18/1985
	6073733	Johnny	Sarah	F	3/16/1988
	6902426	Laframboise	Dionda	F	11/15/1986
	7308405	Guo	Rachel	F	6/30/1984
	7624078	Craig	Amanda	F	8/13/1985
	7762827	Knocke	Ann	F	12/25/1985
	8305904	Warelis	Chris	F	11/13/1985
	8738354	Balog	Robert	M	11/22/1986
	9245913	Catbog	Alexandra	F	5/17/1987
	9249133	Singh	Donna	F	3/19/1987
	9396867	Malik	Sarah	F	3/9/1987
	9848635	Uen	Donna	F	6/7/1986
	9850891	Hoang	Huy	M	11/26/1986

Record: |◀| |◀| 1 |▶| |▶|| |▶*| of 193

Figure 10.5 *Access Student Personal table with Datasheet View.*

Primary Key

Notice the key symbol to the left of the Faculty ID field name. This indicates that the Faculty ID is a Primary Key field. A Primary Key field contains unique identifiers for each record and Access will not allow duplicate primary keys. If the user tries to enter a Primary Key value that is already being used, Access will display an error message and require the user to enter another value.

▶ Close the Faculty table.

Let's open the other two tables and look at the structure of the data in them.

▶ Double-click the Student Personal table name in the academic_records tables window, as shown in Figure 10.2.

The Student Personal table will open in **Datasheet View**, as shown in Figure 10.5.

The Student ID field in the Student Personal table is a Primary Key field. You can confirm this by looking at the structure in **Design View** if you wish.

▶ Double-click the Grades table name in the academic_records tables window, as shown in Figure 10.2.

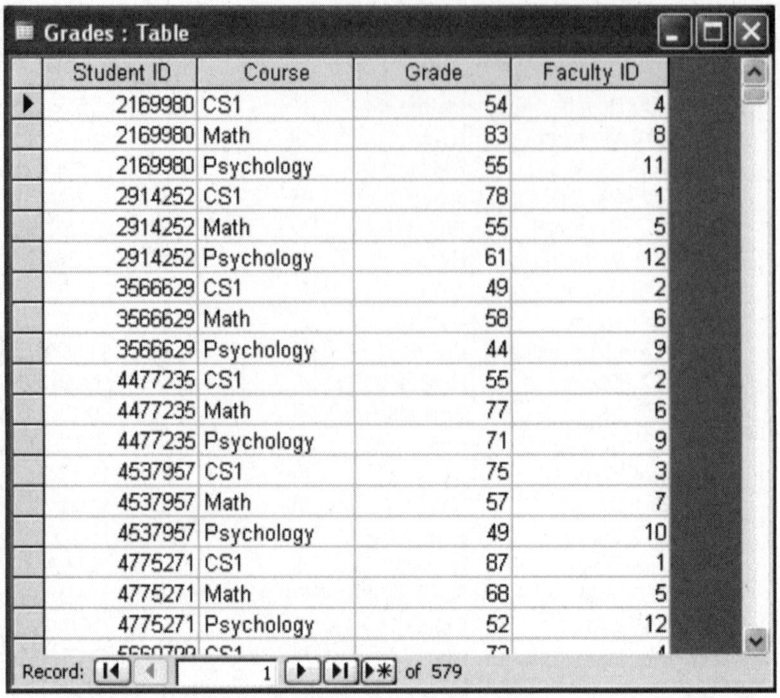
Grades : Table

Student ID	Course	Grade	Faculty ID
2169980	CS1	54	4
2169980	Math	83	8
2169980	Psychology	55	11
2914252	CS1	78	1
2914252	Math	55	5
2914252	Psychology	61	12
3566629	CS1	49	2
3566629	Math	58	6
3566629	Psychology	44	9
4477235	CS1	55	2
4477235	Math	77	6
4477235	Psychology	71	9
4537957	CS1	75	3
4537957	Math	57	7
4537957	Psychology	49	10
4775271	CS1	87	1
4775271	Math	68	5
4775271	Psychology	52	12

Record: 1 of 579

Figure 10.6 *Access Grades table with Design view.*

The Grades table will open, as shown in Figure 10.6.

Notice that the Grades table does not contain student names or faculty names. Instead, it contains Student ID and Faculty ID fields. Also, there is one record for each course grade. If we were to create a table that contained a separate field for each grade, how many fields would we need? For this table, there are three course grades (CS1, Math, and Psychology), but what if another course was added? We would need to add a field for each new course, and this quickly becomes a bad idea. Although there will be many records, if each record contains only one course grade, it's manageable, and expandable. We can add more courses by adding more records, which is easy. Although fields can be added easily, you can imagine a scenario where there could be hundreds of courses, and yet a student would have grades for only a few of them.

Placing the Faculty and Student data in separate tables allows us to change information about the individual faculty or student without having to change that information again in the Grades table. Imagine that the Grades table also included the first and last names of the students and faculty. Scrolling through the table you can see that there are many instances of the same Student ID and Faculty ID. If a faculty member changed his or her last name, you would have to make that change in the Faculty table and in the Grades table for every instance of the Faculty ID. By placing the personal data in a separate table and assigning a unique key, we can "look up" the personal information and join it to the Grades table.

Creating a Query

Let's create a list that contains the Student IDs, students' first and last names, courses, and grades. We will expand on this to add faculty names later. We will use a query to create these tables.

- ▶ Close the Faculty table, the Grades table, and the Student Personal table.
- ▶ Click the Create tab on the Ribbon toolbar, as shown in Figure 10.7.

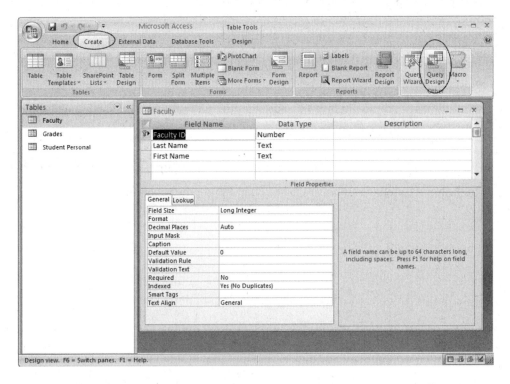

Figure 10.7 *Access Queries object in academic_records.accdb.*

We are going to create a query using Design view so that we can see the relationships between tables.

▶ Click the **Query Design** button as shown in Figure 10.7.

The **Query** window and **Show Tables** dialog box will open, as shown in Figure 10.8.

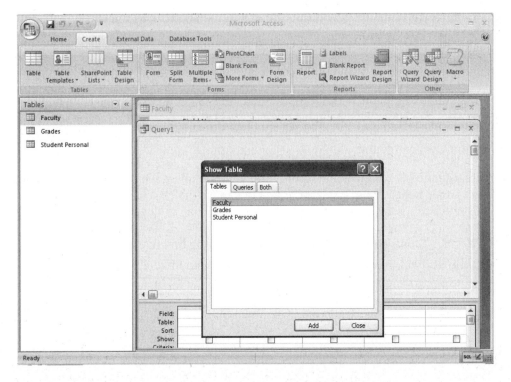

Figure 10.8 *Access Query window and Show Tables dialog box.*

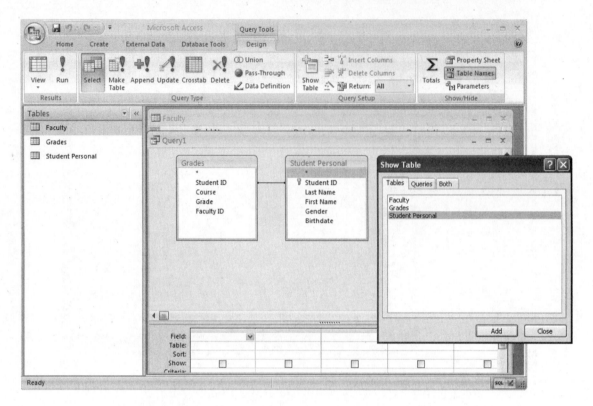

Figure 10.9 *Access Query window with all tables added.*

For the query we are creating, we will need to use only the Grades and Student Personal tables.

> ► Click the Grades table name to select it.
> ► Click the **Add** button to add the Grades table to the **Query** window.
> ► Click the Student Personal table name to select it.
> ► Click the **Add** button to add the Student Personal table to the **Query** window, as shown in Figure 10.9.

Notice the line that has been drawn between the Grades and Student Personal tables. This line indicates that there is a relationship between these tables. A relationship joins two tables on a common field. In this case, the tables are joined on the Student ID field. The Student ID field is a Primary Key in the Student Personal table but is not a Primary Key in the Grades table. The Grades table will contain multiple records with the same Student ID because a student will complete more than one course.

Let's create a query that will generate records containing Student ID, Last Name, First Name, Course, and Grade fields. These fields are found in the two tables. We will need to select each of these fields required for the query.

> ► Click the **Close** button on the **Show Table** dialog box to close it.
> ► In the **Student Personal** window, double click the Student ID field name.

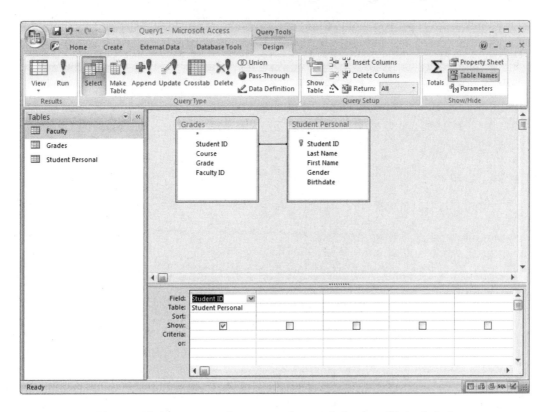

Figure 10.10 *Access Query window with Student ID included.*

Notice that the Student ID field name has been added to the Query, as shown in Figure 10.10.

If we were to run this simple Query now, it would result in a list of the entire Student IDs that are common in the two tables. Since the Grades table contains multiple instances of the Student IDs, the resulting table will also have multiple instances of the Student IDs.

Let's add more fields to the query.

▶ In the Student Personal window, double-click the Last Name field name to add it to the query. The additional fields are shown in Figure 10.11.

▶ In the Student Personal window, double-click the First Name field name to add it to the query.

▶ In the Grades window, double-click the Course field name to add it to the query.

▶ In the Grades window, double-click the Grade field name to add it to the query.

Now that we've added the fields to the query, we can run the query to display the results in a table. The records that satisfy the query are all records that have the Student ID common in both tables.

▶ Click the **Run Query** button, as shown in Figure 10.11.

Access will show the results of the query in a window, as shown in Figure 10.12. The results are shown in **Datasheet** view. The result is a combination of all of the records from the Grades table, which also have Student IDs in the Student Personal table, using the fields specified in the query.

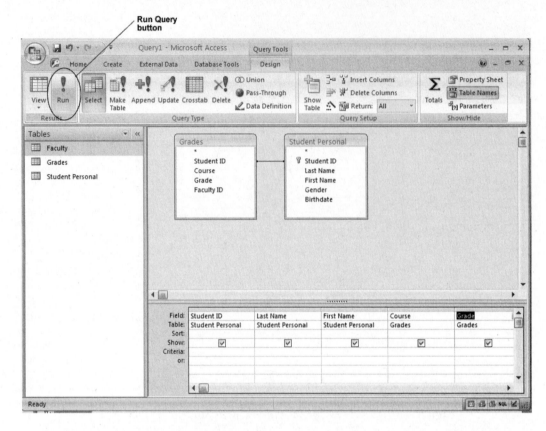

Figure 10.11 *Access Query window showing Student ID, Last Name, First Name, Course, and Grade fields.*

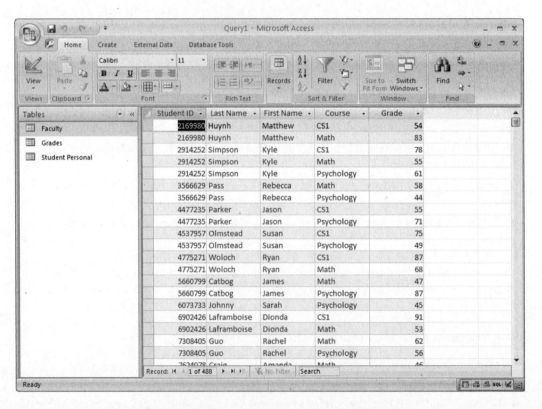

Figure 10.12 *Access grades query results.*

Criteria in a Query

Let's add some criteria to this query. Let's find all records for which the Grade is greater or equal to 90.

▶ Click the **View** drop-down button and select the **Design View**, as shown in Figure 10.13.

▶ Click in the **Criteria** input box in the Grades field and type: >=90, as shown in Figure 10.14.

▶ Click the **Run Query** button to display the results of the query, as shown in Figure 10.15.

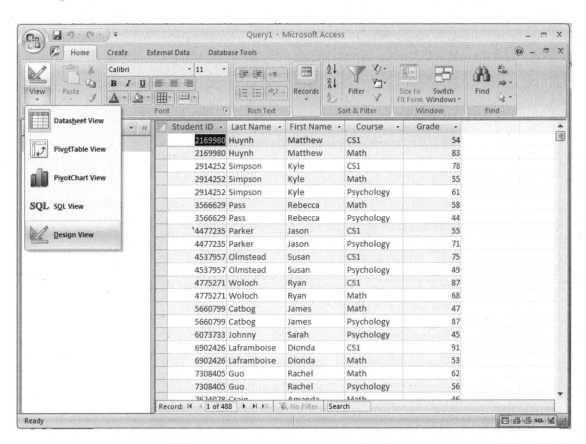

Figure 10.13   *Access view button indicating Design view.*

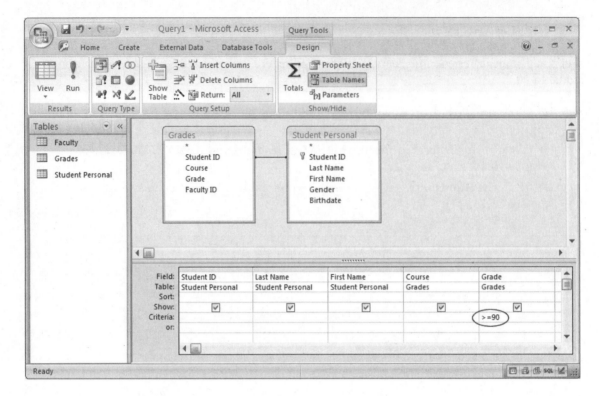

Figure 10.14 *Access query on the Grades field for >=90.*

Notice that each number in the Grade field is greater than or equal to 90. Feel free to scroll through the list to verify this. In the previous query there were 488 records in the results, and in this query there are only 55 records in the results.

Let's add some criteria from another field. Let's find only the records for which the Grade is greater than or equal to 90 and the Course is Math.

▶ Click the **View** drop-down button and select the **Design View** as previously shown in Figure 10.13.

▶ Click in the **Criteria** input box for the Course field and type: Math, as shown in Figure 10.16.

Student ID	Last Name	First Name	Course	Grade
6902426 Laframboise	Dionda	CS1		91
19607736	Hamilton	Ahmed	CS1	93
89347820	Buck	Ryan	CS1	99
66789479	Tang	Amal	CS1	99
63746940	Afonso	Ryan	CS1	96
39778992	Wiseman	Leslie	CS1	97
12587454	Nettleton	Sandra	CS1	92
68640134	Hastings	Daniel	CS1	91
99703902	Bagnowski	Dave	CS1	93
62025731	Durand	Karen	CS1	90
72370077	Yu	Hun	CS1	91
55908079	Dipietro	Nathaniel	CS1	92
19079850	Boutin	Andy	CS1	97
81748236	Nichol	Thomas	CS1	92

Record: 1 of 55

Figure 10.15 *Access query results for Grade >= 90.*

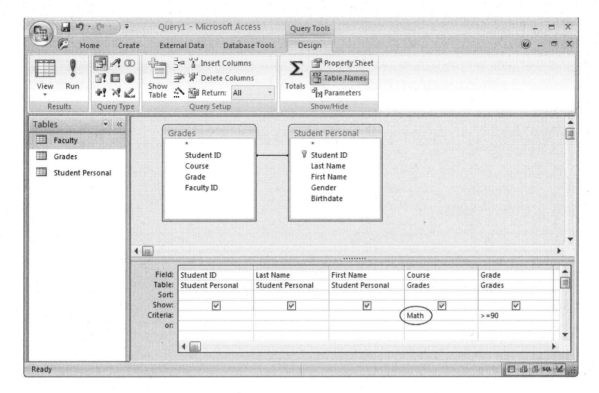

Figure 10.16 *Access query for Grade >=90 and Course = Math.*

Access will automatically put double-quotes around "Math" and you may notice this when you are looking at the criteria grid later.

▶ Click the **Run Query** button to display the results of the query, as shown in Figure 10.17.

Now there are only 13 records that satisfy the criteria where the Course is Math and the Grade is greater than or equal to 90.

We can also add more criteria to a single field. Let's find the records for which the Math Grade is greater than or equal to 80 but less than 90. In this case we will need to use AND criteria where the Math Grade is greater than or equal to 80 AND less than 90.

Student ID	Last Name	First Name	Course	Grade
36459676	Yuan	David	Math	92
89347820	Buck	Ryan	Math	96
59070610	Catbog	Ryan	Math	91
39778992	Wiseman	Leslie	Math	94
24704075	Singh	Lori	Math	93
70155444	Melchior	Ken	Math	95
55908079	Dipietro	Nathaniel	Math	96
22677450	Gecas	Drew	Math	94
52756781	Kamermans	Hanan	Math	92
95740486	Grech	Dustin	Math	98
33184698	El Gharabli	Megan	Math	94
27691684	Martin	Brian	Math	98
51844584	Tarpey	Defrim	Math	95

Record: ◀◀ ◀ [1] ▶ ▶▶ ▶✱ of 13

Figure 10.17 *Access query results for Grade >= 90 and Course = Math.*

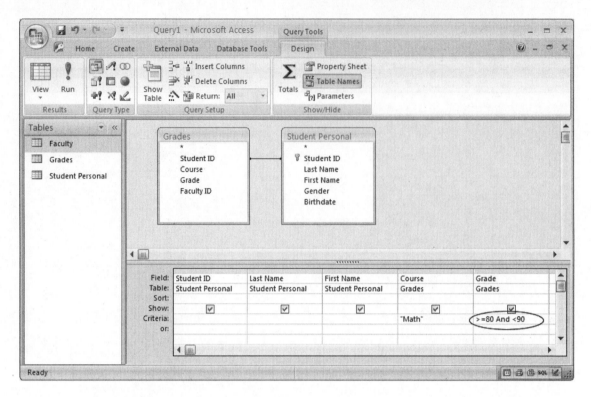

Figure 10.18 *Access query for Course = Math and Grades >=80 And <90.*

▶ Click the **View** drop-down button and select the **Design View**.

▶ Click in the criteria cell for the Grade field and edit the cell as: >=80 And <90, as shown in Figure 10.18.

▶ Click the **Run Query** button to display the results of the query, as shown in Figure 10.19.

As we have seen, records must satisfy all criteria along a row in the criteria grid in order to be included in the results. If there is criteria on separate rows in the criteria grid, this becomes an OR search. In this case, records must satisfy either the criteria on one row or the criteria on the next row. Let's change our criteria to find all records for which the Course is either Math or CS1.

▶ Click the **View** drop-down button and select the **Design View**.

Student ID	Last Name	First Name	Course	Grade
67721910	Markwith	Shawn	Math	87
84552953	Jamieson	Ryan	Math	82
36543580	Harris	Miaolin	Math	87
82039878	Mercer	Megan	Math	84
96913046	Snelling	Urviben	Math	84
95840054	Barker	Michael	Math	83
19090636	Phoummany	Nicholas	Math	83
10066078	Gibbs	Matthew	Math	80
21038349	Kowalchuk	Rebecca	Math	83
42359706	Yeoh	Frank	Math	83
46468638	Mcalpine	Ryan	Math	89
63444819	Robb	Jimi	Math	84
2169980	Huynh	Matthew	Math	83
78814950	Blanco	Joseph	Math	89

Record: I◀ ◀ 1 ▶ ▶I ▶* of 16

Figure 10.19 *Access query results for Course = Math and Grades >=80 And <90.*

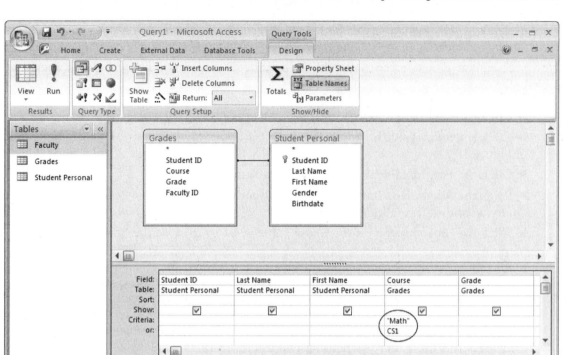

Figure 10.20   *Access query for Course = Math or Course = CS1.*

▶ Click the criteria cell for the Grade and delete the grade criteria, as shown in Figure 10.20.

▶ Click the criteria cell below the Course criteria cell containing "Math" and type: CS1, as shown in Figure 10.20.

▶ Click the **Run Query** button to display the results of the query, as shown in Figure 10.21.

▶ Scroll through the query results to verify that the records contain only "CS1" or "Math" in the Course field.

	Student ID	Last Name	First Name	Course	Grade
▶	67736035	Maltais	Peter	CS1	66
	85040424	Biggar	Nicole	CS1	45
	67721910	Markwith	Shawn	CS1	74
	84552953	Jamieson	Ryan	CS1	46
	6902426	Laframboise	Dionda	CS1	91
	53277628	Blanchette	Larissa	CS1	75
	60561670	Beasley	Grechen	CS1	42
	86862033	Brousseau	Murray	CS1	71
	89075008	Ely	Tyler	CS1	49
	36543580	Harris	Miaolin	CS1	48
	63688148	Wright	Ann	CS1	62
	34303109	Niamat	Edith	CS1	71
	31225104	Houghton	Jonathan	CS1	73
	12637950	Hassnieler	Jennifer	CS1	81

Record: 1 of 326

Figure 10.21   *Access query results for Course = Math or Course = CS1.*

Database Relationships

Now, let's add the Faculty name to the table. In order to do this we will have to add the Faculty table to the query.

▶ Click the **View** drop-down button and select the **Design View**.

▶ Click the **Show Table** button. The Show Table window will appear, as shown in Figure 10.22.

▶ Click the Faculty table in the **Show Table** dialog box to select it.

▶ Click the **Add** button in the **Show Table** dialog box to add this table to the Query, as shown in Figure 10.22.

▶ Click the **Close** button on the Show Table window to close the Show Table window.

We will need to define a relationship, joining the Faculty ID fields from the Grades table and the Faculty table. It's a bit easier to see when the tables are aligned a bit differently.

▶ Drag the Grades and Student Personal tables to the right to make some room for the Faculty table on the left, as shown in Figure 10.23.

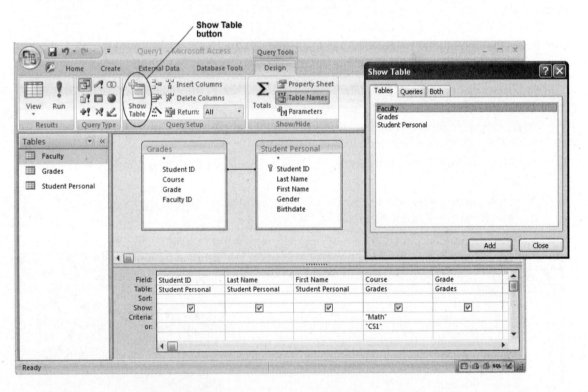

Figure 10.22   *Access query adding Faculty table.*

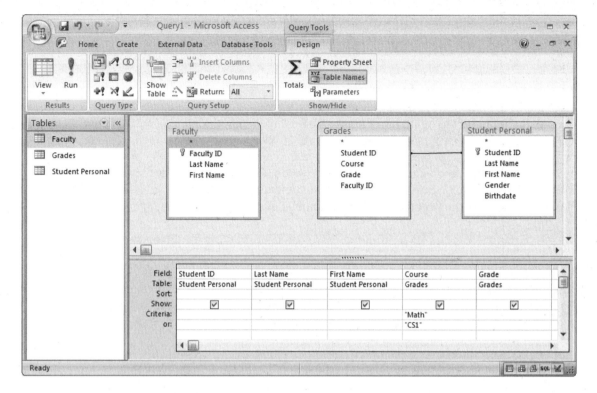

Figure 10.23 *Access query with Faculty table.*

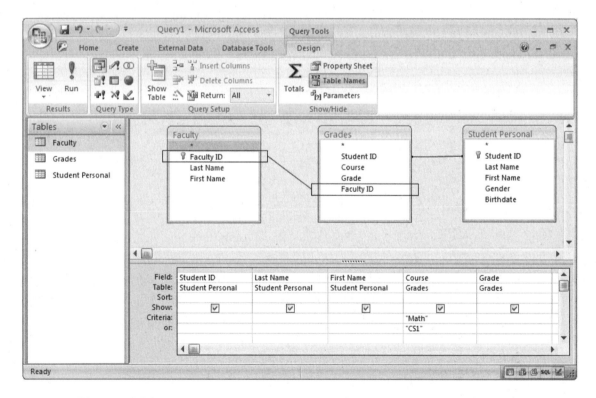

Figure 10.24 *Access query with Faculty table, dragging the Faculty ID field.*

As you drag the tables, the line between the Grades and Student Personal table will "stick" to the tables, preserving the relationship between the Student ID fields.

▶ Drag the Faculty table to the left of the Grades table, as shown in Figure 10.23.

The Faculty ID field in the Faculty table is a Primary Key. There is only one instance of each Faculty ID in the Faculty table. The Faculty ID field in the Grades table is not a Primary Key. There are multiple instances of Faculty IDs in the Grades table because a faculty member has many students and issues many grades. We have the same situation with the Student ID fields in the Student Personal and Grades tables. In the Student Personal and Grades tables, the relationship between the Student ID fields was automatically detected. The relationship of the Faculty ID fields has not been detected and we must establish it manually.

▶ Drag the Faculty ID field name from the Faculty table and drop it onto the Faculty ID field name in the Grades table, as shown in Figure 10.24.

After you've completed dragging the Faculty ID field name, you should notice the relationship line between the Faculty ID fields as shown in Figure 10.25. Figure 10.25 also shows the additional fields from the Faculty table that we will be including in the next query.

▶ Double-click the Last Name field in the Faculty table to add this field to the criteria grid, as shown in Figure 10.25.

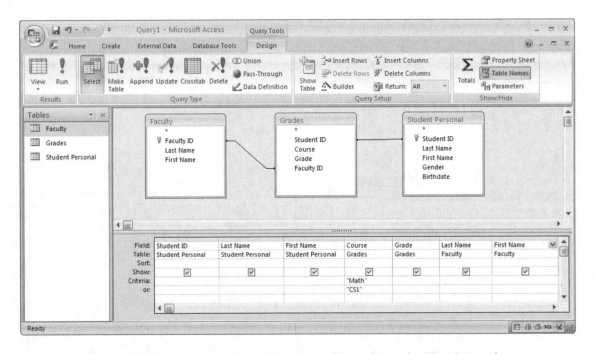

Figure 10.25 *Access query with Faculty table and Faculty ID relationship.*

Query1 : Select Query						
Student ID	Student Personal.Last Name	Student Personal.First Name	Course	Grade	Faculty.Last Name	Faculty.First Name
67736035	Maltais	Peter	CS1	66	Smith	Bob
85040424	Biggar	Nicole	CS1	45	Lew	Marty
67721910	Markwith	Shawn	CS1	74	McDonald	Gina
84552953	Jamieson	Ryan	CS1	46	Digiovanni	Lori
6902426	Laframboise	Dionda	CS1	91	Smith	Bob
53277628	Blanchette	Larissa	CS1	75	Lew	Marty
60561670	Beasley	Grechen	CS1	42	McDonald	Gina
86862033	Brousseau	Murray	CS1	71	Smith	Bob
89075008	Ely	Tyler	CS1	49	Lew	Marty
36543580	Harris	Miaolin	CS1	48	McDonald	Gina
63688148	Wright	Ann	CS1	62	Digiovanni	Lori
34303109	Niamat	Edith	CS1	71	Smith	Bob
31225104	Houghton	Jonathan	CS1	73	Lew	Marty
12637950	Hasspieler	Jennifer	CS1	81	Smith	Bob
21093070	Roussel	Chris	CS1	44	Lew	Marty

Record: I◄ ◄ ☐ 1 ► ►I ►* of 326

Figure 10.26 *Access query results for Math and CS1 courses with Faculty fields.*

▶ Double-click the First Name field in the Faculty table to add this field to the criteria, as shown in Figure 10.25.

▶ Click the **Run Query** button to display the results of the query, as shown in Figure 10.26.

You may have to increase the widths of the columns to see the field names. Since there are two Last Name fields and two First Name fields, the field names are further identified by the name of the table. For instance, Faculty:Last Name and Faculty:First Name indicate that these fields are from the Faculty table.

Let's save this query and generate a report based on it.

▶ Click the **Save** button to save the query. The **Save As** box will appear, as shown in Figure 10.27.

▶ In the **Save As** box, type: Math and CS1, as shown in Figure 10.27.

▶ Click the **OK** button to save the query.

▶ Close the **Query** window.

Figure 10.27 *Access query Save As box.*

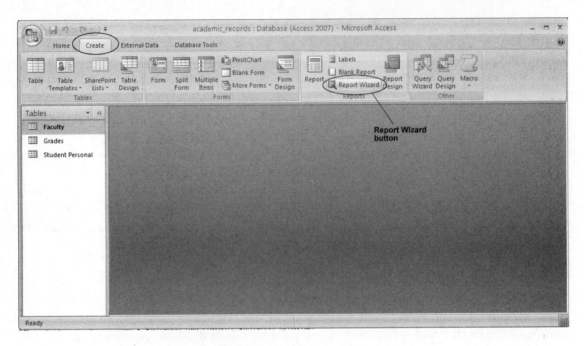

Figure 10.28 *Access create report.*

Creating a Report

We can generate simple reports using fields in tables, or we can use a query as a basis of a report. Let's generate a report based on the Math and CS1 query.

▶ Click the Create tab and then click on the **Report Wizard** button, as shown in Figure 10.28.

▶ In the Report Wizard window, click the drop-down menu for the Tables/Queries and select the Math and CS1 query, as shown in Figure 10.29.

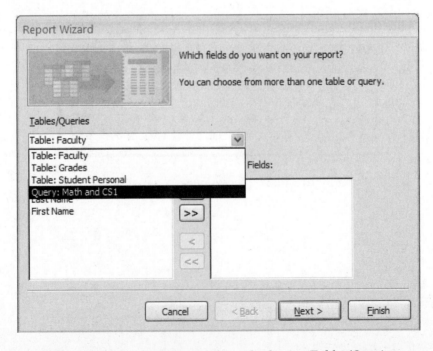

Figure 10.29 *Access Report Wizard selecting Tables/Queries.*

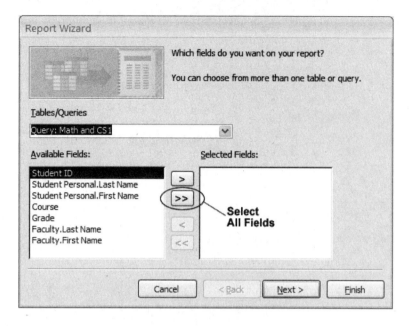

Figure 10.30 *Access Report Wizard with Available Fields from Math and CS1 query.*

The field names used in the Math and CS1 query will be included in the **Available Fields** box, as shown in Figure 10.30.

▶ Click on the **Select All Fields** button, as shown in Figure 10.30.

All of the field names will be placed in the **Selected Fields** box.

▶ Click the **Next >** button to advance to the next step.

We can group the results on any of the fields. Let's group the results on the Faculty Last Name field to see the grades for each Faculty member.

▶ Click on the Course name to select it, as shown in Figure 10.31.

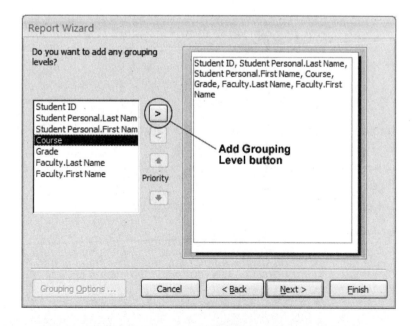

Figure 10.31 *Access Report Wizard grouping dialog box.*

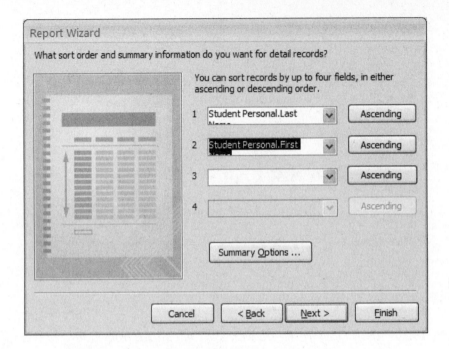

Figure 10.32 *Access Report Wizard sorting dialog box.*

▶ Click on the **Add Grouping Level** button to add the Faculty.Last Name field as a grouping level, as shown in Figure 10.31.

The field name Course will be placed at the top of the grouping pane.

▶ Click the Faculty.Last Name field name to select it.

▶ Click on the **Add Grouping Level** button to add the Faculty.Last Name field as a grouping level, as shown in Figure 10.31.

▶ Click the **Next >** button to advance to the next step.

The next step will allow us to specify the fields to sort.

▶ Click the drop-down arrows and specify the Student.Last name and Student.First name fields for sorting, as shown in Figure 10.32.

▶ Click the **Next >** button to advance to the next step.

We can choose the format for grouping and page setup.

▶ If the **Stepped Layout** radio button is not already selected, click the **Stepped Layout** radio button, as shown in Figure 10.33.

▶ Click the **Portrait Orientation** radio button if it is not already selected, as shown in Figure 10.33.

▶ Click the **Next >** button to advance to the next step.

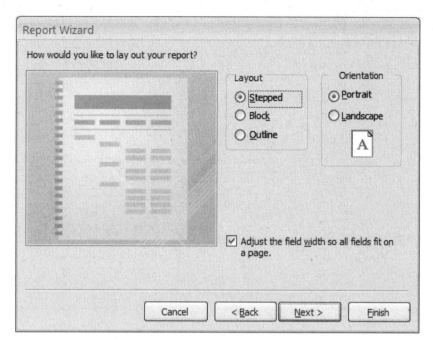

Figure 10.33   *Access Report layout dialog box.*

We can choose a formatting style for the report.

▶ Feel free to click on format style to view the possible styles, as shown in Figure 10.34.

▶ Click on the **Concourse** style to select it, as shown in Figure 10.34.

▶ Click the **Next >** button to advance to the next step.

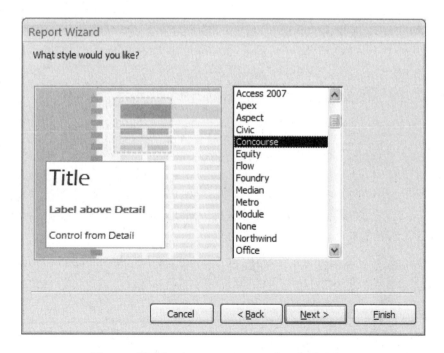

Figure 10.34   *Access report styles dialog box.*

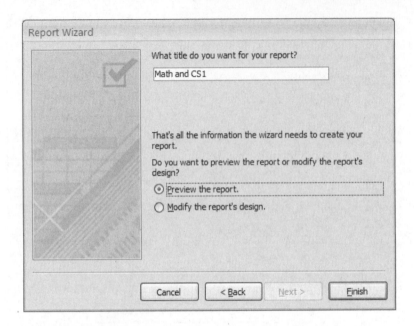

Figure 10.35 *Access report finish dialog box.*

▶ Click the **Report Title** box and edit the name as: Math and CS1, as shown in Figure 10.35.

▶ Click the **Finish** button to complete the report and preview it.

The **Report Preview** window will open, as shown in Figure 10.36. The report is multiple pages.

▶ Click the **Next Page** button to view the subsequent pages of the report, as shown in Figure 10.36.

▶ Close the **Report** window when you have finished viewing the report.

▶ Close the **Access** window.

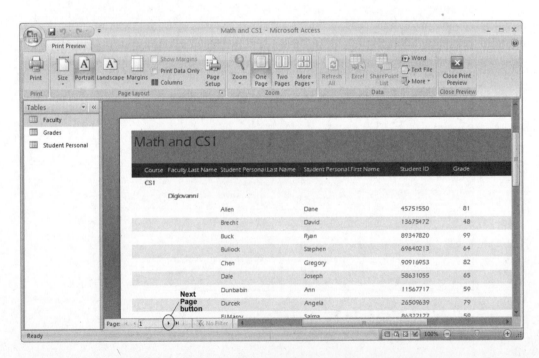

Figure 10.36 *Access Report Preview window.*

Review

This has been a busy lab! We have covered the following topics:

- A review of database terminology including database, table, record, field, and field name
- Data integrity issues and the importance of storing only one copy of data items
- Creating a query using the Design view and multiple tables
- Using multiple criteria in a query
- Adding tables to a query
- Creating a relationship between tables
- Generating a report from a query

Exercises

Use the academic_records.accdb database and perform the following tasks.

1. Create a query using the Faculty and Grades tables only with the following results. Be sure to create the relationship between the Faculty ID fields.
   a. Faculty Last Name, Faculty First Name, Student ID, Course, and Grade showing all grades less than 60. Save this query as Grades Less Than 60.
   b. Course, Student ID, Faculty Last Name, and Faculty First Name showing Psychology and Math courses. Save this query as Faculty Psychology Math.

2. Create a query using the Grades and Student Personal tables with the following results.
   a. Student ID, Student Last Name, Student First Name, Course, and Grade showing all grades greater than or equal to 60. Save this query as All Greater Than 60.
   b. Student ID, Student Last Name, Student First Name, Course, and Grade showing all grades greater than or equal to 60 in Math only. Save this query as Greater Than 60 Math.

3. Create reports for each of the queries. Do not use grouping for the reports.

Presentation Concepts Using Microsoft PowerPoint

Objectives:

Upon successful completion of Lab 11, you will be able to

- Understand some simple tips for effective presentations
- Create slides using a variety of slide layout designs
- Create a table for a slide
- Add a picture to a slide
- Apply a design to all slides
- Apply a transition effect to all slides

Resources required:

- A computer running Microsoft PowerPoint 2007 (PC) or Microsoft PowerPoint 2008 (Mac)

Starter file:

- resort.jpg

Prerequisite skills:

- General keyboarding skills; familiarity with editing keys such as Delete, Backspace, Shift, Caps Lock, and Arrow keys
- Ability to find files using Windows Explorer or Windows search feature
- Ability to open and save a file in a Windows application

NRC's Top Ten Skills, Concepts, and Capabilities:

- Skills
  Use a computer to communicate with others—designing a presentation
  - Create a simple presentation using PowerPoint
  - Slide layout, transitions, animations
  - Insert graphics
- Concepts
  Structuring information
- Capabilities
  Manage complexity

Lab Lesson

At some point in your career you will likely have to make a presentation to someone. Perhaps it will be a sales presentation to a client, a summary for a group of managers, a presentation during a job interview, or a training presentation. If you require some sort of slide show, you can use presentation software such as PowerPoint to create it.

Effective Slide Presentation Techniques

Before we get started creating a slide show, there are a few basic techniques to be aware of when creating a slide presentation.

- Use the same theme for all slides. Background color, font, style, text color, and the general look should be the same for all slides. You don't have to be artistic! There are a variety of templates available to choose from.
- Use images, tables, and charts where appropriate to add interest and clarity.
- Use effective slide titles. It should read like a headline so that the viewer understands what the slide is about by its title.
- Use no more than 5–7 bullets per slide for text information.
- Use short sentences. Think in terms of point form, and not narrative sentences and paragraphs.
- Use a large font, 18–24 point.
- Use a serif font because it's easier to read from a distance.
- Add an empty slide or a simple slide with a "Thank you" message to the end of your presentation so that the viewer is not left looking at your desktop!

Let's create a slide show for Woodland Resort, a new vacation destination. We will create the following slides:

- Title
- Facilities
- Fitness classes
- Contact information

Let's start with the title slide.

▶ Open PowerPoint.

Notice that only one slide is visible, as shown in Figures 11.1a and 11.1b. We will add slides as we need them.

▶ On the Mac, ensure the Formatting Palette is visible as shown in Figure 11.1b. If it is not visible, click the menu options View, Formatting Palette to display it.

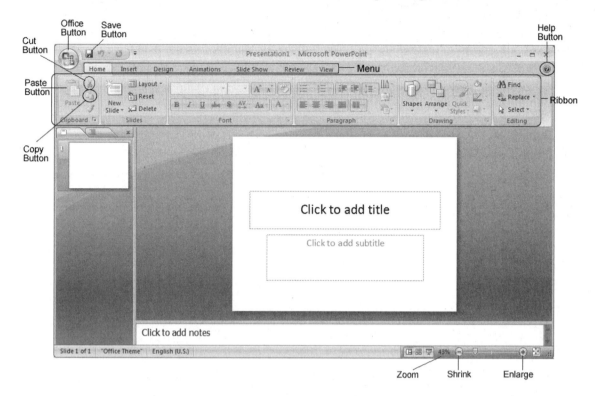

Figure 11.1a *PowerPoint parts of the window for PC.*

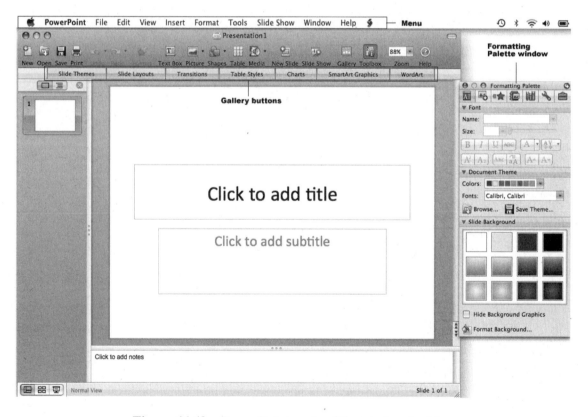

Figure 11.1b *PowerPoint parts of the window for Mac.*

Title Slide

The current slide is a title slide layout. Notice the rectangular areas for title and subtitle. We will click in each area and add content.

▶ Click in the area labeled "Click to add title." A flashing insertion point will appear in the title area.

▶ In the title area type: Woodland Resort, as shown in Figure 11.2.

▶ Click in the area labeled "Click to add subtitle." A flashing insertion point will appear in the subtitle area.

▶ In the subtitle area type: Presentation by

▶ Press the **Enter** key.

▶ Type: Your Name, as shown in Figure 11.2.

▶ Save this file as woodlandresort.pptx.

It's simple, but we'll add some interest later. Let's add a new slide for the facilities listing.

▶ On the PC, click the **drop-down arrow** on the **New Slide** button, as shown in Figure 11.3a.

▶ On the Mac, click the **New Slide button** as shown in Figure 11.3b. Click the **Slide Layouts gallery button** as shown in Figure 11.3b.

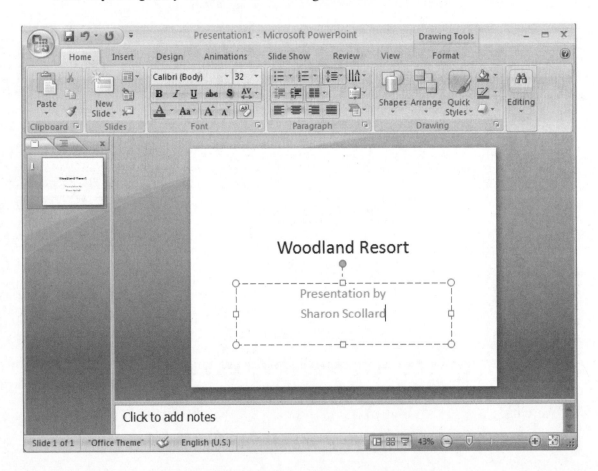

Figure 11.2 *PowerPoint Presentation title slide.*

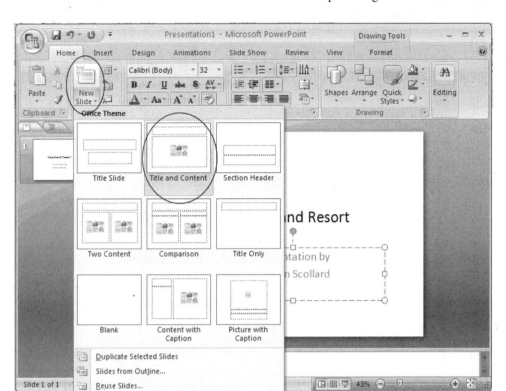

Figure 11.3a   *PowerPoint Insert New Slide for PC.*

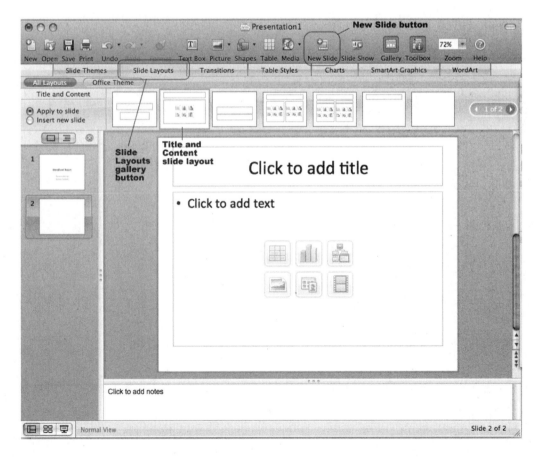

Figure 11.3b   *PowerPoint Insert New Slide for Mac.*

A selection of slide layout options will appear in a gallery, as shown in Figures 11.3a and 11.3b.

Some of the slide layouts have icons for images, charts, two columns, and tables. Some slide layouts are suitable for text.

Bulleted List

▶ Click the **Title and Content** slide, as shown in Figures 11.3a and 11.3b.
▶ Click in the "Click to add title" area.
▶ Type: Woodland Resort Facilities, as shown in Figure 11.4.
▶ Click in the area labeled "click to add text."

PowerPoint automatically places bullets at the beginning of each line and this is exactly what we want for the slide we are creating now.

▶ Type: Tennis
▶ Press the **Enter** key, as shown in Figure 11.4.
▶ Type: Fitness room
▶ Press the **Enter** key, as shown in Figure 11.4.
▶ Type: Spa treatments
▶ Press the **Enter** key, as shown in Figure 11.4.
▶ Press the **Tab** key.

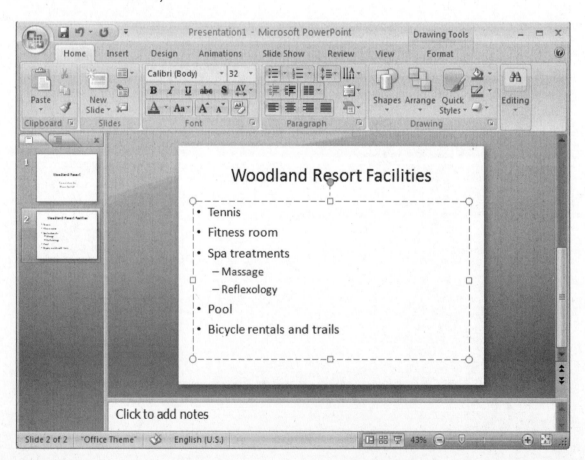

Figure 11.4 *PowerPoint Facilities slide.*

Notice that the bullet has indented and changed to a hyphen bullet symbol.

▶ Type: Massage

▶ Press the **Enter** key, as shown in Figure 11.4.

▶ Type: Reflexology

▶ Press the **Enter** key, as shown in Figure 11.4.

▶ Hold the **Shift** key while you press the **Tab** key, to move the bullet to the left one level.

Notice that this moves the bullet up one level, back to the black dot bullet and to the left margin.

▶ Type: Pool

▶ Press the **Enter** key, as shown in Figure 11.4.

▶ Type: Bicycle rentals and trails

The completed slide is shown in Figure 11.4.

▶ Save the file. Be sure to save your file periodically through the lab exercise.

Adding a Table

Let's add a new slide for the resort events. We will include the Fitness Class schedule as shown below.

	Monday – Friday	**Saturday – Sunday**
10:00 am	Yoga	Dance Fit
1:00 pm	Aerobics	Yoga
7:00 pm	Dance Fit	No Classes

We will use a table for the Fitness Center slide and will choose an appropriate slide layout.

▶ Click on the **New Slide** button and select the Title and Content Slide.

The content area contains icons for different types of content, as shown in Figure 11.5.

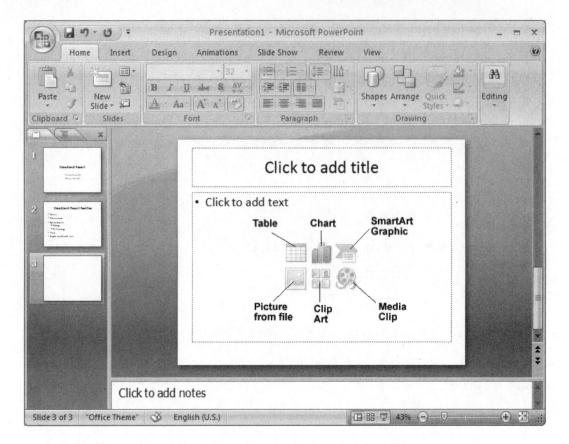

Figure 11.5 *PowerPoint title and table Slide Layout.*

▶ Click in the area labeled "Click to add title."

▶ Type: Fitness Classes, as shown in Figures 11.7a and 11.7b.

▶ Click the table icon.

The **Insert Table** dialog box will appear, as shown in Figure 11.6.

▶ Set the number of columns as 3 and the number of rows as 4 in the **Insert Table** dialog box, as shown in Figure 11.6.

▶ Click the **OK** button to insert the table grid.

To move the flashing insertion point from one cell to another you can either click on a cell or press the **Tab** key.

▶ Enter the data in the table, as shown in Figures 11.7a and 11.7b.

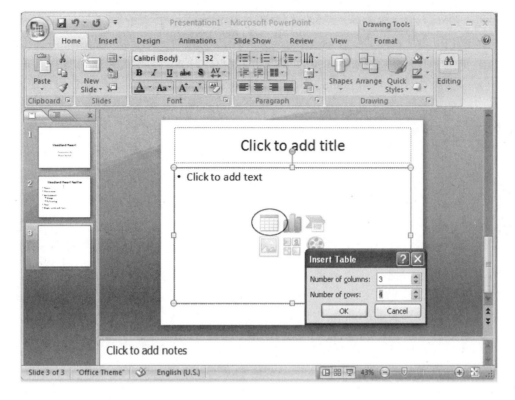

Figure 11.6   *PowerPoint Insert Table.*

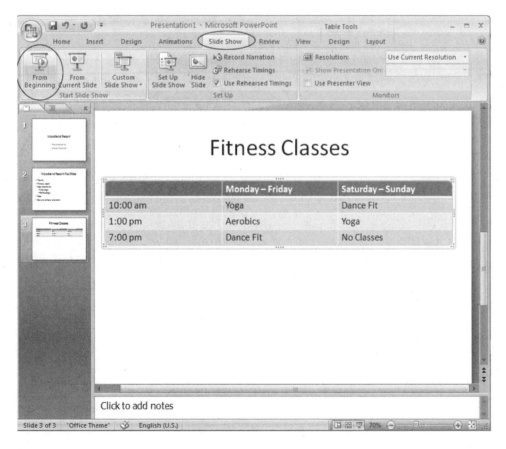

Figure 11.7a   *PowerPoint Fitness Classes slide for PC.*

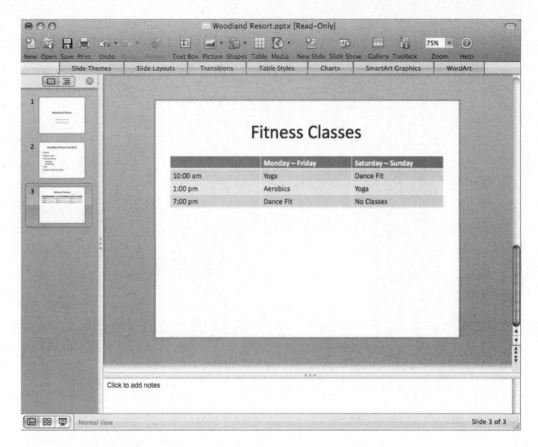

Figure 11.7b *PowerPoint Fitness Classes slide for Mac.*

Playing the Slide Show

Now that we have a few slides, let's preview the slide show.

▶ On the PC, click the **Slide Show** menu option and click the **From Beginning** button as shown in Figure 11.7a.

▶ On the Mac, click the Slide Show button as shown in Figure 11.7b. The slide show will begin to run immediately.

Your slide show will begin with the title slide displayed on the full screen.

▶ Click the **left mouse** button or press the **Enter** key to advance to the next slide.

▶ Press the **Enter** key several times to view each slide. Depending on the version, at the end of the slide show a black slide may appear.

▶ Press the **Enter** key to end the slide show and return to PowerPoint.

We will add some interesting slide transitions later.

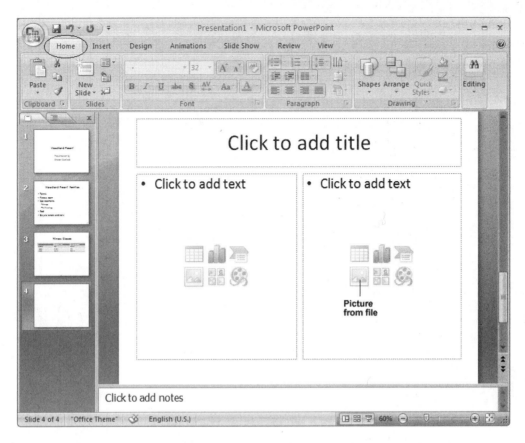

Figure 11.8a   *PowerPoint slide layout for title and content for PC.*

Adding an Image

Let's create the contact information slide and an image of the resort.

▶ On the PC, click the **Home** menu option as shown in Figure 11.8a.

▶ On the PC, click the **New Slide** button and select the **Two Content** slide.

▶ On the Mac, click the **New Slide button**, and click the **Slide Layouts gallery button** as shown in Figure 11.8b.

▶ Click the Insert Picture from File icon in the content area on the right-hand side, as shown in Figures 11.8a and 11.8b.

▶ Select the resort.jpg picture provided with this lab.

The picture of the resort will be inserted, as shown in Figure 11.9.

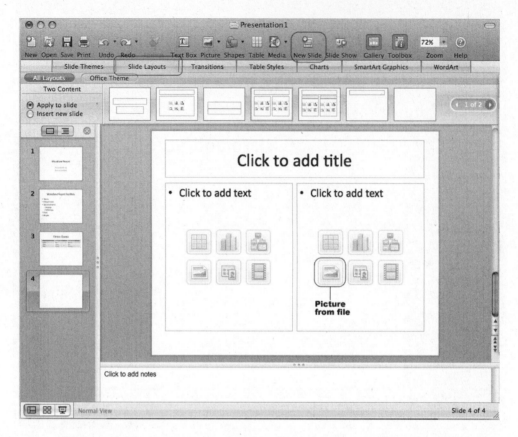

Figure 11.8b *PowerPoint slide layout for title and content for Mac.*

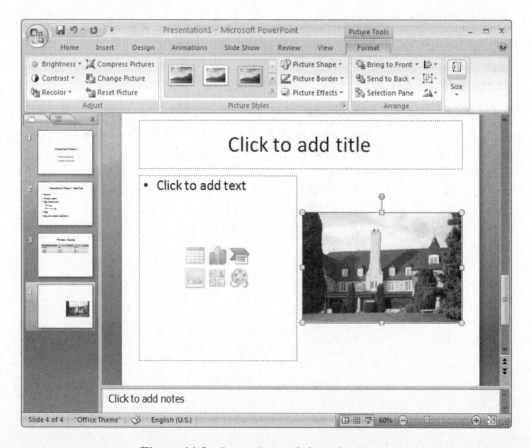

Figure 11.9 *PowerPoint slide with picture.*

The picture is selected and has handles around it. You can resize it by dragging the handles. In this case, we'll leave the default size, as it seems appropriate for the slide.

Let's add the title.

► Click the area labeled "Click to add title."
► Type: Woodland Resort, as shown in Figure 11.10.
► Click the area labeled "Click to add text."
► Type: Phone: (505) 555-1111, as shown in Figure 11.10.

Let's remove the bullet from the text.

► Click the **Bullets** button as shown in Figures 11.10a and 11.10b.

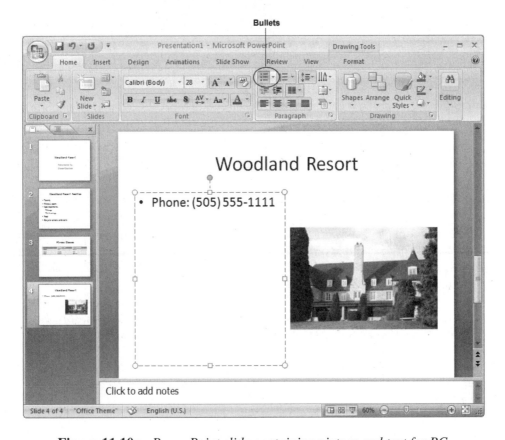

Figure 11.10a   *PowerPoint slide containing picture and text for PC.*

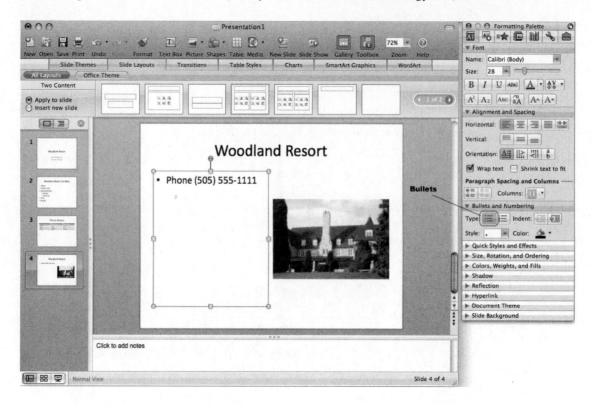

Figure 11.10b *PowerPoint slide containing picture and text for Mac.*

Notice that the bullet has been removed from the text.

We will be adding more contact information but it may be a bit longer than the phone number text. It would be nice if we could avoid wrapping each line. Let's choose a more appropriate slide layout that will accommodate longer lines of text. We can easily change a slide layout by choosing another layout from the gallery.

▶ On the PC, click the **Layout** button and select the **Picture with Caption** slide layout option as shown in Figure 11.11a.

▶ On the Mac, click the page indicator in the gallery to scroll to the next page of layout options and click on the Picture with Caption slide layout as shown in Figure 11.11b.

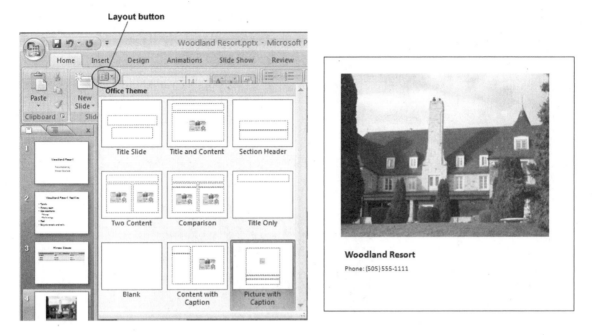

Figure 11.11a   *PowerPoint slide containing picture over text for PC.*

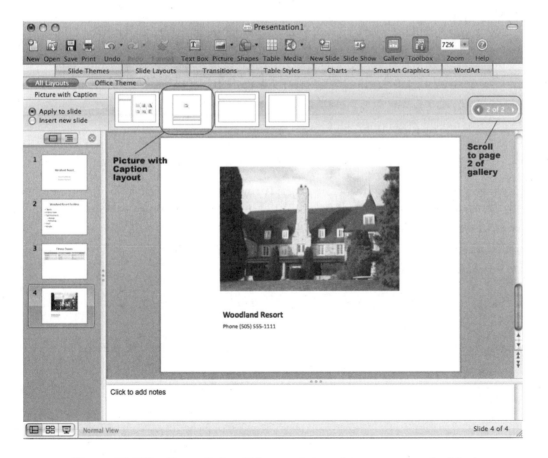

Figure 11.11b   *PowerPoint slide containing picture over text for Mac.*

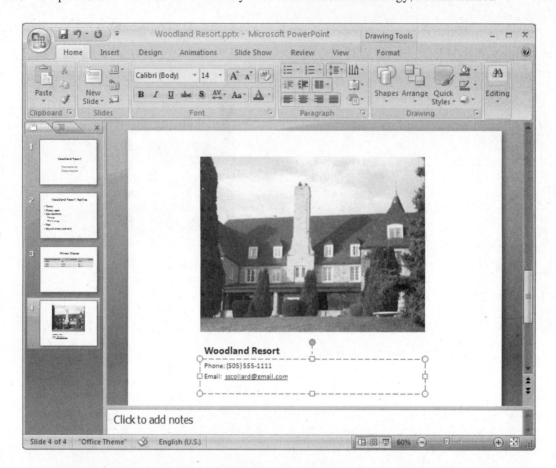

Figure 11.12   *PowerPoint slide containing picture and contact information.*

Let's add some more contact information.

▶ Position the mouse pointer at the end of the phone number and click the **left mouse** button (PC) or mouse button (Mac). This should position the flashing insertion point after the phone number. If the flashing insertion point is not positioned at the end of the phone number, use the arrow keys to position it.

▶ Press the **Enter** key to move the flashing insertion point to the next line.

▶ Type: Email: Your email address, as shown in Figure 11.12.

▶ Press the **Enter** key.

Notice that the email address changes color and becomes underlined. This indicates that the email address has become a link.

Feel free to view the slide show using the **Slide Show** menu as we've done previously.

Slide Designs

The slides are very plain so let's add some visual interest. Although you can certainly define colors and gradients for the background there are also a number of preset designs you can use. Let's browse through the themes and make some selections for our slides.

One of the tips for a professional presentation is to use the same color scheme or design for all slides. We can choose a design and apply it to all slides at once.

▶ On the PC, click the **Design** menu command as shown in Figure 11.13a.

▶ On the Mac, click the Slide Themes gallery button as shown in Figure 11.13b.

▶ On the PC, hover the mouse pointer over each of the themes to see the design applied to all of the slides in the presentation.

▶ On the Mac, click on each of the themes to see the design applied to all of the slides in the presentation.

▶ Feel free to experiment by clicking several design samples.

▶ View the slide show using the **Slide Show menu command** (PC) or **Slide Show button** (Mac), as we have done previously.

Figure 11.13a *PowerPoint Themes for PC.*

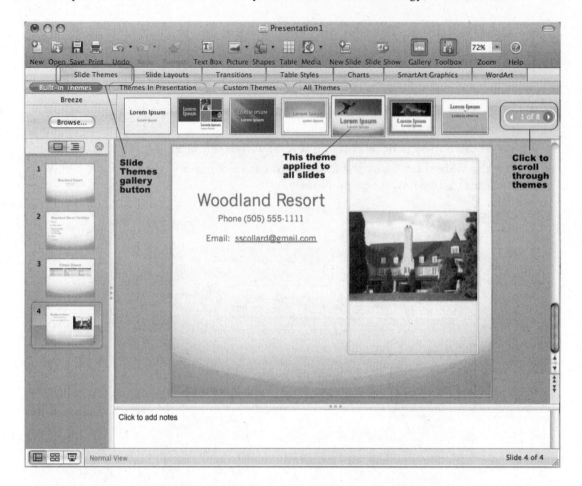

Figure 11.13b *PowerPoint Themes for Mac.*

Slide Transitions

Now that we've settled on a design for the slides, let's add an interesting transition. At the moment, the slides simply appear all at once.

▶ On the PC, click the **Animations** menu command, as shown in Figure 11.14a.

▶ On the Mac, click the Transitions gallery button, as shown in Figure 11.14b.

The slide transitions are animations that will occur during the slide show as one slide unloads and the next slide loads.

On the PC:

▶ Use the **Scroll up** and **Scroll down** buttons to see the available slide transitions.

▶ Hover the mouse pointer over one of the transition icons. PowerPoint will demonstrate the transition.

▶ After you've chosen a transition you like, click the transition icon to select it and click the **Apply to All Slides** button.

▶ View the slide show using the **Slide Show** menu command as we have done previously.

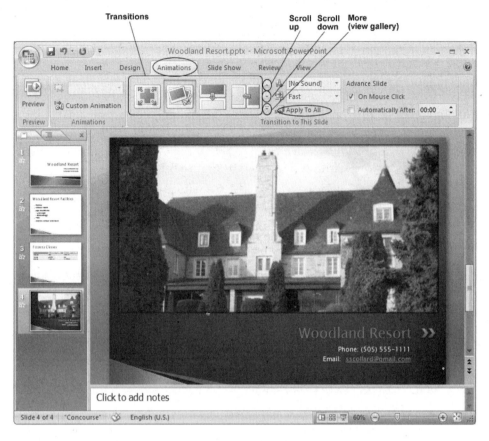

Figure 11.14a *PowerPoint Slide Transitions for PC.*

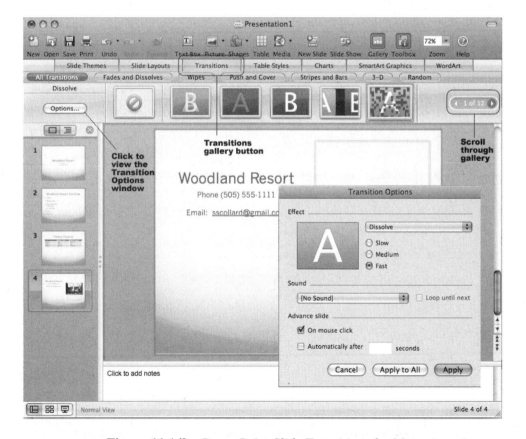

Figure 11.14b *PowerPoint Slide Transitions for Mac.*

On the Mac:

▶ Click the Transitions gallery button to view the transition types in the gallery as shown in Figure 11.14b.

▶ Scroll through the gallery using the scroll arrows as shown in Figure 11.14b.

▶ Click on each of the transition options in the gallery. Powerpoint will demonstrate the transition and apply it to the current slide.

▶ After you've chosen a transition you like, click the Options button to reveal the Transition Options window as shown in Figure 8.14b.

▶ Click the **Apply to All button** to apply the transition to all slides in the presentation, as shown in Figure 8.14b.

▶ View the slide show using the **Slide Show** menu command as we have done previously.

PowerPoint offers a variety of other features including animations of individual objects on a slide, creating charts from a table of data and customized backgrounds.

Review

This has been a busy lab! We have covered the following topics:
- Some simple tips for effective presentations
- A variety of slide layout designs
- Adding a table to a slide
- Adding a picture to a slide
- Applying a design to all slides
- Applying a transition effect to all slides

Exercises

1. Create a slide show for your favorite hobby or recreational activity. Include the following items:
   a. Title slide containing the name of your topic and your name.
   b. Slide containing bulleted points for reasons why you enjoy this hobby or activity.
   c. Slide containing a table of information about your hobby or activity. This could be a list of rules, equipment, or details of features.
   d. Slide containing a picture pertaining to your hobby or activity and some text information about the picture or additional features.

2. Apply a design to all slides in your presentation.

3. Apply a transition to all slides in your presentation.

Image Concepts

Objectives:

Upon successful completion of Lab 12, you will be able to

- Create a simple image using the drawing tools in Windows Paint or Mac Paintbrush including pencil, brush, airbrush, and some filled shapes
- Select and move part of an image
- Select and copy part of an image
- Understand that images are stored in files that can be compressed or uncompressed
- Use the image in a Word document

Resources required:

- A computer running Word, and Windows Paint or Mac Paintbrush

Starter files:

- mountain.jpg (required for Exercise 2)

Prerequisite skills:

- General keyboarding skills; familiarity with editing keys such as Delete, Backspace, Shift, Caps Lock, and Arrow keys
- Ability to find files using Windows File Explorer, Mac Finder or a file search feature
- Ability to open and save a file in a Windows or Mac application

NRC's Top Ten Skills, Concepts, and Capabilities:

- Skills
  Use a graphics or artwork package to manipulate an image
  - Use Paint or Paintbrush to edit an image
  - Use Paint or Paintbrush to create an image
  - Image compression
- Concepts
  Structuring information
  Universality
- Capabilities
  Anticipate technological change

273

Lab Lesson

Pictures and other images can be stored digitally in files. There are examples of this around us every day. The pictures you see on a Web page are stored in separate files. Pictures taken with a digital camera are also stored in files. Documents and pictures can be scanned using a scanner and also stored in files. An image file often contains a picture but can also contain a scanned image of a document, banner advertising used for a Web page, or a company logo.

Let's explore some of the techniques that can be used to create and edit an image. We will use Paint. This is a very simple image editing application and does not have some of the more sophisticated features such as selecting individual objects after they've been drawn, layers, or applying gradient and lighting effects. It accomplishes some very simple drawing and editing. In Windows, we will be using Paint. Mac OS X does not include an application such as paint, however, we will use Paintbrush for Mac, which is a free application.

▶ In Windows, open Paint. You will probably find it in the Windows menus, Start, All Programs, Accessories, Paint. The Paint window is shown in Figure 12.1a.

▶ In Mac OS X, open Safari and download and install the Paintbrush application available at http://paintbrush.sourceforge.net/. Open Paintbrush after it has been installed.

▶ In Paintbrush, set the canvas height to 300 and width to 300 as shown in Figure 12.1b. Click the OK button to set the canvas size. The Paintbrush window is shown in Figure 12.1b.

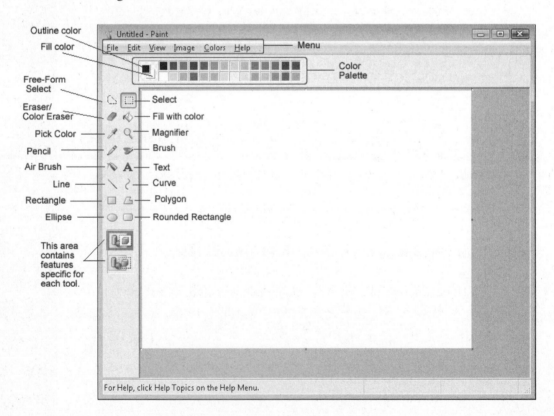

Figure 12.1a *Paint parts of the window.*

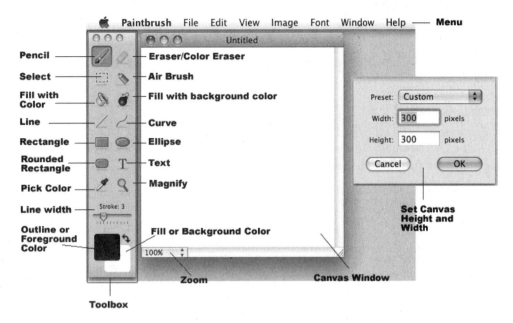

Figure 12.1b *Paintbrush parts of the window.*

The drawing area can be sized to accommodate images of different sizes.

Adjusting the Canvas Size

Let's experiment with some of the drawing tools. First, we'll set the drawing canvas size in Paint. This has already been done in Paintbrush.

In Paint:

▶ Click the **Image**, **Attributes** menu commands.

▶ Click the **Width** box and delete the number in the box.

▶ Type: 300, as shown in Figure 12.2.

▶ Click the **Height** box and delete the number in the box.

▶ Type: 300, as shown in Figure 12.2.

▶ Ensure that the **Pixels** radio button is selected for Units, as shown in Figure 12.2.

▶ Click the **OK** button to set the canvas size.

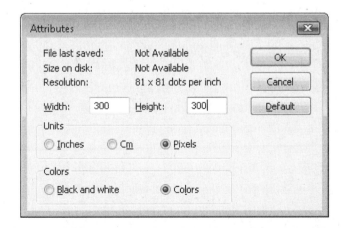

Figure 12.2 *Paint image attributes.*

The Pencil Tool

Let's experiment with drawing some shapes. Do not worry about artistic talent. Keep it abstract and just have fun!

▶ Click the Pencil tool, as shown in Figures 12.3a and 12.3b.

▶ Click one of the colors in the color palette (Paint) or color window (Paintbrush) to select a drawing color.

▶ Drag a path on the canvas with the mouse.

The pencil line will follow the path you draw, as shown in Figures 12.3a and 12.3b.

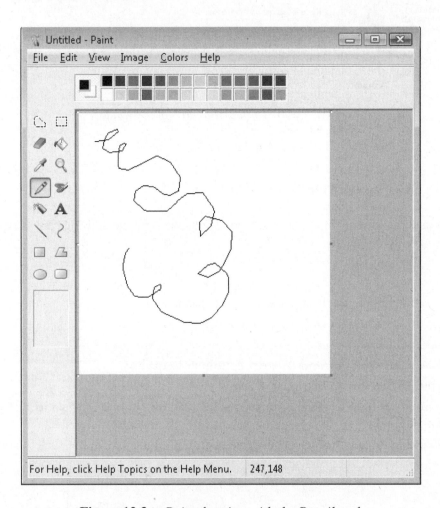

Figure 12.3a   *Paint drawing with the Pencil tool.*

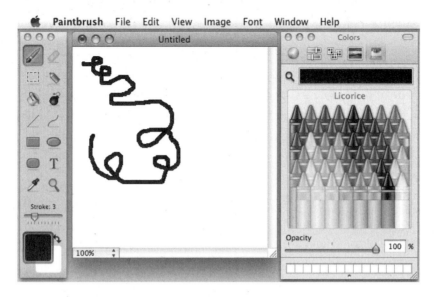

Figure 12.3b *Paintbrush drawing with the Pencil tool.*

The Brush Tool

Paint has a brush tool as well. Paintbrush does not have a brush tool.

In Paint only:

▶ Click the **Brush** tool, as shown in Figure 12.4.

Figure 12.4 *Paint adding the Brush tool drawing.*

Notice that there are a variety of brush tips to choose from that have appeared below the **Tool** buttons.

▶ Click one of the brush tips. The slanted tips will provide a calligraphy effect.

▶ Click one of the colors in the color palette to choose a drawing color.

▶ Again, drag a path on the canvas to draw with the **Brush** tool, as shown in Figure 12.4.

The Air Brush Tool

You will find that it is easier to draw a smooth curve if you move the mouse a bit quickly. You may also find that you have more control over drawing if you put more pressure on the mouse button with your index finger and use that motion to move the mouse rather than using your whole hand to move the mouse.

▶ Click the **Air brush** tool, as shown in Figures 12.5a and 12.5b. In Paint, there are three spray sizes below the tool buttons. In Paintbrush, you can drag the stroke slider to change the size of the spray.

▶ In Paint, click the largest spray size.

▶ In Paintbrush, drag the slider to the right to stroke 7 or larger.

▶ Click one of the colors in the color palette to select the spray color.

▶ Drag a path on the canvas with the mouse. If you hover over a spot for a second or two, the spray will intensify just as if you were using a can of spray paint.

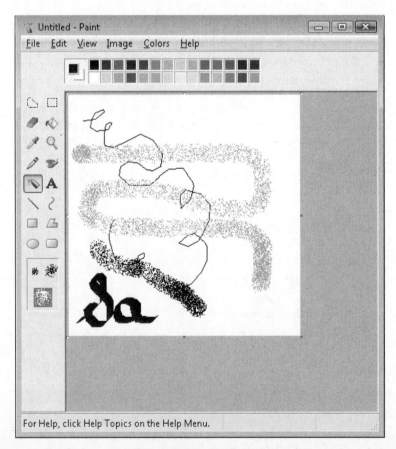

Figure 12.5a *Paint drawing with the Air Brush tool.*

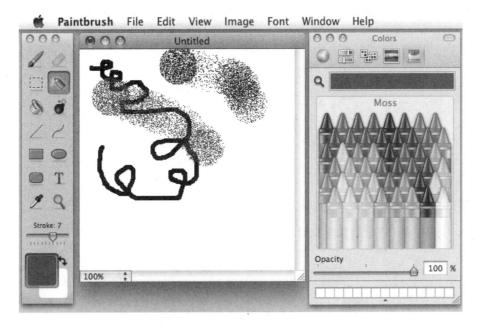

Figure 12.5b *Paintbrush drawing with the Air Brush tool.*

Notice that as you draw over other drawn items, the current item appears on top and may obstruct the other item entirely, as shown in Figures 12.5a and 12.5b.

Notice that the spray is formed, following the path of your mouse, as shown in Figures 12.5a and 12.5b.

Erasing

Paint does not allow us to select and delete a drawn object individually. This is a feature of most other image editing software packages. We can erase parts of the image using an eraser. Let's erase part of the image.

▶ Click the **Eraser** tool, as shown in Figures 12.6a and 12.6b.

In Paint, a variety of eraser sizes appear below the **Tool** buttons. In Paintbrush, you can adjust the size of the eraser with the stroke slider.

▶ In Paint, click the largest eraser size.
▶ In Paintbrush, drag the stroke slider to the right and select stroke size 10.
▶ Drag through parts of your drawn image. Notice that the eraser colors a white path through the image as you drag the mouse. Figures 12.6a and 12.6b show an erased area in the middle of the image.

Figure 12.6a   *Paint with erased portion.*

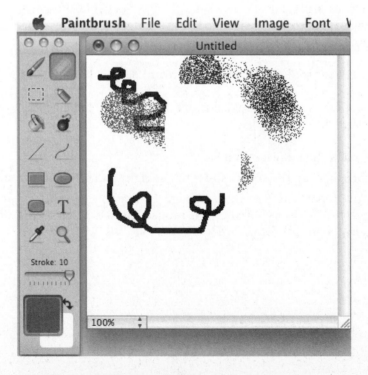

Figure 12.6b   *Paintbrush with erased portion.*

Selecting, Moving, and Copying Part of the Image

We can select part of the image to move or copy it as well. The selection tools allow us to define a rectangular shape or draw a custom shape. Let's select part of the image and move it.

▶ Click the **Select** tool, as shown in Figures 12.7a and 12.7b.

▶ Drag through part of the image to draw a rectangle area, as shown in Figures 12.7a and 12.7b.

▶ Position the mouse pointer inside the selected area.

▶ Drag the selected area to a new location on the canvas, as shown in Figures 12.8a and 12.8b.

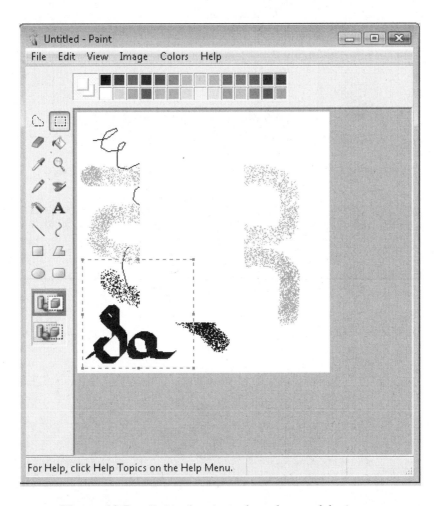

Figure 12.7a *Paint showing selected part of the image.*

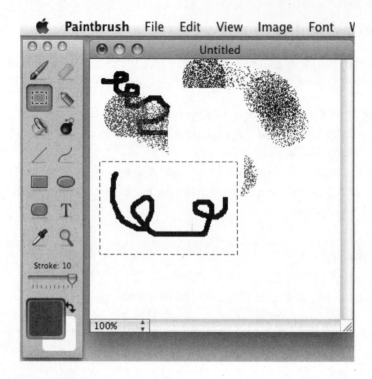

Figure 12.7b *Paintbrush showing selected part of the image.*

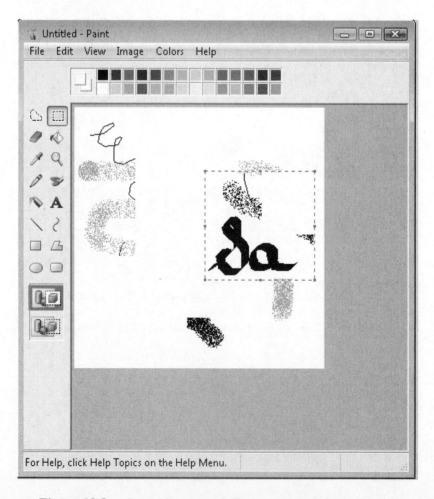

Figure 12.8a *Paint showing selected portion of image moved.*

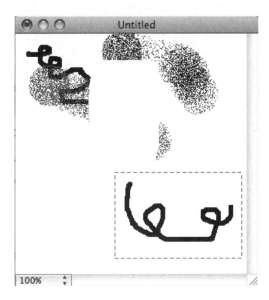

Figure 12.8b   *Paintbrush showing selected portion of image moved.*

We can also copy part of the image as well.

▶ Move the mouse pointer to a new location in the image and drag to select a new portion of the image, as shown in Figures 12.9a and 12.9b.

▶ Click the **Edit**, **Copy** menu commands.

▶ Click the **Edit**, **Paste** menu commands.

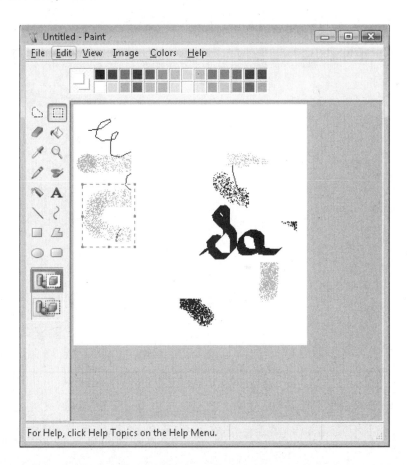

Figure 12.9a   *Paint selected portion of the image.*

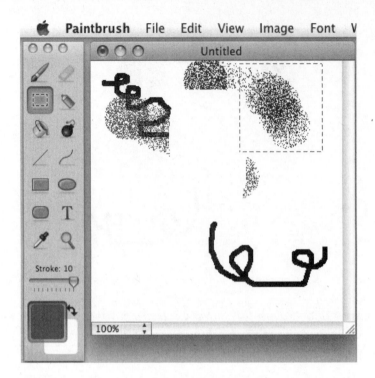

Figure 12.9b *Paintbrush selected portion of the image.*

Notice that a copy of the selection has been pasted in the upper left corner of the image, as shown in Figures 12.10a and 12.10b.

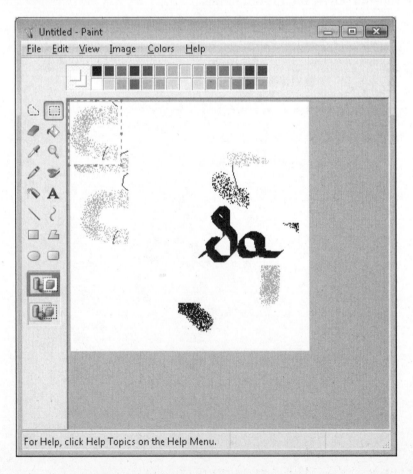

Figure 12.10a *Paint with copied selection.*

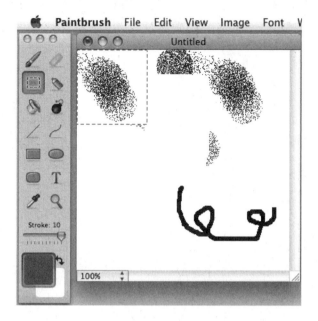

Figure 12.10b *Paintbrush with copied selection.*

▶ Feel free to move the copied selection to a new location on the canvas.

Filled Objects

Let's experiment with a few of the filled objects.

▶ Click the **Ellipse** tool, as shown in Figures 12.11a and 12.11b.

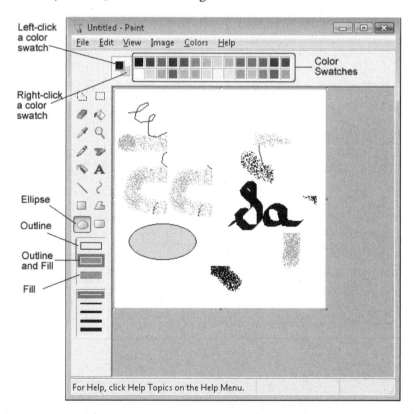

Figure 12.11a *Paint Ellipse drawing options.*

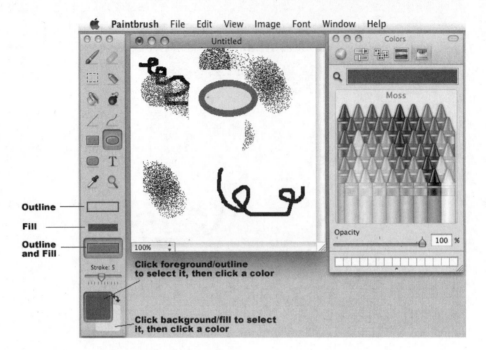

Figure 12.11b *Paintbrush Ellipse drawing options.*

The three options shown below the toolbar include outline, outline and filled, and filled, as shown in Figures 12.11a and 12.11b.

▶ Click the **Outline and Fill** option below the **Tool** buttons, as shown in Figures 12.11a and 12.11b.

We can select the outline and fill colors separately.

▶ In Paint, left-click one of the color swatches.

Notice that the color you have selected appears as indicated by the left-click location in Figure 12.11a.

▶ In Paint, right-click one of the color swatches.

Notice that the color you have selected appears as indicated by the right-click location in Figure 12.11a.

▶ In Paintbrush, click the foreground or outline swatch as shown in Figure 12.11b then click a color in the color window.
▶ In Paintbrush, click the background or fill swatch as shown in Figure 12.11b then click a color in the color window.
▶ Move the mouse pointer to the canvas and drag to form an ellipse.

The method to draw the rectangle and rounded rectangle shapes is identical to drawing an ellipse.

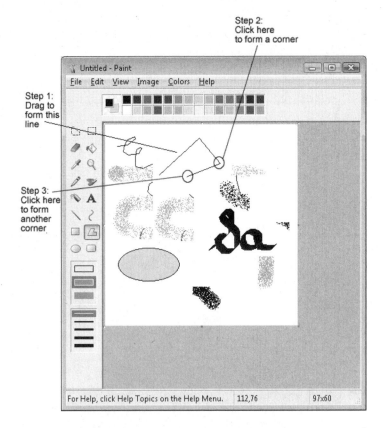

Figure 12.12 *Paint drawing a polygon.*

Drawing a Polygon (Paint only)

Pain has a polygon tool. Paintbrush does not have this tool. A polygon is a multi-sided shape. Again, we will use the **Outline and Fill** option.

▶ Click the **Polygon Shape Tool** button, as shown in Figure 12.12.

▶ Click the **Outline and Fill** option, as shown in Figure 12.12.

▶ Move the mouse pointer into the canvas area and drag to form a line, as shown in Figure 12.12, Step 1.

▶ Move the mouse pointer to another spot on the canvas where the next "corner" for the polygon will be, and click the **left mouse** button as shown in Figure 12.12, Step 2. Do not drag.

▶ Move the mouse pointer again to another point on the canvas and click the **left mouse** button to form another "corner" as shown in Figure 12.12, Step 3.

▶ Hover the mouse pointer over the starting point and double-click to close the polygon, as shown in Figure 12.13.

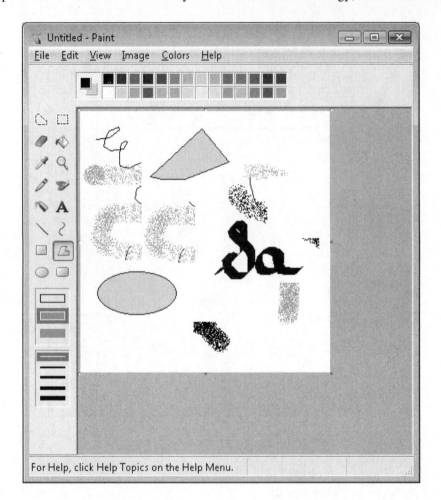

Figure 12.13   *Paint polygon drawing.*

Using the Fill Tool

We can change or add fill color to the canvas or objects. The **Fill with Color** tool will fill a closed area with color. If the area chosen is a closed object, such as the ellipse, it will fill only the inside of the ellipse. If the area chosen is an object that is not closed, the color will spill into all of the open areas. Let's fill the canvas with color to see this effect.

▶ Click the **Fill with Color** button, as shown in Figures 12.14a and 12.14b.

▶ Click one of the color swatches to select the fill color. Figures 12.14a and 12.14b show a grey swatch selected.

▶ Move the mouse pointer to the canvas but not inside a filled object.

▶ Click somewhere on the canvas to fill the canvas with the selected color.

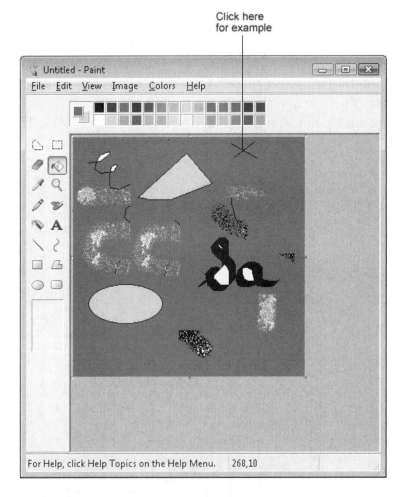

Figure 12.14a *Paint filling the canvas with color.*

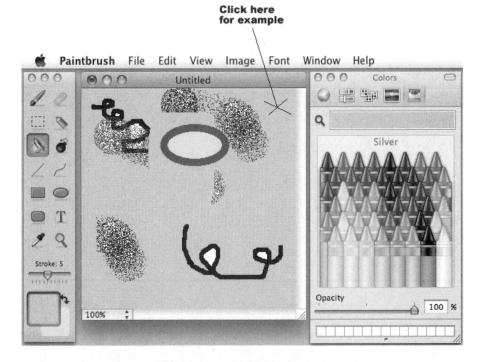

Figure 12.14b *Paintbrush filling the canvas with color.*

The effect is shown in Figures 12.14a and 12.14b.

Notice that some of the filled shapes have not been filled with color. They will need to be filled separately. Let's try another one.

▶ Click one of the color swatches to select a different color.

▶ Move the mouse pointer to the middle of the ellipse and click to fill the ellipse with the new color, as shown in Figures 12.15a and 12.15b.

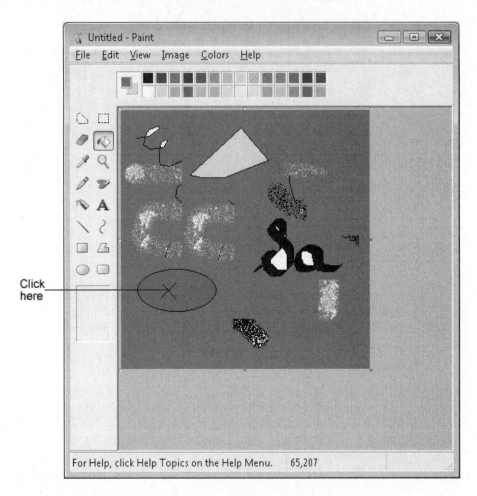

Figure 12.15a *Paint with fill color in the ellipse.*

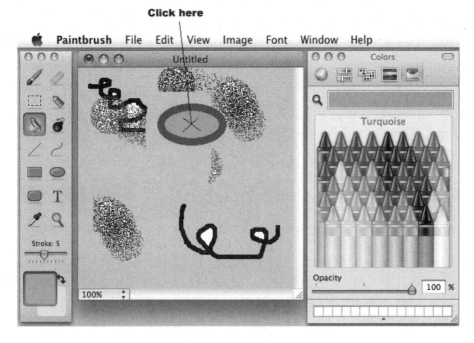

Figure 12.15b *Paintbrush with fill color in the ellipse.*

Image File Types

There are a variety of image file types used to store images. Let's look at just a few of them.

▶ Click the **File**, **Save** menu commands.

Windows may automatically choose the **Pictures** folder, as shown in Figure 12.16a.

▶ Click the **File name** box and type: test, as shown in Figures 12.16a and 12.16b.

The default file type for an image created in Paint is jpg. The default type for an image created in Paintbrush is png. We will save this file again using different file types and compare.

▶ In Paintbrush, click the drop-down arrow for the file format and select JPEG as shown in Figure 12.16b.

▶ Click the **Save** button to save the file.

Figure 12.16a *Save As dialog box default as jpg.*

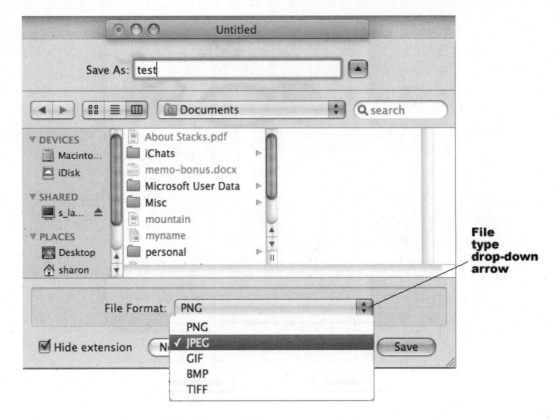

Figure 12.16b *Save As dialog box showing file save as JPEG.*

There are a variety of compressed image formats that may consolidate pixels that have the same color in the internal storage, or limit the number of colors that are used. One of the most popular image formats for displaying an image in a Web page is jpg. A bitmap file type uses an uncompressed format and stores a color number for each pixel. Let's store our image as a bitmap image and look at the difference in file size.

▶ Click the **File**, **Save As** menu commands.

▶ Click the **Save as type** drop-down menu, as shown in Figures 12.17a and 12.17b.

▶ In Paint, select 24-bit Bitmap as shown in Figure 12.17a.

▶ In Paintbrush, select BMP as shown in Figure 12.17b.

▶ Click the **Save** button to save the file.

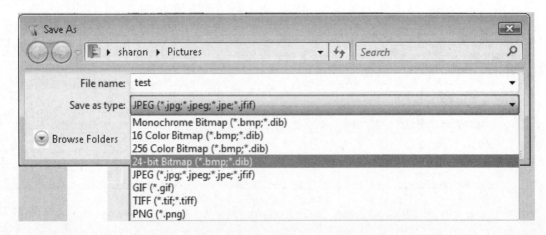

Figure 12.17a *Paint Save As 24-bit Bitmap.*

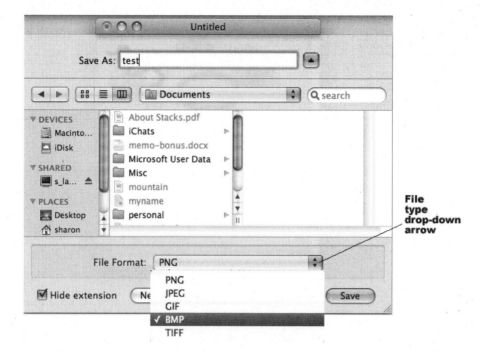

Figure 12.17b *Paintbrush Save As BMP.*

Saving in some formats produces an alert message that there may be some color loss. You may find this to be the case with gif images. Let's look at the difference in file size.

▶ In Windows, click the **Start** button and click the **Pictures** menu option to display the folder list for the folder containing the images, as shown in Figure 12.18a.

▶ In Mac OS X, click Finder on the Dock to display the list of files in the Documents folder, as shown in Figure 12.18b.

▶ In Windows, click the **Views** button and select the **Details** option to see the listing shown in Figure 12.18a.

▶ In Windows, hover the mouse pointer over each file name to see the detailed information including file type.

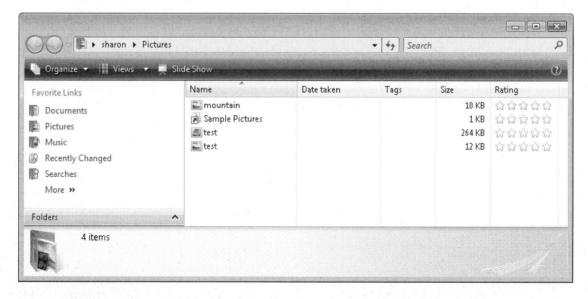

Figure 12.18a *Windows File Explorer showing the list for the image files created.*

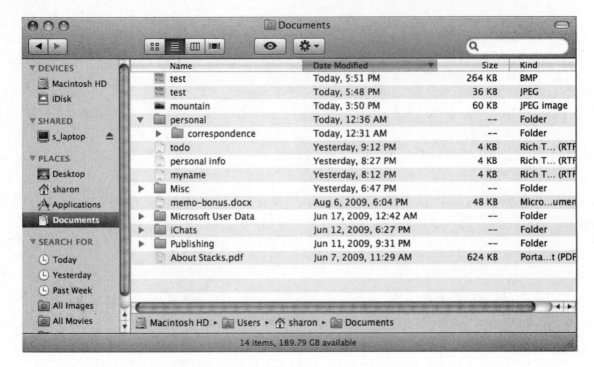

Figure 12.18b *Mac Finder showing the list for the image files created.*

In the example shown in Figure 12.18a, the test.bmp file is 264 KB and the test.jpg file is 12 KB. In the example shown in Figure 12.18b, the test.bmp file is 264 KB and the test.jpg file is 36 KB. That's quite a difference. The jpg image is more suitable for a Web page where download time is a concern and file sizes should be as small as possible.

Now that we have an image, we can use it in a document such as a Word, Excel or PowerPoint file. We can also include it in a Web page.

Let's add our image to a document.

▶ Open Windows Word 2007 or Mac Word 2008.

▶ In Windows, click the **Insert** menu command. In the **Picture** button, select the folder containing your image files and select the test.bmp image file from the list, as shown in Figure 12.19a. The file list in Figure 12.19a is shown using the medium icons view.

▶ In Mac OS X, click the menu options **Insert, Picture, From File.** Select the test.bmp image from the list, as shown in Figure 12.19b. The file list in Figure 12.19b is shown using the columns view.

▶ Click the **Insert** button to insert the test.bmp picture into the Word document.

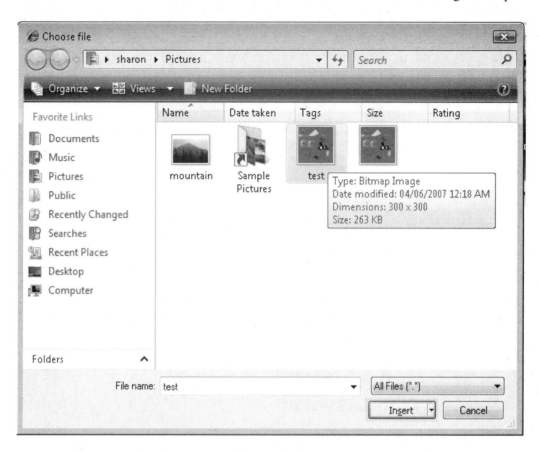

Figure 12.19a *Windows Word 2007 Insert Picture dialog box showing file list from Pictures.*

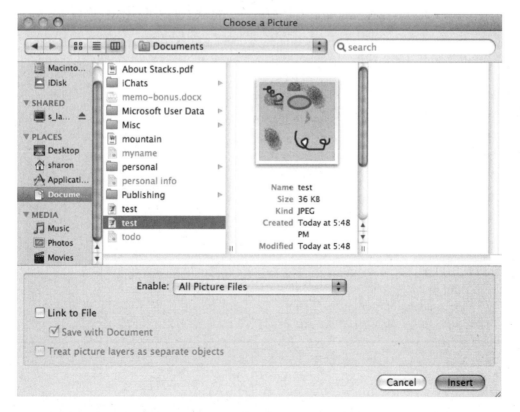

Figure 12.19b *Mac Word 2008 Insert Picture dialog box showing file list from Documents.*

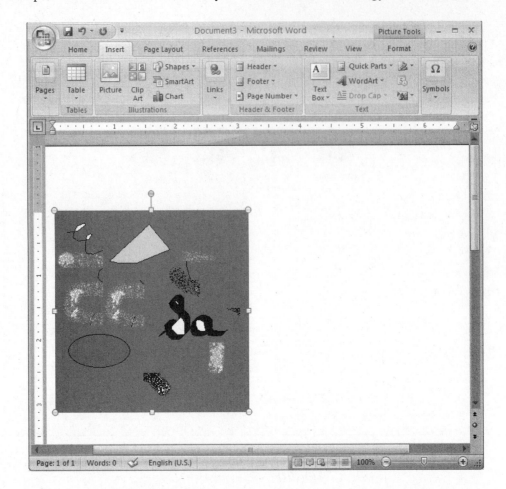

Figure 12.20a *Windows Word 2007 document with test.bmp.*

The image should appear in the Word document, as shown in Figures 12.20a and 12.20b.

Review

This has been a busy lab! We have covered the following topics:

- Creating a simple image using some of the drawing tools in Paint
    - Pencil
    - Brush (Paint only)
    - Airbrush
    - Filled shapes
- Selecting and moving part of an image
- Selecting and copying part of an image
- Storing an image in a file
    - Bmp as a large uncompressed file
    - Jpg as a smaller compressed file
- Using the image in a Word document

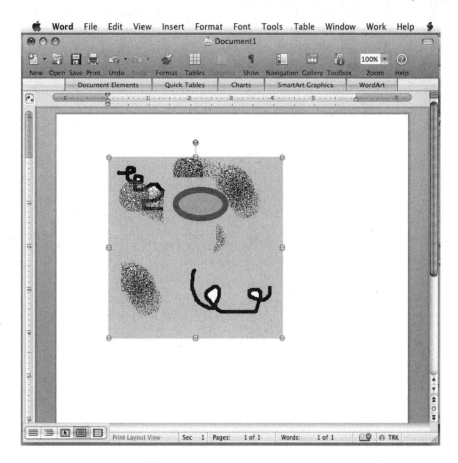

Figure 12.20b   *Mac Word 2008 document with test.bmp.*

Figure 12.21   *Paint with stick figure drawing.*

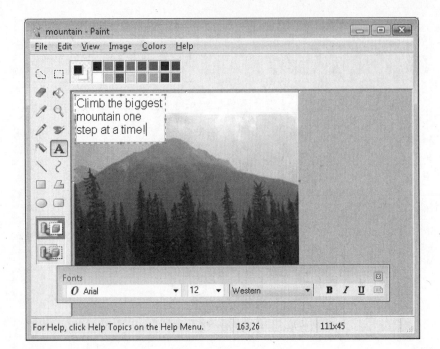

Figure 12.22 *Paint with mountain picture and text.*

Exercises

Use Paint to create the following effects:

1. Draw a picture of some people stick figures. Be creative! Figure 12.21 is a small example.

2. We can open an image file in Paint or Paintbrush and add enhancements to it or clip out parts. Open the mountain.jpg file in Paint or Paintbrush, as shown in Figure 12.22.

   a. Click the **Text** tool to add text.

   b. Drag to form a rectangle in the upper left corner, as shown in Figure 12.22.

   c. From the Fonts toolbar choose the Arial font, size 12.

   d. In the new text box, type: Climb the biggest mountain one step at a time! This is shown in Figure 12.22.

The World Wide Web Using Microsoft Internet Explorer

Objectives:

Upon successful completion of Lab 13, you will be able to

- Define the terms "World Wide Web" and URL
- Use a Web browser to load a Web page from the World Wide Web and navigate using hypertext links and Back and Forward navigation buttons
- Find and load previously viewed Web pages using the History list
- Set the homepage
- Store and organize Favorites
- Understand that information on Web pages may not be reliable and describe some questions that should be answered to determine if the information is likely to be reliable

Resources required:

- A computer running Internet Explorer (PC) or Safari (Mac) and an Internet connection

Starter files:

- None

Prerequisite skills:

- General keyboarding and mouse skills; familiarity with editing keys such as Delete, Backspace, Shift, Caps Lock, and Arrow keys

NRC's Top Ten Skills, Concepts, and Capabilities:

- Skills
    Use the Internet to locate information
    - Use Internet Explorer to surf the Web
    - Use a portal to find information
    - Assess information for reliability
- Concepts
    Social impact of computers and technology

- Capabilities
  - Navigate a collection and assess the quality of the information
  - Engage in sustained reasoning
  - Think abstractly about Information Technology
  - Anticipate technological change

Lab Lesson

When people talk about "surfing the Web" they are referring to a portion of the Internet called the **World Wide Web**. The World Wide Web (WWW) is a collection of files stored on computers called **Web servers** that are located all over the world. A Web **server** is a computer that is able to accept a request for a Web page and send the Web page to the computer that requested it. Without getting into the intricacies of how this happens, suffice it to say that each Web server is identified by a unique address and the request is sent by a software program called a **Web Browser**. There are a variety of Web browsers available including Microsoft's Internet Explorer, Apple's Safari, and other lesser known Web browsers such as Netscape, Firefox, and Opera. We will be exploring the World Wide Web using Internet Explorer.

Let's load the USA.gov Web page to start exploring the WWW.

▶ Open Internet Explorer (PC) or Safari (Mac).

You may find that a Web page automatically loads into the browser.

▶ Click the address bar, as shown in Figures 13.1a and 13.1b.

The Web page address in the address bar should be selected. If it is not selected, drag with the mouse to select it.

▶ Press the **Delete** key to delete the address.
▶ Type: www.usa.gov
▶ Press the **Enter** key to request the Web page, as shown in Figures 13.1a and 13.1b.

Let's look at the Web page in the Internet Explorer window.

▶ Move the mouse pointer across the Web page.

At some point you will notice that the pointer changes from an arrow to a hand symbol, as shown in Figures 13.1a and 13.1b. When the pointer becomes a hand symbol, it is hovering over a hypertext link. When you click on a hypertext link, most often another Web page will load. A hypertext link could be text or a picture. The text is often underlined. There may also be a change when the mouse pointer hovers over a hypertext link. The text may change color or size, or a picture may appear or change. You may also notice that a message or Web page address appears on the Status Bar of the Web browser window as the pointer changes to a hand.

▶ Move the mouse pointer to hover over one of the hypertext links on the Web page and click the **left mouse button** (PC) or **mouse button** (Mac).

You should notice that a new Web page loads in the Web browser window.

We will be using some of the buttons on the toolbars shown in Figures 13.2a and 13.2b.

Address Bar

Figure 13.1a *Internet Explorer showing USA.gov Web page for PC.*

Address Bar

Figure 13.1b *Internet Explorer showing USA.gov Web page for Mac.*

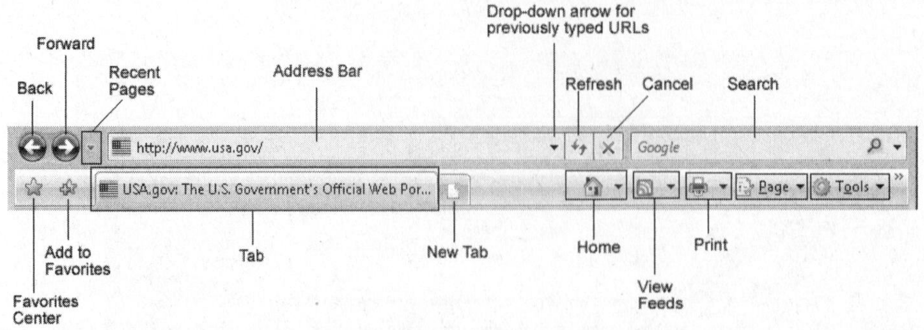

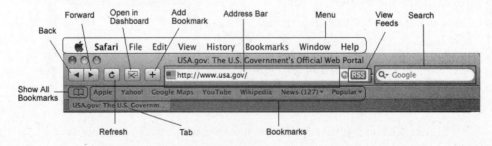

Figure 13.2a *Internet Explorer toolbar buttons for PC.*

As you view Web pages, from time to time they seem to stall. In Internet Explorer, if this happens, click the **Cancel** button shown in Figure 13.2a to halt the loading of the Web pages, and type the Web page address in the address bar again. In Safari, click in the address bar, and press the Enter key to reload the page. Also, from time to time you may wish to refresh the Web page so that it loads again. For instance, you may be viewing a news Web page and want to see if there are new headlines. In Internet Explorer, to reload a Web page, you can click the **Refresh** button, as shown in Figure 13.2a and in Safari you can click in the address bar and press the Enter key

▶ Take a few moments to click on the hypertext links on a few more Web pages. Feel free to follow your interests and view an assortment of Web pages.

The URL

Let's look at the structure of a Web page address. A Web page address is called a **Uniform Resource Locator (URL)**. A URL has the following form:

transfer-type://name-of-computer/foldername/filename

Oh, this looks so technical. Let's break it down. The transfer type for a Web page is generally "http." **Http** is an acronym for HyperText Transfer Protocol and that refers to the method of transfer for a Web page. Web browsers will allow you to omit typing http:// in the URL, which is why we were able to type www.usa.gov as the Web page address. The address we used, www.usa.gov, is rather simple and does not contain a folder name or file name. A more complex Web page address might be something like the following:

http://www.usa.gov/Agencies/Federal/All_Agencies/index.shtml

The URL above contains references to the folders, Agencies, Federal, and All_agencies. It also contains a reference to the actual Web page file, index.shtml. Web pages are files that are stored in folders on Web servers. The images contained in a Web page are also stored as files on a Web server.

Figure 13.2b *Internet Explorer toolbar buttons for Mac.*

The name-of-computer portion of the URL is a combination of the name of a particular computer at a domain, in a top level domain (TLD). For example, www.usa.gov has the following components:

www   This is the name of the actual Web server.
usa.gov   This is the domain, representing the institution, company, or organization location.
gov   This is the top level domain (TLD).

There are many TLDs including com, edu, org, net, and mil. Each of these TLDs, including gov, represent the type of organization as follows:

com   commercial for-profit organization or company
edu   educational institution such as a school district, elementary school, or university
org   organization, typically non-profit
gov   government organization
mil   military installation

By far, the most popular TLD is "com." You will also see region codes such as country, state, and province, including the following:

us   United States
ca.us   California, United States
mx   Mexico
uk   United Kingdom
ca   Canada
on.ca   Ontario, Canada

You will also see combinations such as "www.gov.on.ca". The TLD can give you a clue to the geographic location of an organization if there is a region code included.

One convention that was adopted early was to use some form of a company name or organization as the domain name. You can try a URL such as "www.companyname.com" for a for-profit company, for instance.

Try viewing the following Web sites. To view the Web site, type the URL in the address bar of the Web browser and press the **Enter** key to load the Web site.

▶ www.whitehouse.gov
▶ www.disney.com
▶ www.cnn.com
▶ www.utoronto.ca

If you know another URL, feel free to type it into the address bar and press the **Enter** key to display the page.

Back, Forward, and History

Let's explore some more of the toolbar buttons, as shown in Figures 13.2a and 13.2b.

▶ Click the **Back** button to display the previous Web page.

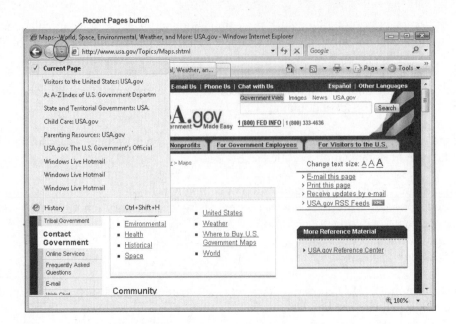

Figure 13.3 *Internet Explorer History list shown via the Recent Pages button.*

Web browsers keep track of the Web pages you visit in the History list. You can click on the **Back** button to go backward through the History list and reload Web pages.

▶ In Internet Explorer, click the **Recent Pages** button, as shown in Figure 13.3.

▶ In Safari, click the menu option **History** to reveal the list of recently visited pages.

Notice that the list of visited Web pages is displayed as a menu below.

▶ Click on one of the Web page names on the menu to reload a Web page.

The **Forward** button also allows you to reload Web pages from the History list. The **Back** and **Forward** buttons combined scroll backward and forward through the History list.

▶ Click on the **Recent Pages** button (Internet Explorer) or the History menu command (Safari).

Notice the active page is indicated by a checkmark in the list of visited pages.

In Internet Explorer, from time to time you may notice an information bar appear under the toolbars, perhaps with a message window as shown in Figure 13.4.

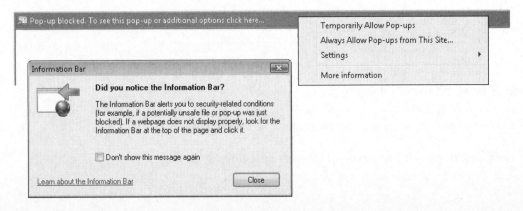

Figure 13.4 *Pop-up warning and Information Bar with menu.*

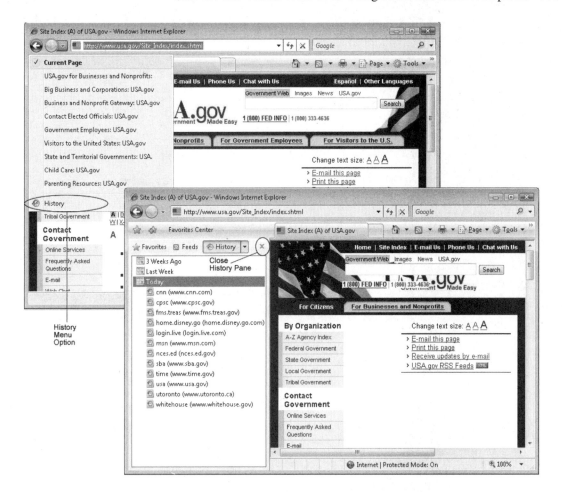

Figure 13.5a *Internet Explorer History pane for PC.*

This indicates that a pop-up window has been suppressed. Safari will simply block the pop-ups without an information notice. Often these pop-up windows contain advertising but sometimes they contain useful information. In Internet Explorer, if you wish to see the pop-up window that has been suppressed, simply click on the Information Bar and select a menu choice such as **Temporarily Allow Pop-ups**. The menu is shown in Figure 13.4. In Safari, you can use the menu commands **Safari, Block Pop-Up Windows** to turn the blocking feature off/on.

The History list can accumulate for days, weeks, or months depending on the configuration setting in the Web Browser. Let's view the History list.

> ► In Internet Explorer, click the **Recent Pages** button and select the **History** option, as shown in Figure 13.5a.

> ► In Safari, click the menu options **History, Show All History,** as shown in Figure 13.5b.

Notice that the History pane appears on the left side of the Internet Explorer window, and as the current window in Safari. The listing indicates days of the week, weeks ago, and perhaps months ago. You can click on any of the options to expand the History list, as indicated in the Today list shown in Figures 13.5a and 13.5b.

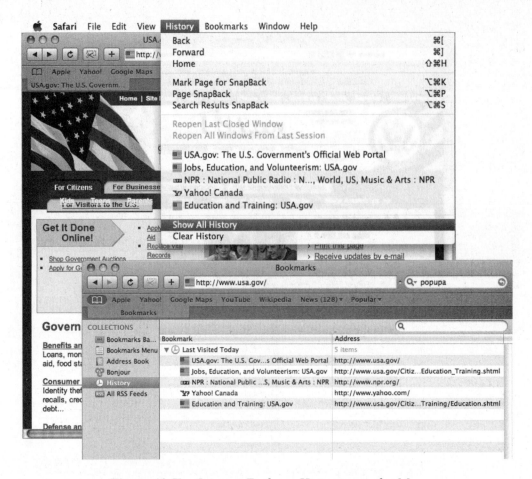

Figure 13.5b *Internet Explorer History pane for Mac.*

In Internet Explorer:

▶ Click on the **Last Week** link.

You may see a list of Web sites viewed during the past week.

▶ Click on one of the Web sites listed.
▶ Click on one of the Web pages listed under the Web site name.

In Safari:

▶ Double-click on one of the Web sites in the list. This will replace the history listing with the Web page.

Notice that the Web page corresponding to the link displays in the Web browser window. There are several View options available as well. If you are looking specifically for a Web page that you know you have viewed often, you can organize the History list by most often viewed pages, for instance.

▶ In Internet Explorer, click the **Close** button for the History pane, as shown in Figure 13.5a.

Setting the Home Page

When you first open the Web browser, you may wish to have a particular Web page load, or you may wish to start with a blank page. The page that is loaded when the browser opens is called the "Home Page." Internet Explorer has a **Home** button. This is a shortcut to load the Web page you set as the home page.

▶ Load one of your favorite Web pages into the browser. Either type the URL or use the History list to find the Web page again.

In Internet Explorer:

▶ Click the drop-down arrow to the right of the **Home** button as shown in Figure 13.6a.
▶ Click the **Radio** button for the option **Use this Web page as your only home page** as shown in Figure 13.6a.
▶ Click the **Yes** button to set the Home Page.

In Safari:

▶ Click the menu options Safari, Preferences as shown in Figure 13.6b.
▶ Click the Set to Current Page button as shown in Figure 13.6b.
▶ Click the Close button to close the General window.

Let's see if the new home page setting works!

▶ Click the **Back** button to display a different Web page in the browser.
▶ In Internet Explorer, lick the **Home** button to display the new home page.
▶ In Safari, click the menu options **History, Home** to display the new home page.

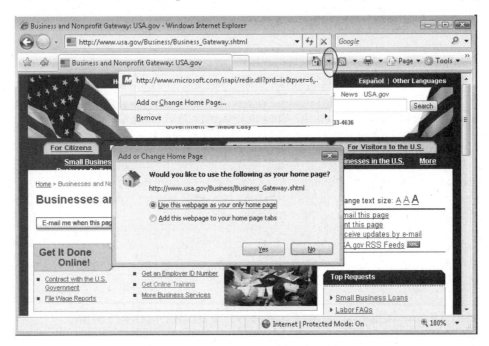

Figure 13.6 *Internet Explorer, setting the Home Page.*

Figure 13.7 *Internet Explorer showing www.usa.gov with "arizona" as a search term.*

Using a Text Box

There are many instances when you may wish to use a **Search** box or there may be a form on a Web page used to collect information. Text boxes are very common, particularly for entering search terms. Let's look at a sample search.

▶ Load the Web page www.usa.gov.

Notice that there is a **Text** box and **Search** button on the upper portion of this Web page, as shown in Figure 13.7.

▶ Click the **Text** box to activate it.

▶ Type the name of your state in the **Text** box, as shown in Figure 13.7 using "arizona" as an example.

▶ Press the **Enter** key or click the **Search** button to perform the search. The search results are shown in Figure 13.8.

This search was a specialized search designed to search only government Web sites. There are many general search sites available that will produce results from a large pool of Web sites. There is no centralized index of all Web pages since they can come and go so quickly. One of the most popular search sites is Google. Let's have a quick peek.

▶ Load the Web page www.google.com in the Web browser.

▶ Feel free to type a search term in the **Search** box and click the **Search** button to reveal the results.

Organizing Favorites (Internet Explorer) or Bookmarks (Safari)

As you come across useful Web pages, you will want to be able to revisit them. You could write down the URLs on paper or try to remember them, but you can use the Favorites (Internet Explorer) or Bookmarks (Safari) to organize your favorite Web sites. Let's add some Web pages to the Favorites/Bookmarks and organize them into folders as well.

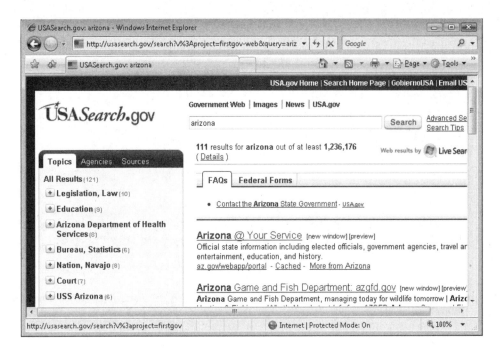

Figure 13.8 *Internet Explorer showing the results of the search at www.usa.gov for the term "arizona."*

▶ Load the Web page www.whitehouse.gov.

▶ In Internet Explorer, click the **Favorites** button and the **Add to Favorites** command, as shown in Figure 13.9a.

▶ In Safari, Click the **Add Bookmark button** as shown in Figure 13.9b.

Notice that the **Add a Favorite** dialog box appears, as shown in Figure 13.10a, or the Bookmark dialog box as shown in Figure 13.10b.

▶ Edit the title in the **Name** box as: whitehouse.gov, as shown in Figures 13.11a. and 13.11b.

▶ Click the **Add** button to set the Favorite/Bookmark entry.

Figure 13.9a *Internet Explorer, partial window showing the Favorites menu for PC.*

Figure 13.9b *Internet Explorer, partial window showing the Favorites menu for Mac.*

Figure 13.10 *Internet Explorer Add a Favorite dialog box.*

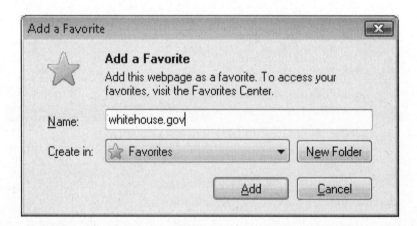

Figure 13.11a *Internet Explorer Add a Favorite dialog box with whitehouse.gov title for PC.*

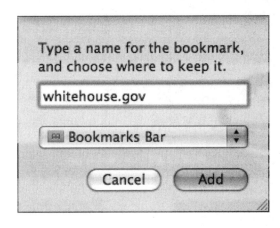

Figure 13.11b *Internet Explorer Add a Favorite dialog box with whitehouse.gov title for Mac.*

Let's verify that the Favorite/Bookmark entry was created.

▶ In Internet Explorer, click the **Favorites Center** button, and click the **Favorites** button in the pane on the left as shown in Figure 13.12a.

▶ In Safari, notice the bookmark entry on the bookmark bar, as shown in Figure 13.12b.

In Internet Explorer, your list may look different as it may already have a few different folders and Favorites entries. Notice that the whitehouse.gov entry is at the bottom of the list. Let's test it out. We'll load the home page, and then use the Favorite/Bookmark entry to load the whitehouse.gov page.

▶ In Internet Explorer, click on the **Home** button to load the home page. Click the **Favorites Center** button and the link for **whitehouse.gov**.

▶ In Safari, click the menu options **History, Home,** to load the home page. Click the **whitehouse.gov bookmark** on the Bookmark Bar.

Notice that the whitehouse.gov page loads in the Web browser.

Figure 13.12a *Internet Explorer, window showing the Favorites for PC.*

New Bookmark on Bookmarks Bar

Figure 13.12b *Internet Explorer, window showing the Favorites for Mac.*

Once you start to accumulate a few Favorites/Bookmarks, you'll need to organize them into folders. Let's create a folder and move the new entry into it.

► In Internet Explorer, click the **Add to Favorites** button and click the menu option **Organize Favorites** as shown in Figure 13.13a.

► In Safari, click the menu options Bookmarks, Show All Bookmarks, as shown in Figure 13.13b.

► In Internet Explorer, click the **New Folder** button.

► In Safari, click the menu options **Bookmarks, Add Bookmark Folder.**

A new folder will be created, as shown in Figures 13.14a and 13.14b.

► In the new folder type: government, as shown in Figures 13.14a and 13.14b.

► In Internet Explorer, click the whitehouse.gov Favorite entry once to select it.

Figure 13.13a *Internet Explorer Organize Favorites menu and dialog box for PC.*

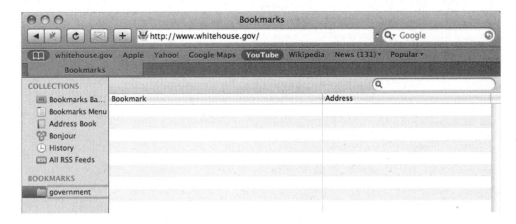

Figure 13.13b   *Internet Explorer Organize Favorites menu and dialog box for Mac.*

You can drag the selected Favorite entry to the government folder, but we will use a more manual method in the Internet Explorer instructions. We will use the dragging method in the Safari instructions.

In Internet Explorer:

▶ Click the **Move** button. The **Browse for Folder** dialog box will appear, as shown in Figure 13.15.

▶ Click the **Government** folder, as shown in Figure 13.15.

▶ Click the **OK** button in the **Browse for Folder** dialog box.

Figure 13.14a   *Internet Explorer Organize Favorites dialog box with government folder for PC.*

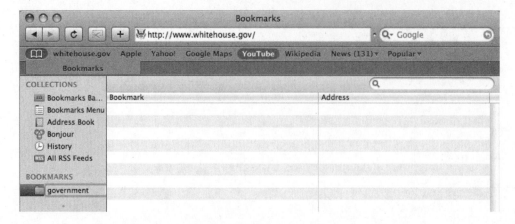

Figure 13.14b *Internet Explorer Organize Favorites dialog box with government folder for Mac.*

The whitehouse.gov Favorite entry will move below the government folder.

▶ Click the **Close** button to close the **Organize Favorites** dialog box.

▶ Click the **Favorites Center** button and the **government** link, as shown in Figure 13.16.

In Safari:

▶ Click the Bookmarks Bar collection in the left pane and click the whitehouse.gov bookmark to select it as shown in Figure 13.16b.

▶ Drag the whitehouse.gov bookmark to the government folder as shown in Figure 13.16b.

Figure 13.15 *Internet Explorer move Favorite entry to folder.*

Figure 13.16a *Internet Explorer, Favorites menu with government link for PC.*

▶ Drag the government folder into the Bookmarks Bar area as shown in Figure 13.16b.

▶ Click the menu options **Bookmarks, Hide All Bookmarks** to close the bookmarks pane. Notice that the government folder is now on the Bookmarks Bar in the Safari window.

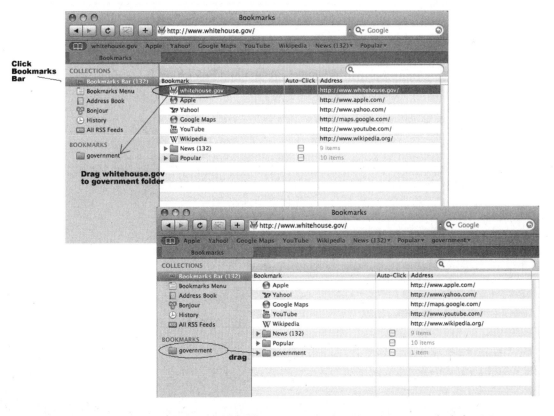

Figure 13.16b *Internet Explorer, Favorites menu with government link for Mac.*

Bookmarks/favorites can be deleted in the organize window by selecting the bookmark/favorite, then hitting the Delete key.

Assessing Web Pages for Reliability

The World Wide Web is a rich resource of information and misinformation. Literally, anyone can publish a Web page. Since publishing Web pages is so accessible, it is important to critique the information on a Web page before you rely on it.

You can ask yourself several key questions to help you decide whether the information might be reliable.

- How current is the information? If there is no indication of copyright date or other clues, you have no way of knowing if the information is five days old or five years old.
- Find a second source or more to corroborate the information. If you can find several sources with the same information, there's a better chance that the information is reliable.
- Who created and published the Web page? If you're looking for medical information and you've come upon a hospital or medical university Web site, the information is likely very reliable. If the author is trying to sway you for financial or other purposes, think about the bias and consider using other sources.

Review

This has been a busy lab! We have covered the following topics:

- Discussion of the terms "World Wide Web" and URL
- Using a Web browser to load a Web page from the World Wide Web and navigate using hypertext links and Back and Forward navigation buttons
- Finding and loading previously viewed Web pages using the History list
- Setting and using the home page
- Storing and organizing Favorites
- Understanding that information on Web pages may not be reliable and listing some questions that should be answered to determine if the information is likely to be reliable

Exercises

1. Use Internet Explorer to view each of the following Web pages. Feel free to click on any hypertext links that interest you!
   a. www.yahoo.com
   b. www.mapquest.com
   c. www.reference.com

2. Use the History list to revisit www.yahoo.com.

3. Add www.yahoo.com to the Favorites/Bookmarks list.

4. Choose one of the Web pages you've found and answer the following questions:
   a. Who is the Web page author?
   b. When was the Web page updated or created?
   c. Should you rely on the information on this page?

Email Using MSN Hotmail

Objectives:

Upon successful completion of Lab 14, you will be able to

- View email messages received in the Inbox
- Send email messages using the To, Cc, and Bcc fields
- Reply to a received email message
- Forward a received email message to another email address
- Delete unwanted email messages from the Inbox
- Send an email message with a file attachment
- Understand the risk of viruses in file attachments

Resources required:

- A computer running Windows with a Web Browser and an Internet connection

Starter files:

- None

Prerequisite skills:

- General keyboarding and mouse skills; familiarity with editing keys such as Delete, Backspace, Shift, Caps Lock, and Arrow keys

NRC's Top Ten Skills, Concepts, and Capabilities:

- Skills
  Use a computer to communicate with others
  - Use Internet Explorer and acquire a hotmail account
  - Send and receive email messages
  - File attachments
  - Risk of virus
- Concepts
  Universality
  Social impact of computers and technology
- Capabilities
  Communicate using IT about IT

Lab Lesson

Electronic mail, or email, has rapidly become a very popular form of communication for business and personal use. Email messages may contain text only or they may include file attachments in order to send pictures, documents, video files, or sound files.

If you subscribe to an Internet service, your Internet Service Provider (ISP) provides an email address and instructions for connecting to the email service. You may require email software such as Microsoft Outlook or your ISP may provide a Web site where you can view your email messages and send messages. If you use email software such as Microsoft Outlook, you can download your email messages and store them on your computer. Your ISP will provide a small amount of storage space only. Therefore, you will have to delete messages periodically if you choose not to use email software and download messages.

Subscribing to an ISP is not necessary in order to be able to send and receive email messages. There is a wide variety of free Web-based email services. We will explore email features using a free service, MSN Hotmail.

You will have to register for a Hotmail account if you do not already have one. The procedure is very friendly.

> ▶ Open Internet Explorer.
> ▶ In the address bar, type: live.hotmail.com
> ▶ Press the **Enter** key to load the Hotmail Web page.

You should find a **Sign Up** button on the Hotmail Web page. Because these Web pages change frequently, you may not see the Web page in Figure 14.1 exactly as shown.

> ▶ Click the **Sign Up** button to begin the registration process.
> ▶ Follow the instructions to sign up for a Hotmail account.

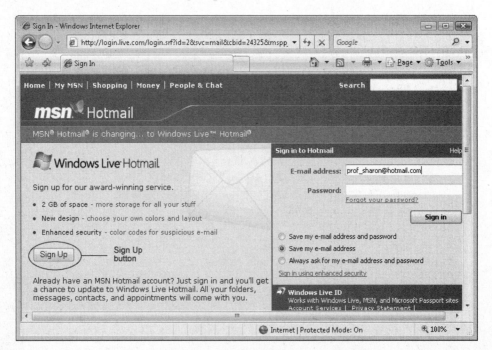

Figure 14.1 *MSN Hotmail homepage.*

Figure 14.2   *Hotmail Web page showing the Today information.*

You will find that at some point you may have to be creative about choosing an email address. As the Hotmail service is very popular your first few choices will likely already have been taken. People often combine their name with numbers and Hotmail will also suggest some names that are available.

Once you've completed the registration procedure, your account is active immediately.

▶ Sign in using your new Hotmail address and password.

If there is no sign in information visible, return to the www.hotmail.com page and sign in from there.

After you sign in, the Hotmail Web page will load, as shown in Figure 14.2. The design of these Web sites frequently changes, so yours may not look identical to Figure 14.2 but it will have the same functionality or more.

Notice that there are tabs for Today, Mail, Calendar, and Contacts. The **Today** tab shows the available storage space and a count of new messages. Let's look at the email page.

Viewing Email Messages

▶ Click the **Inbox** link (or if your Web page looks different, find the link for the mail folders). The Inbox Web page is shown in Figure 14.3.

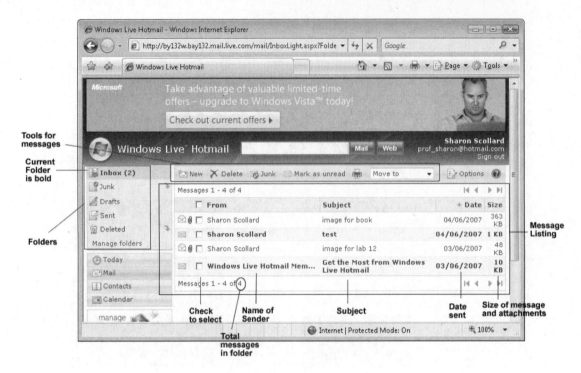

Figure 14.3   *Hotmail Mail window.*

Figure 14.3 shows several messages in the Inbox including one from Hotmail Member Services. You will likely have at least one message in your Inbox from Hotmail Member Services. Incoming email messages are placed in the **Inbox** folder. Many email software packages will allow you to set filters or rules to route incoming messages to specific folders. We will view incoming messages from the **Inbox** folder only. Let's view the message in the **Inbox** folder.

▶ Click the name of the sender of the email message.

The email message will display, as shown in Figure 14.4.

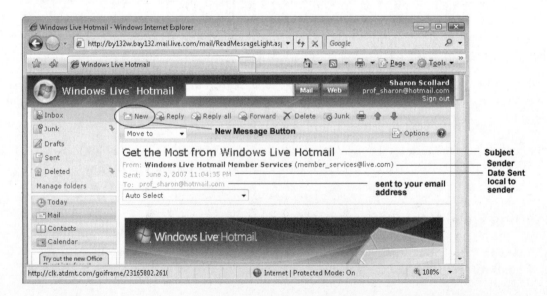

Figure 14.4   *Hotmail displaying a message from Hotmail Member Services.*

Notice the message header information, From, Sent, To, and Subject. The From heading indicates the sender. It should contain the email address and perhaps the name as well. In Figure 14.4, the sender is Hotmail Member Services and the email address is indicated. The Sent heading indicates the date and time when the message was sent. This date and time is usually the date and time on the sender's computer, but when a Web-based email service is used, the date and time is from the service. If the service is based in California, then the time will be Pacific Time, for instance. The To field indicates your email address and will also indicate others if the message was sent to more than one address in the To heading. The Subject heading contains the subject that was created by the sender. The message is displayed below the header information.

▶ Scroll down to see the rest of the message if it is not visible.

Sending an Email Message

Let's start by sending an email message to you! You can send an email to yourself!

▶ Click the **New**, **Mail Message** commands, as shown in Figure 14.4.

An email composition window will appear, as shown in Figure 14.5.

Let's compose the message, as shown in Figure 14.6.

▶ Click in the **To** input box.
▶ Type: your hotmail email address
▶ Click in the **Subject** input box.
▶ Type: first message
▶ Click the large message area.
▶ Type a message to yourself. Feel free to use the editing tools to add formatting and color.

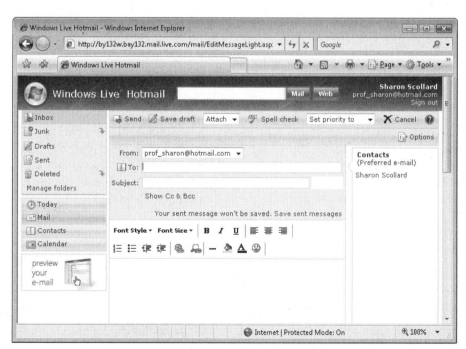

Figure 14.5 *Hotmail, new email message composition.*

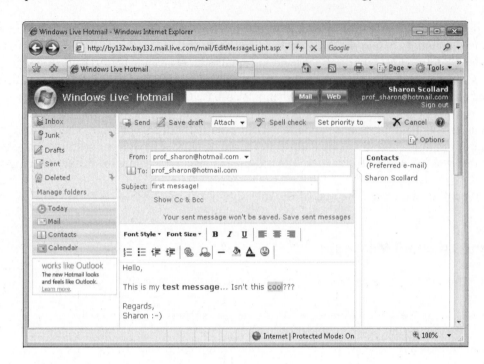

Figure 14.6 *Hotmail email composition window containing a message.*

There are several heading fields that we did not use. There are fields for Cc and Bcc. **Cc** means "computer copy" and email addresses can be entered in the Cc field. **Bcc** means "blind computer copy" and email addresses can be entered in the Bcc field. A copy of the email will be sent to all email addresses in the To, Cc, and Bcc fields. We will use these later.

Multiple email addresses can be entered by separating each with a comma (,). People who receive a copy of the email address will be able to see all email addresses in the To and Cc fields. The Bcc field will not be displayed on any email messages. Bcc is used when you wish to send a copy of the email message but do not wish others to see the Bcc recipient. For instance, perhaps you are sending a message to a group of clients and do not wish the clients to see the email addresses of other clients. In that case, put your email address in the To field, and all your clients' email addresses in the Bcc field.

The subject should be short and to the point. Creating a good subject title can be something of an art form. Try to indicate the main purpose of the email message in the subject field.

The message body contains the text you wish to send. Some email software packages allow you to add formatting to the message including font changes and background images. Notice the special characters that appear at the end of the email message in Figure 14.6. They are :-) and represent a **smilie**. Tilt your head to the left. Can you see two eyes, a nose, and a smile? This was the method used to convey some emotion years ago when email messages could contain text only. The smilies have evolved and are still used today.

▶ Click the **Send** button on the message toolbar to send the message.

A message should appear indicating that the email message was sent, as shown in Figure 14.7.

▶ Click the **Return to Inbox** link, as shown in Figure 14.7. If your window looks different, look for a link that will return you to the Inbox list.

Your new email message should appear in your Inbox, as shown in Figure 14.8.

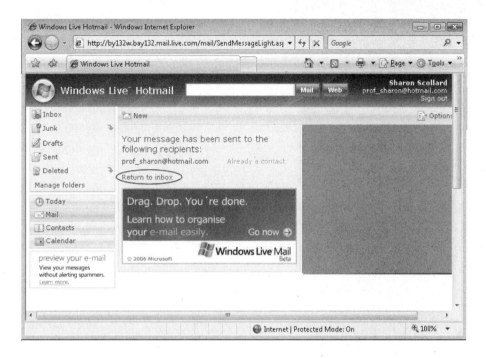

Figure 14.7   *Hotmail confirmation of sent email message.*

Notice that the new message appears at the top of the list. The number of messages indicated below the list shows a total of 2 messages and 1 unread message. The closed envelope image indicates that the message is unread.

▶ **Click the name of the sender to read the new message, as shown in Figure 14.9.**

Reply and Forward

You may wish to reply to an email message. When you reply to an email message the sender's email address will automatically appear as the To address in the heading area.

▶ Click the **Reply** button. This is shown on the **Message** toolbar in Figure 14.9.

A reply email composition window will be displayed, as shown in Figure 14.10.

Notice the subject heading now includes RE: to the left of the original subject. This indicates that the message is a reply. Also notice that the message body includes the original heading information (From, To, Subject, and Date) and the original message is indented. Some email software programs include a symbol such as a vertical bar (|) or > symbol to indicate the original message and some do not include any special symbol.

	From	Subject	↓ Date	Size
Messages 1 - 2 of 2			⏮ ◀ ▶ ⏭	
✉ ☐	**Sharon Scollard**	**first message!**	11:17 AM	2 KB
✉ ☐	Windows Live Hotmail Member ...	Get the Most from Windows Live Hotmail	03/06/2007	10 KB
Messages 1 - 2 of 2			⏮ ◀ ▶ ⏭	

Figure 14.8   *Hotmail email message list in the Inbox.*

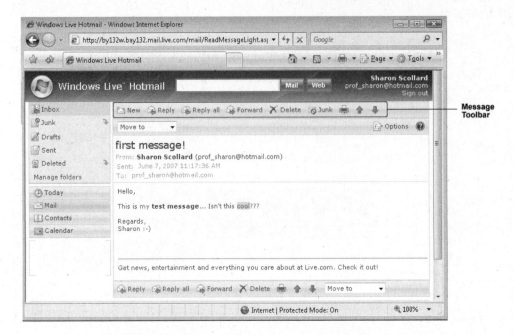

Figure 14.9 *Hotmail displaying the message sent to you.*

You can add your reply above the original message. If the original message is long you can insert your reply throughout the message or delete parts of the original message. Let's add a reply above the message.

▶ Click in the message area above the original message.
▶ Type an appropriate reply, as shown in Figure 14.11.
▶ Click the **Send** button to send this reply email message.

Figure 14.10 *Hotmail Reply message composition window.*

Figure 14.11   *Hotmail Reply message.*

The confirmation window will appear, similar to that shown in Figure 14.7.

▶ Click the **Return to Inbox** link.

The new reply message should appear in the Inbox, as shown in Figure 14.12.

At some point you may wish to send a copy of an email message to someone else. Sending a copy of an email message is done using the Forward feature. Let's forward the new reply message. If you know another email address, perhaps a friend, you can use that address as the To address, if you wish.

▶ Click the name of the sender on the newest message to view it.
▶ Click the **Forward** button on the message toolbar.

The mail composition window will open, as shown in Figure 14.13.

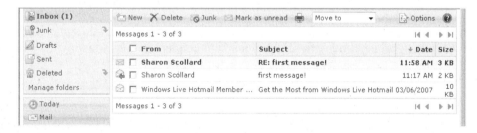

Figure 14.12   *Hotmail Inbox list.*

Figure 14.13 *Hotmail email to forward.*

Notice that the subject now includes FW:, as shown in Figure 14.13. This indicates that this message has been forwarded, or in this case, is about to be forwarded. The original message has been included in the message area, as was the case with the reply message. We will send a copy of this email message to someone else as well.

▶ Click the link **Show Cc & Bcc** as shown in Figure 14.13. This reveals the Cc and Bcc text boxes.

▶ In the To location, type the email address of your friend. If you do not have another email address, type your own email address.

▶ In the Cc location, type your email address, or the email address of another friend, as shown in Figure 14.13.

▶ In the message area type a short message, as shown in Figure 14.13.

When you forward an email message to someone, it is a good idea to include some explanation above the message. This is particularly important if the recipient is not expecting the message.

▶ Click the **Send** button to send the message.

Again, the message confirmation window will appear.

▶ Click the **Return to Inbox** link in the message confirmation window.

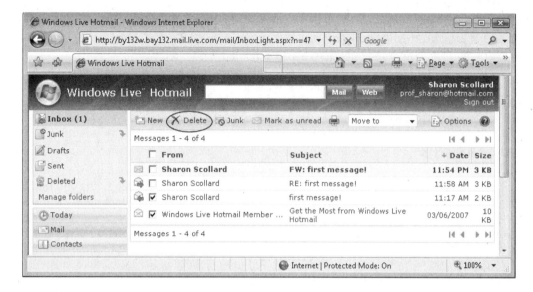

Figure 14.14   *Hotmail select messages.*

Deleting Messages

As you accumulate email messages you may wish to delete old messages. Let's delete some messages.

▶ Click the checkboxes beside the last two messages in the Inbox list, as shown in Figure 14.14.

Adding a check mark to a checkbox selects that email message. Once an email message has been selected, you can delete it, put it in another folder, or mark it as unread. Let's delete the selected email messages.

▶ Click the **Delete** button on the message toolbar, as shown in Figure 14.14.

The selected messages will be removed from the Inbox list. They're not quite gone yet, though! They're in the Deleted mailbox. Let's look at the messages in the Deleted mailbox.

▶ Click the **Deleted** button in the folder list, as shown in Figure 14.15.

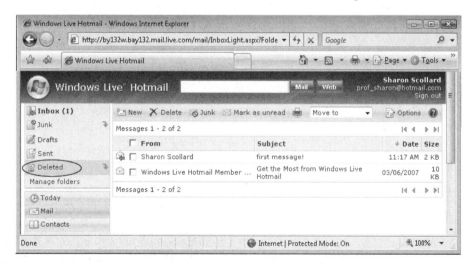

Figure 14.15   *Hotmail Trash Can list.*

Some email services require you to delete messages or empty the trash periodically. The Hotmail email service indicates that trash is automatically emptied each day. You can leave these messages in the Deleted mailbox and they will be deleted within a day.

In addition to deleting messages, you can also organize your messages by moving them into folders and creating folders of your own. This procedure is beyond the scope of this lab.

File Attachments

We've been exploring sending text email messages. You can also send documents and images as file attachments that will be sent with the text message. Let's send a file attachment.

> ► Click the **New** button, as shown in Figure 14.15.
> ► In the To field, type: your email address.
> ► In the Subject field, type: file attachment
> ► In the **Message** box, type a quick message explaining that you are sending a file attachment, as shown in Figure 14.16.
> ► Click the **Attach**, **File** menu commands, as shown in Figure 14.17.
> ► Click the **Browse** button.

The **Choose File** dialog box will appear, as shown in Figure 14.17.

> ► Select a file from the file list, as shown in Figure 14.17.
> ► Click the **Open** button to add the selected file to the attachment window.
> ► Click the **Attach** button as shown in Figure 14.17.

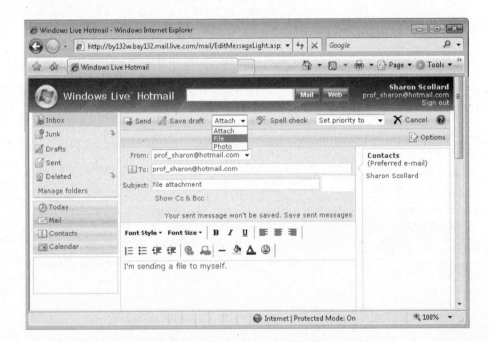

Figure 14.16 *Hotmail file attachment message.*

Figure 14.17   *Hotmail attach file with Browse window.*

The message composition window will appear again. If you click the **Attach**, **File** commands again you will see the attached file listed and you could delete it from the message if you wish. Some email services have limits for the size of file attachments. Let's send the file with the attachment.

▶ Click the **Send** button.
▶ Click the **Return to Inbox** link in the confirmation window.

The new message will appear in the Inbox, with a paperclip icon indicating that a file is attached, as shown in Figure 14.18.

▶ Click the name of the sender on the most recent email message.

Figure 14.18   *Hotmail Inbox list showing file attachment.*

Figure 14.19   *Hotmail view email with attachment.*

The file attachment is also indicated in the message, as shown in Figure 14.19.

▶ **Click on the name of the attached file, as shown in Figure 14.19.**

The file attachment may be scanned for viruses and a link will be displayed for download, as shown in Figure 14.20.

▶ Click the **Save** button to save the file.
▶ Choose a folder location and click the **Save** button to save the file.
▶ Click the **Close** button after the download is complete.
▶ Click the **Mail** tab to return to the email message listing.

Viruses

The risk of infecting your computer with a virus becomes greater when you receive file attachments. A virus cannot hide in the text of an email message but it can certainly hide in a file attachment. It is important to use good antivirus software and update it regularly. Although many email services provide automatic antivirus protection, your computer can acquire a virus from other sources. Some antivirus software can scan all of your outgoing email as well as your incoming email. If you are scanning your computer for viruses regularly it may not be necessary to scan all outgoing email, as you would be attaching files that have already been scanned during your routine scanning. It is important to scan incoming file attachments, even if you have been assured by the sender that the attachment does not contain a virus. People unknowingly send infected file attachments.

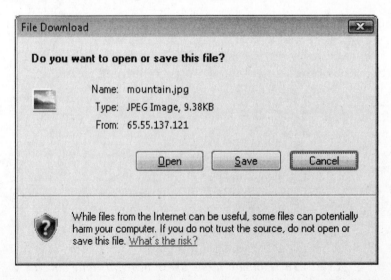

Figure 14.20   *Hotmail file attachment download window.*

Review

This has been a busy lab! We have covered the following topics:
- Viewing email messages received in the Inbox
- Sending email messages using the To, Cc, and Bcc fields
- Replying to a received email message
- Forwarding a received email message to another email address
- Deleting unwanted email messages from the Inbox
- Sending an email message with a file attachment
- The risk of viruses in file attachments

Exercises

1. Compose an email message to one of your friends, and Cc yourself. The message should describe an event that happened today. If you do not have email addresses for friends, compose this message to yourself. Include an appropriate subject such as "something happened today." Save a copy of the email message in the sent folder.

2. Reply to the above message, adding another event that happened today.

3. Forward the replied message to your instructor and include a small file attachment.

4. Delete the original message.